The Essential Díaz

Selections from *The True History of the Conquest of New Spain*

BERNAL DÍAZ DEL CASTILLO

The Essential Díaz

Selections from *The True History of the Conquest of New Spain*

Edited and Translated, with an Introduction, by
Janet Burke and Ted Humphrey

Hackett Publishing Company, Inc.
Indianapolis/Cambridge

Copyright © 2014 by Hackett Publishing Company, Inc.

17 16 15 14   1 2 3 4 5 6 7

For further information, please address
  Hackett Publishing Company, Inc.
  P.O. Box 44937
  Indianapolis, Indiana 46244-0937

  www.hackettpublishing.com

Cover design by Abigail Coyle
Interior design by Elizabeth L. Wilson
Composition by Aptara, Inc.
Maps by Lynne Donovan

Library of Congress Cataloging-in-Publication Data

Díaz del Castillo, Bernal, 1496–1584.
  [Historia verdadera de la conquista de la Nueva España. Selections. English]
  The essential Díaz : selections from the True history of the conquest of New Spain / Bernal Díaz del Castillo ; edited and translated, with an introduction, by Janet Burke and Ted Humphrey.
       pages cm
  Includes bibliographical references.
  ISBN 978-1-62466-002-3 (pbk.) — ISBN 978-1-62466-003-0 (cloth)
  1. Mexico—History—Conquest, 1519–1540. 2. Cortés, Hernán, 1485–1547. I. Burke, Janet, 1943– editor, translator. II. Humphrey, Ted, 1941– editor, translator. III. Title.
  F1230.D56513 2014
  972′.02—dc23   2013030782

CONTENTS

THE TRUE HISTORY OF THE CONQUEST
OF NEW SPAIN

[Bracketed Roman numerals refer to chapters in the Guatemalan
manuscript of the *True History*.]

PREFACE

Bernal Díaz del Castillo's experiences as a foot soldier in the conquest of New Spain had their origins in a number of social, economic, and political changes in fifteenth-century Europe. These included the desire on the part of Europeans for the new tastes and textures first introduced by Crusaders returning from the East during the several centuries before the encounters with the Americas and its peoples; the rise of strong new monarchies in Europe; the sense of mission to convert non-Christian peoples to Christianity that arose during the final stages of the struggle between Christians and Muslims for territorial domination of the Iberian Peninsula; and the scientific and technological developments that sprang from the burst of intellectual energy that accompanied the reintroduction into Europe of ancient mathematical and philosophical texts that had been held primarily in the East. The factors that enter into an event of such enormous proportions as the European movement to the Americas are so many and so diverse—including, for example, the discovery of the patterns of trade winds, the European fascination with and devotion to the spirit of adventure, and the restlessness that arose among sons who were not first in line to inherit a given family's lands and goods, all which played an important role—that they do not permit here the examination they might otherwise deserve. With these forces in play the stage was set for a new era of European discovery and territorial expansion.

Goods from the East. Europeans' experience of luxuries first brought to Europe by returning Crusaders, such as silk, porcelain, jewelry, perfume, tapestries, sugar, and, especially, spices, created demand for these goods. To satisfy this demand, Europeans at first dealt with Arab traders who brought the goods from the East, mostly overland, a long and expensive process. European traders thus longed for their own routes to the East, thereby avoiding having to deal with middlemen.

The Rise of New Monarchies in the Middle of the Fifteenth Century. In various parts of Europe after 1475, monarchs appeared who solidified their positions by siphoning power from the nobility and quelling violence in their countries. In return for peace and stability, cash-rich urban citizens and some of the nobility were prepared to pay higher taxes and allow greater monarchical dominance. With these tax monies, monarchs were able to raise fighting forces, which allowed for war with ever more sophisticated weaponry. The new monarchies included England with the Tudor dynasty, France with the Valois line, and Spain's union of Aragon and Castile through the marriage of Fernando and Isabel. In the German states, which included the Netherlands and some non-Germanic peoples, the Habsburgs were in the process of solidifying power.

The Reconquista. The event historians often refer to as the "Reconquista" was, in fact, the culmination of a centuries-long struggle between European Christians and Muslims, mostly north African Berbers, who in the early part of the eighth century had entered the Iberian Peninsula by crossing the Strait of Gibraltar and ranging as far as and even beyond the Pyrenees. From that point on, Christian powers began a long, slow process of pushing those they regarded as invaders south and eventually back across the strait. The contest was long and often in doubt, with alliances shifting among Muslim caliphs and Christian monarchs and their lesser nobles—sometimes Muslims and Christians formed alliances through marriage and other means—but, slowly, from the late eighth century on, European Christian rulers began to reclaim territories of the Iberian Peninsula, which effort culminated on January 2, 1492, in the fall of Granada, the last remaining stronghold of the Muslim emirate on the Iberian Peninsula. Credit for the Christian victory fell to Fernando and Isabel, whose marriage brought their respective kingdoms, Aragon and Castile, together and whose combined forces laid siege to the city. The final stages of this effort of reconquest were accompanied by papal exhortations not just to rid Europe of nonbelievers, most particularly Muslims and Jews, but to carry on a campaign to convert non-Christians to the faith. As a consequence of their success in pushing the last Muslims occupying the Iberian Peninsula back across the Strait of Gibraltar, Fernando and Isabel came to hold the papal designation of "their most Catholic Majesties."

The end of the struggle between Muslims and European Christians for dominance on the Iberian Peninsula coupled with papal exhortations to extend Christianity's domain through conversion and conquest, if necessary, opened the way for the Spanish Crown's sponsorship of Christopher Columbus's exploration for a new sea route to the Indies and, shortly after his landfall in the Antilles, the voyages that would bring the sons of those Spaniards from Extremadura and Andalusia who had been involved in the Crusades and struggles against the Iberian Muslims to the Americas.

Technological Advance and Borrowing in Europe. The rise of science and a spirit of inquisitiveness and improvements in navigation, all of which came at about this time, laid the foundation for a European race to explore the world and open new territories and trade routes. Some of the early improvements included adoption of the mariner's compass, improvements in ship architecture, and innovation in the use of sails. With these advances, the Portuguese, under the leadership of Henry the Navigator, began to work their way down the west coast of Africa until in the 1490s Vasco da Gama rounded Cape of Good Hope, entering the Indian Ocean, allowing the Portuguese to establish a trading empire. The price of Asian goods dropped dramatically, and European demand and consumption increased equally dramatically. This economic situation led to increases in the rates of exploration by other Europeans who wanted a share of the trade. During the same decade, the Spanish were striving to reach the East, particularly China, before da Gama and the Portuguese.

Atlantic Exploration. A new era of Atlantic history was about to begin, fueled by demands for goods from the East and the great promise held out by the first sea route to the East; with the new monarchies strong and poised to go after these trade routes, but also attracted by gold and slaves that from the 1450s had been coming from Africa as a result of Portuguese explorations and opening of trade routes; with the missionary zeal for saving souls unleashed by the Spanish expulsion of the Muslims from the Iberian Peninsula; and with the improvements in navigation that made exploration possible.

The 1490s was the crucial decade for the European encounter with the Atlantic and the Americas. Columbus sailed with the backing of Queen Isabel of Castile, but other expeditions, including English expeditions under the Cabots (1497), a Spanish expedition led by Magellan (1519) that circumnavigated the globe for the first time, and a French expedition under Jacques Cartier (1534), were all looking for routes to the East. Once Amerigo Vespucci ascertained in 1502 that Columbus had not reached Asia, exploration focused on finding a northwest or southwest passage to Asia through or around the landmasses he had actually discovered. The fascinating story of the encounter between the Old World and the New World is an Atlantic story, not the story of one country over another. To be sure, it is tale of Spain exploring and colonizing Central and South America and parts of North America; but it is also the tale of the pope and the Treaty of Tordesillas, in which he divided the world between Spain and Portugal, leading ultimately to Portuguese occupation of Brazil; and, finally, it is the tale of England, France, and, briefly, the Netherlands, exploring and colonizing North America. Although these latter European nations would not be present in the New World for some time after the Spaniards had invaded Mexico, the foregoing constitutes the overarching context of Bernal Díaz del Castillo's dramatic account of the conquest of Mexico.

Once Europeans encountered the Americas, the time had come for the New World to exert its influence on the Old. Beyond the story of the cataclysmic effect of colonization on the indigenous peoples of the New World, one finds that the encounter of these two cultures had profound effects on Europe as well, including the heated philosophical and theological debate about what constitutes being human, the rise in Europe of the concept of the noble savage, and the entire economic restructuring of Europe with such New World goods as timber for shipbuilding and furs, which had tremendous economic influence on England and France respectively. The greatest impact came with the extraction of gold and silver from the mines of New Spain (Mexico) and South America, riches Spain used to fund its wars, reshaping the contours of European and global finance. One can see in Bernal Díaz del Castillo's story some of the first steps in the changes that would overtake Europe in the century that followed the conquest of Mexico.

INTRODUCTION

The Conquest in Context

Because the Spanish conquest of New Spain, of Moctezuma (referred to by Bernal Díaz del Castillo as Montezuma) and the Aztecs of Mexico, is so prominent in the popular mind, people have been tempted to take it for a singular event that occurred not long after Christopher Columbus's landfall in the Americas. In fact, the Spaniards set foot on the Yucatan about twenty-five years after Columbus landed on Hispaniola (now home to the Dominican Republic and Haiti), and much had happened in that quarter century. Most importantly for our present purposes, the pattern of events that emerged as the Spaniards imposed control on the natives of Hispaniola, Cuba, and Tierra Firme (modern-day Panama) set the stage for the more widely known occupations of what are now Mexico and, a bit later, Peru, patterns we briefly examine in what follows.

Columbus and his crew first sighted the lands of the New World on October 12, 1492, and after some relatively cursory explorations of a number of islands in the Lesser and Greater Antilles, he settled a party of thirty-nine men on Hispaniola before returning to Spain to report his findings and fit out for a second voyage. The second voyage involved seventeen ships and some twelve hundred men of diverse backgrounds and skills, who came with the explicit purpose of colonizing the recently discovered lands. Among those who came on that second voyage was Diego Velázquez, who would be centrally involved in settling first Cuba and then, at least indirectly, the Mexican mainland. Arriving for the second time at Hispaniola, Columbus and those with him found the fort he had originally built destroyed and more than a quarter of the men he had left behind dead, having been overrun by the native Taino people. In the face of this destruction, Columbus determined to establish a settlement some sixty miles to the north, still on Hispaniola, but in what is today the Dominican Republic. That location also proved unsuitable for permanent occupation because it could provide few of the resources necessary to maintain a large colony. The site was inhospitable, with difficult weather and little of the gold necessary for trade with Spain to secure the goods the settlers needed to make the kind of life they desired in coming to the Americas. Internal strife among the settlers with respect to *encomiendas*—officially sanctioned rights to demand the labor of native peoples[1]—as well as a desire for greater independence in establishing domains of power and influence led to the final breakdown of the settlement. Almost immediately, parties went off to Tierra Firme and, under the leadership of Diego Velázquez, to Cuba to establish new colonies and subject further native peoples to their control.

The goal of these expeditions was not to establish trade relations with the native peoples, but to establish dominance over a territory and its population for purposes of extracting resources of value, for example, gold that could be traded for goods produced in the metropolis. These expeditions, then, followed a standard pattern, one originally developed during Spain's successful reconquest of the Iberian Peninsula from the Muslims. In this pattern, a senior but subordinate member of a given settlement group would, with the permission and support of the settlement's leader, form a party to underwrite the costs of an expedition to new

---

1. The reference here is to the *encomienda* system, in which the Spanish Crown assigned an indigenous sociopolitical unit under its ruler, the cacique, to an individual Spaniard primarily to receive labor from the native peoples, but also increasingly other benefits, and, on the mainland, tribute in whatever they had, from precious metals to food and supplies. At the time of the conquest of Mexico, everyone spoke of *repartimientos*, units given out in distribution, and not of *encomiendas*, but by the time Bernal Díaz wrote his chronicle, *encomienda*, which had become current in public decrees and disputes, had displaced *repartimiento*.

territories. In the Americas, the requirements for such an expedition included ships, horses, and supplies necessary for bringing a territory under control and properly settling it. Those participating in such an expedition were effectively investors in the enterprise, not paid soldiers. The rewards they received by way of position and rank—encomiendas of Indian labor and, indirectly, land and estates—were largely a function of what they were able to invest of themselves and what goods they could devote to the enterprise. Such goods included horses, arms, and other resources necessary to the expedition's success, as well, of course, as the esteem in which the expedition's leader held them. Thus, in 1511, with the permission of the governor of Hispaniola, fray Nicolás de Ovando, Diego Velázquez formed a company of some three hundred thirty men to make an expedition to the island of Cuba. But Diego Velázquez soon slipped out from under the control of the governor of Hispaniola and, after seeking endorsement from the Spanish Crown, claimed the governorship of Cuba and set up his own court and entourage, which included many of the individuals who populate Bernal Díaz's narrative. In forming these companies, family and other personal relations—relations arising from being a member of a household, rendering prior loyal service and being from a given Spanish city or region, all relations to which Bernal Díaz refers—were of utmost importance.[2] They were fundamental social binders, even if they did not guarantee continued loyalty; one is, after all, dealing with men who were proud, adventurous, and, above all, interested in securing their fortunes. Finally, being the designated organizer and leader of a company gave primacy to the individual, as did serving as a captain of men and simply being among the first to enter and subdue a given area.

---

2. Bernal Díaz notes that he was a member of Diego Velázquez's household. Further, Diego Velázquez offered the captaincy generalship of the third expedition to three relatives, all of whom declined because they already had comfortable situations on Cuba. Even Diego Velázquez's offer of the post to Hernando Cortés was based on relationships of prior loyal service and Cortés's marriage to a member of Velázquez's extended family.

Even before Cortés's expedition to the Mexican mainland, the process for taking control of new territories had been well established. The matter of first importance was to subdue the native populations by capturing their leaders and, if possible, subordinating those leaders to the Spaniards' control, thereby making the native peoples they ruled sources of labor, both for mining and for providing agricultural and household labor. The Spaniards much preferred working through native leaders, as the latter had already established authority within their communities and were thus in the best position to communicate the Spaniards' desires and keep their subjects compliant. The Spanish leader of a given expedition, or *entrada*, controlled the distribution of Indian labor; this control was one source of significant influence and power. An individual Spaniard's allocation of Indian labor determined to a large degree his or her prospects for wealth, prosperity, and political position—particularly in dominating the municipal councils. Such allocations were not entirely arbitrary inasmuch as those Spaniards who contributed most to an expedition were able to lay claim to at least proportional shares of the spoils it produced. In this way, senior leaders of expeditions—captains who normally had wealth sufficient to own a horse—gained wealth, influence, and even property, often leading to conflicts with the original leader—the designated captain general—of the expedition, conflicts that led to enmities, divisions and, ultimately, to further expeditions in search of lands and populations of which the subordinate might himself become principal leader. This was the situation with Governor Ovando and Diego Velázquez when the latter organized his expedition to Cuba, and it would be the situation when, finally, Velázquez named Cortés captain general of the third expedition to Mexico. Cortés maneuvered his independence from Velázquez when he, Cortés, contrived to found Villa Rica de la Veracruz and have himself named captain general and *justicia mayor*.

The other major factor that drove the exploration and settlement of new territories was the decline of productivity in already established ones. The fundamental reason for declining productivity was the decrease in native populations whose labor the Spaniards could exploit. The native populations suffered enormously under the kinds of labor—mining and sugarcane cultivation, in particular—to which the Spaniards subjected them, and they were also particularly susceptible to such viral diseases as smallpox that the Spaniards brought from Europe, diseases to which the native populations had not yet been exposed. With the drastic decline in the populations native to a given area, the Spaniards sought not just new territories with populations sufficient to carry out the work they required, but also other sources of labor, such as that provided by enslaved Africans. The Spaniards, having arrived on Hispaniola in relatively large numbers in 1493, had to a great extent exhausted its human resources by 1501. They moved on to Puerto Rico and then, in 1511, to Tierra Firme under Pedrarias Dávila and, a bit later, to Cuba under Diego Velázquez. Accompanying Velázquez were Cortés and Pánfilo de Narváez, both of whom figure significantly in Bernal Díaz's account of the conquest of Mexico. One sees, then, that the expeditions to Mexico fall into a larger pattern of Spanish expansion in the Americas. By 1518, a generation after the Spaniards had arrived in the Americas, they found it necessary and possible to move on from the islands of the Caribbean to the mainland.

Diego Velázquez initiated three expeditions to the mainland, the first led by Francisco Hernández de Córdoba, which made its way up the coast of the Yucatan but finally suffered defeat at the hands of the natives at Champoton, where they had landed in search of water. Juan de Grijalva led the second expedition, which left Cuba in 1518 and retraced much of the route Córdoba followed, encountering many of the same obstacles. He became convinced, however, that the land had great promise and should be settled, although he had neither the men nor the resources to carry out that task. Instead, he sent Pedro de Alvarado back to Cuba to let Diego Velázquez know of his findings.

In the meantime, fearing that the Spanish Crown might grant rights of exploration and settlement to some other, more preferred person, Diego Velázquez had already begun to organize a third expedition, the one to be led by Hernando Cortés, who, as Bernal Díaz's account makes clear, assiduously set about organizing the largest, most experienced, and best outfitted company yet to set out for the mainland, a company that included almost one-third of Cuba's Spanish population and greatly diminished the island's food and other supplies.[3] Although large, the Cortés expedition was not the first or a particularly innovative effort to reach and settle the mainland, but rather one that built upon the efforts and information of other attempts to establish a foothold on the continent. One sees throughout Bernal Díaz's account that Cortés judiciously used the information he had gleaned, taking (if not seeking) the advice of those among his company who had participated in earlier expeditions. Further, Cortés's strategies of seeking interpreters and large populations with whom he could establish alliances, as well as founding Villa Rica de la Veracruz, by which he established a claim to independence from Diego Velázquez, were ones he must have observed among earlier expedition leaders, since they had all become part of standard Spanish practice in settling the Caribbean. None of the foregoing detracts from the skill and forcefulness of Cortés's leadership nor of the accomplishment of those who either set out with him or later joined the expedition, but it does show that his effort built upon established practice. Nonetheless, nothing in Cortés's previous experience of the New World could have fully prepared him for what he and the company of men he was able to raise were about to meet. The mainland on which they were soon to disembark had for many centuries, since before the Christian Era in fact, been home to civilizations that by the sixteenth century had developed high degrees of cultural sophistication and extraordinary material cultures, as the accounts of Díaz and others record.

In the one hundred years prior to the Spanish arrival on the Mexican mainland, the Mexica, a Nahuatl-speaking people who in the thirteenth century migrated from a mythic northwestern

---

3. Robert Himmerich y Valencia, *The* Encomenderos *of New Spain, 1521–1555* (Austin: University of Texas Press, 1996), 10.

home they referred to as Aztlán, had established a hegemony in central Mexico. Upon their initial arrival in the Central Valley of Mexico, they settled in less desirable parts of the valley, but by the end of the first quarter of the fourteenth century they had moved to marshy lands adjoining Lake Texcoco, on and around which other migrant peoples before them—the Otomi, Tarascan, and Totonacs, for example—had established themselves. The Mexica, of course, had their own origin myths, namely, that they had been brought or led to the Central Valley and Lake Texcoco by their particular deity—Huichilobos (Huitzilopochtli). The peoples established in the area, seeing the Mexica as interlopers, tended to disregard them but also used them as mercenaries in their struggles for supremacy, the Mexica thereby developed a strong warrior ethos. By the beginning of the fifteenth century, they had become one of the more important military powers in the region, and somewhat after mid-century, with strong leadership from Itzcoatl (d. 1440) and Moctezuma I (d. 1468)—two *tlatoani*, the chief ruler of the Mexica or Aztecs—the Mexica had become the Central Valley's dominant power, and they were able to collect tribute and gather resources all the way east to the gulf coast and its Totonac peoples, the Mixtecs in Oaxaca, as well as from nearer Nahuatl-speaking groups, namely the Tlaxcalans, the Cholulans, and the Huetzozincans.

By the time the Spaniards disembarked on the coast of Mexico, the Mexica, then, having allied as the principal power in Tenochtitlan with Texcoco and Tlacopan, were at the center of a thriving empire built on strong warrior and priestly classes, trade and communication routes throughout central Mexico, and an impressive material culture featuring cities with distinctive religious, administrative, and domestic structures, all of which Bernal Díaz notes in his narrative. Nonetheless, the hegemony the Mexica had established was fragile. In Tenochtitlan, members of the nobility from the constituent cities of the triple alliance were constantly maneuvering among themselves for ascendency. Beyond Tenochtitlan, tribute-paying states chafed under the cloak of their colonization, as one also reads in Díaz's account, although, as with his portrayals of Nahuatl material culture, one suspects he is able to observe only just beneath the surface. Despite the sophistication of the cultures of central Mexico and the obvious military power and skill with which the Mexica were able to deploy against the invading Spaniards, the maneuvering among the Tenochtitlan and Tlatelocan nobility and the resentments of peoples the Mexica had conquered and subjected to paying tribute and providing victims for sacrifice at religious festivals through, for example, flower wars, created fissures in the Mexica empire that would contribute significantly to its ultimate downfall.

The record indicates that Moctezuma became aware of the Spanish at the time of the Grijalva expedition and that he had its progress followed as it moved up the eastern coast of the mainland. He became alarmed when he learned of Cortés's even larger expedition, and it is clear he gathered increasingly detailed information about it. Cortés, meanwhile, upon disembarking at San Juan de Ulúa, set out not only to find a location suitable for establishing a settlement, but also to discover what substantial populations of native peoples might be located in the area. In fact, he did not so much come across them as they came to him, and he soon began to seek information about the dominant power in the region, the Aztecs, and to establish alliances with those peoples who had become subject and tribute payers to them. Because territorial and other divisions existed among the peoples native to Mexico, the Spaniards were able to assert themselves and establish alliances that would ultimately restructure the balance of power among the indigenous groups in central Mexico. During the course of the conquest, the Totonacs and, especially, the Tlaxcalans, who had been under pressure from the Aztecs for more than one hundred years, became allies without whom Cortés very likely could not have succeeded in overcoming the Aztecs and their central city, Tenochtitlan. That is, those native peoples, far from foreseeing the future destruction of their indigenous civilizations, based their decisions to form alliances with the Spaniards on their desire to overthrow Aztec dominance.

In conquering the Aztecs and other peoples native to Mexico, Cortés employed several strategies that had proven effective in the

Caribbean campaigns. Beyond establishing alliances with local populations, the most important of these was capturing and placing Moctezuma under house arrest, an event that, taken in itself, seems enormously audacious—as indeed it probably was, given the total set of circumstances—but which represents a tactic that had proven possible and effective in earlier Spanish conquests. Most importantly, the Spaniards, greatly outnumbered in general, enjoyed a substantial advantage with respect to the technology of arms: First, they had forged steel for their swords, shields, and armor, although the latter proved so burdensome that they soon adopted the native habit of wearing quilted cotton. Second, their horses served as sixteenth-century equivalents to tanks, giving them advantages in mobility on a relatively level and open battlefield, where they typically sought to engage the enemy. Third, the Spaniards had crossbows, *escopetas*—short matchlock scatter guns—and cannons that shot both steel balls and balls fashioned from stone. All three, with crossbows being the most accurate, gave the Spaniards an advantage at long range. For the native peoples, these were completely new weapons of war. Fourth, the Spaniards had the experience not only of prior conquests in the Caribbean but also of the wars against the Muslims; the men who journeyed to the Americas came from those parts of Spain where the majority of Spaniards who fought the Arabs and the Italians had lived. They were battle wise and battle hardened. Finally, they fought to kill and to subdue. Still, for all their advantages on open battlefields—witness the Battle of Otumba[4] in which the Spaniards with diminished forces, most of whom were wounded, routed the Aztecs—the Spaniards and their horses were vulnerable in closed spaces, either within the walls of a city or in mountain passes that did not afford ready escape routes and where indigenous warriors had the advantage of numbers, as the events of the *Noche Triste*[5] amply show.

By the time the Spaniards arrived on the Mexican mainland, the native populations had developed battle traditions that, in the

---

4. See Chapter 12 below.
5. See Chapter 11 below.

beginning at least, disadvantaged them in their engagements with the invaders. First, their weapons technology had not reached that of the Bronze Age, meaning that their armaments were produced using natural products—cotton, leather, wood, and various kinds of stones and obsidian—from which they crafted highly effective weaponry and armor. They had knives and spear-throwers, but their spears and darts had only fire-hardened tips, which, to be sure, could penetrate cotton and even leather armor, but not steel. Their battle clubs and swords had inset obsidian edges, which, although fragile, were devastatingly sharp, as Bernal Díaz notes in several places. The war clubs, or *macanas*, with their rows of inset obsidian blades on either side of the club, were capable of decapitating even a horse and of inflicting deep bleeding wounds. The native peoples fought in tightly organized groups led by warriors who had proven themselves in previous battles and who wore livery that made it easy to identify them, that is, feathered insignias attached to rods bound to the body and rising above the bearer's head. When those leaders were wounded, captured, or killed, the groups they led tended to become disorganized and ineffective as a fighting force. Further, as Ross Hassig points out, in battling one another the native peoples had developed a fundamental strategy of attacking in full force, hurling masses of spears, darts, and rocks from slings at the opponents to stun and disorganize them.[6] They followed this barrage with an assault to capture, not kill, the enemy, for, in the end, the objective of warfare on the Mexican mainland was first to reduce the enemy peoples to payers of tribute and, second, to secure men, women, and children for sacrifice at the major religious festivals—in the Aztec cosmology the return of human blood to the cosmos was essential to sustaining it. Although the Aztecs did not give up their fundamental strategy of seeking to capture Spaniards for sacrifice, particularly those they perceived to be their leaders, they saw quickly that this strategy tended to disadvantage them in their engagements. In fact, as Bernal Díaz's narrative proceeds, one

---

6. Ross Hassig, *Mexico and the Spanish Conquest*, 2nd ed. (Norman: University of Oklahoma Press, 2006), 30ff.

observes that the Aztecs adapted to the new battle conditions they faced. They learned to lure the Spaniards into mountain passes and narrow passageways or streets and throw rocks down on them. To the very end, they brought every human and natural resource at their disposal in their opposition to the Spaniards, even using captured Spanish swords, crossbows, and other weaponry, and one can only admire their courage and resoluteness in seeking to maintain their independence.

None of the foregoing mentions the impact of the new viral diseases the Spaniards brought to the Americas, particularly smallpox, which by the time Cortés and his followers began their second assault on Mexico had devastated native populations, making it increasingly difficult to form the large bodies of warriors that might more effectively have resisted the Spaniards. Smallpox first appeared in the Americas on Hispaniola in 1518, apparently having been carried there by unsuspecting immigrants from southwest Spain. By the end of that year, the disease had nearly wiped out the indigenous population of that island, a fact that indicates the virulence of the disease and the lack of resistance to it among New World peoples. Smallpox rapidly spread from Hispaniola to Cuba, where it first emerged in November 1519. From Cuba, the disease seems to have been spread by members of Pánfilo de Narváez's expedition, and it took hold first in Cozumel, where it decimated the native population, and then, in 1520, on the Mexican mainland, spreading rapidly through the Mayan population and then to Nahuatl-speaking territories, infecting the Tlaxcalans and the Mexica. Its ravaging of native populations did not stop there, for it spread south to indigenous populations of the coastal and Andean regions of Ecuador and Peru. Having been transmitted to the Americas, one can reasonably assert that it was a major contributing factor to the Spaniard's conquest of the great civilizations native to the Americas.[7]

---

7. See Hugh Thomas, *Conquest: Montezuma, Cortés, and the Fall of Old Mexico* (New York: Simon & Schuster, 1993), 340, 359–60, 443–46; and Matthew Restall, *Seven Myths of the Spanish Conquest* (Oxford, Oxford University Press, 2003), 140–41.

The goal of the Spaniards involved in the conquest, of course, was to establish a place for themselves in the newly subdued territories, using the native peoples to extract resources, primarily gold (and silver), that could be readily traded in Spain, the metropolis, for goods that would allow them to have the kind of lives they would have had in Spain. Some of the more successful conquistadors returned to Spain and set up rich households using the wealth they had gained in the Americas, but most remained in the territories they had conquered. Those who came with Cortés and those who later allied themselves with him were able to claim important rights when it came time to distribute captured lands, peoples, and goods. The leader of the company, in this instance Cortés, was the one to reward them, with the confirmation of the Spanish Crown to be sure, first in rough proportion to what each had invested in and otherwise contributed to the enterprise and, second, with respect to when they joined the conquest company. Those who were able to provide a boat, food, or other supplies for the expedition, perhaps particularly a horse, received the largest shares; a man and a horse, for instance, were held equivalent to at least two men.

One sees, as the Spanish advance across the Americas progressed, not only that successful strategies came to be repeated, but also that those undertaking the next stage of expeditions had, in fact, served the leaders of the preceding expeditions well. Certainly one sees such a dynamic between Diego Velázquez and Governor Ovando, and the dynamic repeated itself when Cortés, who was among Velázquez's most important captains, either threw over or subverted the latter's control and authority. Cortés established the town and town council of Villa Rica de la Veracruz and sent certain members of his company to Spain with presents for the Spanish Crown; he also charged them with pleading the priority of Cortés and his company before the Crown and its court, even as Velázquez was himself waiting to be confirmed as governor of Cuba with rights to explore the Yucatan and Mexico. That Cortés was successful in pressing his case before the Crown stems to a high degree from the great importance attached to being a "first conqueror." This position of seniority in the community carried a presumption that one could both claim the use of land and labor—note that all land was claimed in the name of the Crown and thus, strictly speaking, belonged to it—and also its distribution to those who contributed to its capture on behalf of the Spanish Crown. This fact helps one understand the alarm Velázquez showed when he came to suspect that Cortés intended to go off on his own, and the alarm that Cortés and the leaders and members of his company felt when they learned that Velázquez had sent Pánfilo de Narváez to capture and, if necessary, kill Cortés and his men. Narváez, along with Cortés, had been one of Velázquez's leading captains when Velázquez subdued Cuba. It also illuminates the anger the men in Cortés's company felt when Cortés seemed so willing to include as members of the company certain men in Narváez's company and latecomers who brought important supplies with them. Doing so threatened the potential rewards for the efforts of the original members of the company, that is, the original investors of their wealth and persons.

Each stage of the conquest brought its own further expansions. The captains of one stage became leaders of the next. The fall of Tenochtitlan having been accomplished, Cortés granted Pedro de Alvarado substantial encomienda rights to Guatemala, Gonzalo de Sandoval similar rights in Oaxaca, and Cristóbal de Olid such rights in Honduras, although Olid soon betrayed Cortés, at least as Cortés saw the matter, and Cortés had him captured and killed. Bernal Díaz accompanied Pedro de Alvarado to Guatemala and received encomienda rights there, rights that he and other first conquerors believed were to be held in perpetuity. As times and events would have it, however, the extension of those rights to his heirs came to be challenged; latecomers wanted to claim rights to the use of the land and Indian labor for themselves, and took their case to Spain. This challenge, Bernal Díaz's narrative reveals, becomes one motive for his taking pen in hand.

Bernal Díaz del Castillo

At the outset of the *True History,* Bernal Díaz del Castillo introduces and provides a provenance for himself and, then, in the course of his account, gives other details regarding his life and person, all of which cast his story and its motivations in a particular light. The reader can garner this self-disclosure for him- or herself. Clearly, Bernal Díaz led a rich, robust, and uncommonly long life for a man of his time, outliving the vast majority of those with whom he came to the Americas. Because he does tell us so much about himself in the course of his narrative, one can be brief in providing his biography, even though, having lived as long as he did after the fall of Mexico, a great deal further happened to him. Bernal Díaz del Castillo was born in Medina del Campo in 1492 to a family that was not wealthy, although his father held a position of some importance on the town council, suggesting that he did exercise some influence. Bernal Díaz left his home town and homeland in 1514 at age twenty-two to seek his fortune in the Americas. He came to the Americas with Pedrarias Dávila on the expedition to settle Tierra Firme, that is, the territory we now know as Panama. He became discouraged at this settlement attempt and soon decided to go to Cuba, where he spent a relatively impoverished three years before signing on as a member, first, of Francisco Hernández de Córdoba's expedition to the Yucatan and, second, of Juan de Grijalva's expedition. Surviving those two dangerous and unsuccessful expeditions, Bernal Díaz demonstrated his sheer will and desire to establish a place for himself by joining the company formed by Cortés; the *True History* is an account of this expedition and its aftermath. Following the fall of Mexico, Bernal Díaz joined Pedro de Alvarado's expedition to Guatemala, where he ultimately settled and established himself as a first conqueror with encomienda rights and land holdings, which, in turn, led to his serving as a prominent and respected member of the town council.

Bernal Díaz undertook writing the *True History* sometime during the 1550s, but these efforts were sporadic, and he did not complete the project until the late 1560s; even then he did not send a copy to Spain for publication until the 1570s. His *True History* falls into a genre of writing that had arisen and taken root on the Iberian Peninsula during the period when Europeans were fighting to reclaim the territory from the Muslim emirate. Leaders who had waged successful campaigns wrote to the Crown to give an account of their activities and lay claim to territories and their resources, as well as to seek rewards of status in the form of titles, offices, and sinecures. These documents, called *probanzas de merito*, originally took the form of relatively short letters, but as the form evolved it included letters (*cartas*), and *cartas de relación*, of which the best known are the ones Cortés directed to the Spanish Crown regarding his leadership in the conquest of Mexico. Although one can regard these documents as instances of special pleading on behalf of the author, they became the stuff from which histories could be created. Even a casual reading of Bernal Díaz's *True History* reveals that it has the character of a *probanza*, a demonstration of the author's participation in and contribution to the conquest of Mexico.[8] Thus, although Bernal Díaz might present his account as fact and as correcting the accounts of other authors, particularly Francisco López de Gómara, one must understand that he was laying claim to special consideration for his accomplishments. The work nonetheless provides us with a continuous and often compelling account of one of the world's most significant events. The text was not published until 1632 and then only in a form that fray Alonzo Remón had significantly altered. Not until the middle of the first decade of the twentieth century, when Mexican historian Genaro García discovered Díaz's original manuscript in Guatemala, did the world have an edition of the *True History of the Conquest of New Spain* that conformed to Bernal Díaz's intentions. That edition is the one on which the present translators have based this abridgement of Bernal Díaz's extraordinary account.

---

8. See Restall, *Seven Myths*, 11ff.

FIGURES PROMINENT IN BERNAL DÍAZ DEL CASTILLO'S *TRUE HISTORY*[1]

Aguilar, Jerónimo de (1489–1531) Spaniard who went to the colony of Santo Domingo la Antiguedad de Darien in 1510 but then, after a dispute arose among leaders of the colony, left with sixteen other people in 1511. They were shipwrecked and eventually captured or enslaved by the Maya. During his captive years he learned a Mayan dialect that allowed him initially to serve as intermediary interpreter between Marina and Cortés and Nahuatl speakers.

Alaminos, Antón de (1482–1520) The chief pilot of Cortés's fleet. He had served as a pilot on two of Columbus's voyages and on the two voyages and attempted *entradas* led by Francisco Hernández de Córdoba and Juan de Grijalva respectively to the Yucatan. He was generally knowledgeable regarding sailing conditions in the Caribbean.

Alvarado, Pedro de (1485–1541) One of the three captains who led companies of men during the final siege of Tenochtitlan. Cortés left him in charge of the men who remained in Tenochtitlan while Cortés went to subdue Narváez; Alvarado was responsible for the attack on the Aztecs during their Toxcatl celebration. After Cortés, the most prominent member of the company of men who came with Cortés. Pedro de Alvarado is generally credited with

---

1. The following is only a brief list of the figures who populate Bernal Díaz's narrative. In the instance of native figures, one finds the name Bernal Díaz uses most often in the text followed by the now more commonly used name. The quoted sentences describing the Spanish figures are from Bernal Díaz's text itself.

leading the conquest of Guatemala. A good horseman and talker, brave but rash.

Coadlavaca (Cuitlahuac) The ruler of Iztapalapa who succeeded Montezuma, his brother, as *tlatoani*, cacique, of Mexico. He died of smallpox within eighty days of being raised up to chief ruler.

Cortés, Hernando (1485–1547) Born in Medellín, Spain, he came to Hispaniola in 1504 and participated with Pánfilo Narváez under Diego Velázquez in settling that island and then Cuba. Ultimately rebelling against Diego Velázquez, he led the third expedition from Cuba to the Yucatan and Mexico, laying siege to and conquering Tenochtitlan in 1521, the height of his career. He spent the rest of his life defending his accomplishments and seeking preferment from the Spanish Crown.

Díaz del Castillo, Bernal (1495–1583) Came to Cuba in 1514 and claims to have been the only one of the conquistadors who participated in all three initial expeditions to the Yucatan and Mexican mainland. Not able initially to afford a horse, he fought afoot and wrote of his experiences in the conquest from that point of view.

Escalante, Juan de (n.d.) Close friend of and advisor to Cortés, to whom the latter gave the order to disable the ships on which the Cortés expedition came. Cortés named him captain general and justicia mayor of Villa Rica de la Veracruz, and he in turn warned Cortés at the arrival of Narváez and his fleet.

the fat cacique Cacique of the Totonac peoples, who were among the first allies of the Spaniards in their conquest of Mexico.

Gómara, Francisco López de (1511–1566) Secretary to and biographer of Cortés after the latter's return to Spain. Wrote *Historia de la conquista de México*, one of the works to which Díaz's *True History* is a reaction and response.

Guatemuz (Cuauhtemoc) Succeeded Coadlavaca (Cuitlahuac) as cacique of Tenochtitlan and led the resistance of the Aztecs during the siege undertaken by Cortés after returning from Tlaxcala.

Huichilobos (Huitzilopochtli) The patron god of the Aztec, the god of war whose name signifies either "the left-handed hummingbird" or "the humming bird from the south."

Lugo, Francisco de (d. 1548?) One of Cortés's captains, known for bravery. Saved Cortés from capture during the battle at San Juan de Ulúa and apprehended for execution the leader of a group who conspired to assassinate Cortés.

Marina (La Malinche; Malintzin) Nahuatl-speaking cacica enslaved by Mayan caciques who presented her to Cortés as a gift of friendship. With Jerónimo de Aguilar, she served as interpreter for Cortés, assuming that role almost exclusively over time. Marina knew Nahuatl and Yucatec Mayan and could communicate with Aguilar, who knew Yucatec Mayan and Spanish.

Maseescaci (Maxixcatzin) Tlaxcalan cacique, rough contemporary of Xicotenga the elder. Initially opposed the Spaniards on their first entry into Tlaxcalan territory but subsequently allied with them in their battle against the Aztecs.

Montezuma (Moctezuma/Motecuhzoma) The fifth *tlatoani*, cacique, of Tenochtitlan who ruled from 1502 to 1520. He reputedly was killed accidentally at the hands of his own people while a captive of Cortés and his men.

Narváez, Pánfilo de (1478–1528) Loyal to Diego Velázquez, whom he helped conquer Cuba, Narváez led a large expedition to Mexico to stop Cortés and those with him from claiming and establishing themselves on the Mexican mainland. Cortés defeated his party and convinced many of its members to join his effort to conquer Mexico. Narváez led a later expedition, which met with disaster, to Florida.

Olid, Cristóbal de (1488–1524) One of Cortés's three captains who led a group of men during the final siege of Tenochtitlan. After the fall of Tenochtitlan, he "died in Naco, beheaded [at Cortés's command] because he revolted with a fleet that Cortés had given him." (CCV)

Ordaz, Diego de (1480–1532) Majordomo to Diego Velázquez, who charged him with keeping track of Cortés to make sure he did not rebel against and steal from Velázquez. "He was about forty when he came to [New Spain]; he was captain of soldiers with sword and shield because he was no horseman, a brave man of good counsel." (CCVI)

Sandoval, Gonzalo de (1498–1529) One of the three captains who led a group of men during the final siege of Tenochtitlan. Loyal to Cortés, he was "a very brave captain of about twenty-four years when he came here to [New Spain].... He had the best horse, the best galloper and the most easily turned from one side to the other." (CVI)

Tezcatapuca (Tezcatlipoca) A central Aztecan deity associated with the night sky, night winds, the north, the earth, and obsidian. His Nahuatl name is often translated "smoking mirror." Bernal Díaz consistently refers to this Aztec god in conjunction with Huichilobos, referring to it as the "god of the inferno," imposing his own Christian perspective on it.

Velázquez, Diego (1465–1529) Came to Hispaniola with Columbus on his second voyage in 1493, conquered Cuba, and subsequently became governor. He was responsible for initiating the voyages to the Yucatan and the Mexican mainland of Francisco Hernández de Córdoba, Juan de Grijalva, Hernando Cortés, and Pánfilo de Narváez.

Xicotenga the elder (Xicotencatl; don Lorenzo de Vargas) Cacique of the Tlaxcalans, traditional enemies of the Aztecs, allied with the Spaniards in the conqest of Mexico.

Xicotenga the younger (Xicotencatl the younger) Son of Xicotenga the elder, opposed Cortés and led the Tlaxcalans against the Spaniards when they initially entered Tlaxcalan territory. Later, at the siege of Tenochtitlan, he was executed at Cortés's orders.

TIMELINE FOR THE CONQUEST OF MEXICO

1492	Columbus makes landfall and sets foot on an island, probably Hispaniola, now called Santo Domingo.
1502	Moctezuma II becomes *tlatoani*, or ruler, of Tenochtitlan and its vast empire in Mexico.
1511–1514	Spaniards enter Cuba and establish themselves on the island.
1517	Francisco Hernández de Córdoba leads the first Spanish expedition to explore Mexico; Aztecs reported to have observed omens of change and disruption to their world.
1518	Juan de Grijalva explores the Yucatan but suffers defeat in an encounter with its peoples and eventually returns to Cuba.
Late 1518	Smallpox emerges on Hispaniola and rapidly spreads through the native population and to other Caribbean islands and Cuba.
Late 1518	Diego Velázquez, governor of Cuba, selects Hernando Cortés to lead the third expedition to explore Mexico.
February 10, 1519	Defying Governor Velázquez's orders withdrawing Cortés's leadership of the third expedition, Cortés leaves Cuba to explore and settle Mexico.
June 3, 1519	Under Cortés's leadership, the Spaniards arrive at Cempoala and establish an alliance with the Cempoalans.

June 28, 1519	Villa Rica de la Veracruz is founded as a municipality.
September 2–20, 1519	The Spaniards encounter and fight the Tlaxcalans but end by establishing an alliance with them.
October 1519	The Spaniards enter Cholula and on reports that the Cholulans intend to trap and kill them, carry out a countermassacre of the Cholulans.
November 8, 1519	The Spaniards arrive at and enter Tenochtitlan.
November 14, 1519	Cortés puts Moctezuma under house arrest.
Early 1520	Smallpox is brought to Mexico by a member of Pánfilo de Narváez's company.
May 1520	Cortés leaves Tenochtitlan to fight men sent by Diego Velázquez under the leadership of Pánfilo de Narváez.
May 1520	Pedro de Alvarado and the Spaniards remaining in Tenochtitlan carry out an attack on the celebrants at the Toxcatl festival.
June 24, 1520	Cortés returns to Tenochtitlan with his men and reinforcements from men who came with Narváez.
June 1520	Cuitlahuac becomes *tlatoani*, or ruler, of Tenochtitlan.
June 1520	Moctezuma is struck by hurled rocks while speaking to his people and soon dies.
June 30, 1520	*La noche triste*, the Night of Sorrows; the Spaniards suffer heavy losses of men and treasure fleeing Tenochtitlan.
July 1520	After staving off numerous attacks and fighting the Battle of Otumba on July 14, the Spaniards reach and are welcomed in Tlaxcala.
October 1520	Smallpox ravages Tenochtitlan.
December 1520	Cuitlahuac dies from smallpox.

February 1521	Cuauhtemoc becomes *tlatoani*, or ruler, of Tenochtitlan.
May 1521	The Spaniards lay siege to Tenochtitlan.
May 1521	The Spaniards cut off water to Tenochtitlan.
June 1521	The Spaniards attempt to enter Tenochtitlan.
July 1521	The Spaniards decide to destroy Tenochtitlan.
August 7, 1521	Pedro de Alvarado and his men suffer heavy losses trying to take the marketplace of Tlatelolco.
August 13, 1521	Cuauhtemoc is captured, ending the battle for Tenochtitlan.

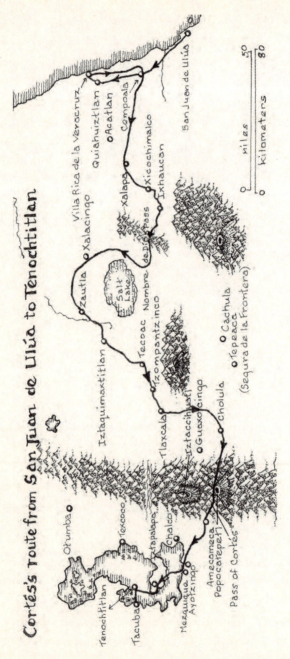

Cortés's route from San Juan de Ulua to Tenochtitlan.

SOURCES AND FURTHER READING

The Spanish conquest of Mexico is one of the most discussed of all topics regarding the encounter between Europeans and the peoples of the Americas; consequently, the bibliography of available materials is enormous. What follows is a brief list of materials that can provide the interested reader with a baseline of information regarding the conquest and many of its major figures, as well as guidance to further study.

Berdan, Frances F. *The Aztecs of Central Mexico: An Imperial Society,* 2nd ed. Belmont, CA: Thompson Wadsworth, 2005.

Clendinnen, Inga. *Ambivalent Conquests: Maya and Spaniard in Yucatan, 1517–1570.* Cambridge: Cambridge University Press, 1988.

———. *Aztecs: An Interpretation.* Cambridge: Cambridge University Press, 1991.

de Fuentes, Patricia, ed. and trans. *The Conquistadors: First-Person Accounts of the Conquest of Mexico.* New York: Orion Press, 1963.

Díaz del Castillo, Bernal. *Historia verdadera de la conquista de la Nueva España (Manuscrito Guatemala).* Edición crítica de José Antonio Barbón Rodríguez. México City: El Colegio de México, 2006.

———. *Historia verdadera de la conquista de la Nueva España,* 20th ed. Edited by Joaquin Ramirez Cabañas. Mexico City: Editorial Porrúa, 2002.

———. *The Conquest of New Spain,* 5 vols. Translated by Alfred Percival Maudslay, M.A. Liechtenstein: Kraus Reprint Limited, 1967.

Cortés, Hernando. *Cartas de relación*. Edited by Ángel Delgado Gómez. Madrid: Editorial Castalia, 1993.

———. *Letters from Mexico.* Translated and edited by Anthony Pagden. New Haven: Yale University Press, 1986.

Elliott, J. H. *Empires of the Atlantic World: Britain and Spain in America 1492–1830.* New Haven: Yale University Press, 2006.

Fernández de Oviedo, Gozalo. *Writing from the Edge of the World: The Memoirs of Darién, 1514–1527.* Translated by G. F. Dille. Tuscaloosa: University of Alabama Press, 2006.

Hassig, Ross. *Mexico and the Spanish Conquest*, 2nd ed. Norman: University of Oklahoma Press, 2006.

Himmerich y Valencia, Robert. *The* Encomenderos *of New Spain, 1521–1555.* Austin: University of Texas Press, 1996.

Léon-Portilla, Miguel, ed. *The Broken Spears: The Aztec Account of the Conquest of Mexico*, rev. edition. Boston: Beacon Press, 2007.

———, ed. and trans. *We People Here: Nahuatl Accounts of the Conquest of Mexico.* Eugene, OR: Wipf & Stock, 2004.

Lockhart, James, and Stuart B. Schwartz. *Early Latin America: A History of Colonial Latin America and Brazil*, Cambridge Latin American Studies no. 4, Cambridge and New York: Cambridge University Press, 1983–1999.

López de Gómara, Francisco. *Historia de la conquista de México*, 3rd ed. Edited by Juan Miralles Ostos. México City: Editorial Porrúa, 1997.

———. *Cortés: The Life of the Conqueror by His Secretary.* Translated and edited by Lesley Byrd Simpson. Berkeley: University of California Press, 1966.

Prescott, William H. *History of the Conquest of Mexico and History of the Conquest of Peru.* New York: Modern Library, n.d.

Restall, Matthew. *Seven Myths of the Spanish Conquest.* Oxford: Oxford University Press, 2003.

Restall, Matthew, and Florine Asselbergs. *Invading Guatemala: Spanish, Nahua, and Maya Accounts of the Conquest Wars*. University Park: University of Pennsylvania Press, 2007.

Thomas, Hugh. *Conquest: Montezuma, Cortés, and the Fall of Old Mexico*. New York: Simon & Schuster, 2005.

Townsend, Camilla. *Malintzin's Choices: An Indian Woman in the Conquest of Mexico*. Albuquerque: University of New Mexico Press, 2006.

Bernal Díaz del Castillo

The Essential Díaz

Selections from *The True History of
the Conquest of New Spain*

Chapter 1

Bernal Díaz del Castillo, an Introduction

[I] I am Bernal Díaz del Castillo, citizen and member of the town council of the most loyal city of Santiago de Guatemala, one of the first discoverers and conquerors of New Spain and its provinces and the Cape of Honduras and Higueras—as it is called in this land—a native of the most noble and distinguished town of Medina del Campo, son of Francisco Díaz del Castillo, former member of that town's council, who was also called the Gallant, and María Díez Rejón, his lawful wife—may they have blessed glory. I write about what concerns me and all the true conquerors, my companions, who have served His Majesty in discovering, conquering, pacifying, and settling all the provinces of New Spain, one of the best parts of the New World, which we discovered at our expense without His Majesty knowing anything about it. I am also speaking here in response to what some people have said and written, people who had no knowledge of it, nor saw it, nor had real information about what they have put forward on this matter except to speak of what is to their taste, in order to obscure, if they can, our many and remarkable services, so they might not be renowned or held in the high esteem they deserve. And as human malice is of such a nature, those evil slanderers do not even want us to be given the preference and recompense His Majesty has ordered his viceroys, presidents, and governors to give. Leaving these arguments aside, I am writing so that such heroic things as I will talk about will not be forgotten, or even more, so that they will not be reduced to nothing; so that the truth of these things might clearly be known; so that the books now written on this subject will be rejected and shown to be nothing because they pervert and obscure the truth; and so that there might be notable fame for our conquests, for it is only just that such illustrious feats as ours be placed, in the histories of heroic deeds, among the

1

most famous in the world. For we have ventured our lives and run excessive risks of death and wounds and countless miseries, both by sea discovering lands that were completely unknown and from battling day and night with a multitude of aggressive warriors, so far from Castile[1] without help or aid of any kind save the great mercy of Our Lord God, who is the true help, whom it has pleased that we conquer New Spain and the very famous and great city of Tenochtitlan, Mexico—for thus it is named—and so many other cities and provinces that I will not mention their names here. After we had pacified the lands and settled them with Spaniards, as good and loyal vassals and servants we sent to give and deliver those lands with much respect to our king and natural lord through our ambassadors to Castile, and from there to Flanders where His Majesty was at that time with his court. Then, as I will tell further on, many good results have come from it, including the conversion of a huge number of souls that have been saved and are being saved every day, earlier lost to hell. Besides this holy work, I will call attention to the great riches we sent from these parts as gifts, which have gone and go daily to His Majesty as royal fifths[2] as well as what was taken by many other people of all conditions. I say that I shall tell in this account who was the first discoverer of the province of Yucatan and how we went about discovering New Spain, who were the captains and soldiers who conquered and settled it, and many other things we experienced during such conquests, which are worthy of being known and of not being forgotten, all of which I will tell as briefly as I can and, above all, with very certain truth, as an eyewitness.

---

1. Castile was the largest of the four Spanish kingdoms of the fifteenth and sixteenth centuries, occupying the central portion of present-day Spain with access to oceans or seas on three sides.

2. The royal fifth, or *quinto,* was a tax levied by the Spanish Crown initially on mined gold but eventually on most goods extracted, captured, or produced in the Americas. This form of taxation originated in the Caribbean and then extended into the rest of the territories that came under Spanish domination.

Bernal Díaz continues, stating that he participated in two previous voyages staged from Cuba at the behest of its governor, Diego Velázquez, to determine precisely what lay to the west. Francisco Hernández de Córdoba, a wealthy Cuban encomendero,[3] led the voyage. Departing February 8, 1517, from Santiago de Cuba, this expedition had its first hostile engagement with mainland peoples at Cape Catoche, lured into an ambush by a seemingly friendly cacique.[4] The Spanish party quickly defeated the attackers, taking two prisoners, who, upon being baptized, were named Julián and Melchorejo. Continuing to sail west for two weeks, the party cautiously disembarked at Campeche to replenish its drinking water. While there, Bernal Díaz states, the Spaniards heard the Indians calling out, "Castilan, Castilan," but they did not understand the meaning of the word Castilan. *Forced again to stop for water in Chanpoton, the Spaniards found themselves surrounded, vastly outnumbered, and under attack. In an hour-long battle, they saw "two of their soldiers carried off alive, their captain with ten arrow wounds, almost all the rest of the men with two or three arrow wounds, and more than fifty dead." The survivors barely escaped with their lives. With this encounter, the Córdoba expedition was effectively at an end and made its way back to Cuba by way of Florida.*

Having been told and believing that the mainland overflowed with great riches, Diego Velázquez immediately began to organize another expedition, which departed from Santiago de Cuba on April 8, 1518, with Juan de Grijalva as captain general. Although the Spaniards met resistance that left "seven soldiers dead, Juan de Grijalva with three arrow wounds and two broken teeth, and seventy of us wounded," the Indians nonetheless fled.

---

3. An *encomendero* held rights to the labor of an allotment of Indians living within a given area; an *encomienda* consisted of the rights to such labor, normally granted by the individual who led the taking of the land and its population.

4. Cacique is a Caribbean term for a chief or leader.

*Working westward, with the aid of Julián and Melchorejo, now
serving as interpreters, Grijalva and his men carried on trade.
The expedition continued northward exploring the coast, and
then returned to Cuba. In the meantime, Diego Velázquez,
fearing that something had befallen the Grijalva expedition, had
sent a party in search of it and also began to organize the next
expedition, of which Hernando Cortés was to be named captain
general.*

I came the third time with the successful and courageous captain don Hernando Cortés. I say that no captain or soldier went
to New Spain three times in succession, one after another, as I did.
Therefore, I am the most senior discoverer and conqueror who has
been or is in New Spain.

I was at that time about twenty-four years old, and the governor of the island of Cuba, my relative Diego Velázquez, promised me he would give me Indians from among the first that
became available, but I did not want to wait until he gave them
to me. I always had zeal for being a good soldier, both to serve
God and our king and lord and to try to win honor, as noble
men should do in life, and to go from good to better. I put out of
my mind the death of the companions they killed in those times
as well as the wounds they gave me and the fatigues and hardships I experienced, which those who go to discover new lands
experience as we put ourselves at risk, being so few companions
entering such great towns filled with a multitude of aggressive
warriors. From the year 1514 when I came from Castile and
began to serve as a soldier in the army of Tierra Firme[5] and to
discover the Yucatan and New Spain, I was always in front and I

---

5. Tierra Firme, sometimes called the "Spanish Main," literally means
"mainland" and referred to a long stretch of the Caribbean coast of what
we now call South and Central America, but centered on Panama and
extended across the Caribbean Sea from Hispaniola south to Cape Vela
in present-day Venezuela and west roughly to what is the border between
present-day Honduras and Nicaragua. These boundaries delineated
rights to exploration and exploitation granted by the Spanish Crown.

did not fall into the many vices there were on the island of Cuba. As my ancestors and my father and brother were always servants of the Royal Crown and the Catholic kings, don Fernando and doña Isabel of most glorious memory, I wanted to be a little like them.

[XVIII] While writing this, my chronicle, I happened to see what Gómara, Illescas, and Jovio wrote about the conquest of Mexico and New Spain.[6] When I read their words and considered how polished they were and how crude and unrefined mine, I stopped writing my chronicle because such good histories were available. With this in mind, I began to read and look very closely at the conversations and arguments in their histories, but neither in the beginning nor the middle nor the end do they talk about what really happened in New Spain. In general, what they write is completely faulty. And why am I so involved in writing, in telling each thing as it actually happened, which wastes paper and ink? I am cursing what they wrote because they had such good style. I decided to proceed with my account because the true polish and grace of composition is to tell the truth. Contemplating this, I decided to go ahead with my attempt, using the order and conversations you will see, so that it might be published and the conquests of New Spain will appear clearly, as they should. With pen in hand, I want to return like the good pilot sounding the depths, revealing shoals in the sea ahead when he senses they are there.

------

6. Bernal Díaz refers here to Francisco López de Gómara's *Historia de la conquista de México*, 1552, Gonzalo de Illescas's *Historia pontifical y catolica*, 1554, and Paolo Jovio's *Elogios or vidas breves de los cavalleros antiguos y modernos*, 1568.

Chapter 2

The Captain, Hernando Cortés

[XIX] When the captain Juan de Grijalva returned to Cuba, Governor Diego Velázquez began to understand how rich the lands were; so he ordered a substantial fleet to be sent, much larger than earlier ones, and he already had ten ships ready in the port of Santiago de Cuba where he lived. Four of those ships were ones in which we had returned with Juan de Grijalva, which he immediately had careened,[7] and the other six they gathered from throughout the island. He had them provisioned with cassava bread and salt pork, because at that time there were neither cattle nor sheep on the island of Cuba, as it had been recently settled. These supplies were sufficient only to get to Havana[8] where we had to secure all the provisions, which we did.

Two great favorites of Diego Velázquez, Andrés de Duero, secretary to the governor himself, and Amador de Lares, accountant to His Majesty, kept secret company with a gentleman named Hernando Cortés, native of Medellín, who had Indians in encomienda on that island, and who a short while before had married a woman named doña Catalina Suárez, the Marcaida. These favorites of Diego Velázquez agreed that they would have Velázquez give the captaincy general of the entire fleet to Hernando Cortés, and among the three of them they would divide the profits from Cortés's share of the gold, silver, and jewels because, secretly, Diego Velázquez was sending the fleet not to settle, as he had announced and proclaimed, but to trade, as became clear from the instructions he later gave for the trip. This agreement made,

---

7. Careening a ship involves grounding and tipping it on its sides to scrape it clean of accumulated moss, sea grasses, and barnacles and then caulking it.

8. The Havana to which Bernal Díaz refers is not modern-day Havana, which is on the northern coast of Cuba, but to an earlier site on the south coast of the island and a bit to the east.

Duero and the accountant used all means possible on Diego Velázquez. They spoke fine and honeyed words to him, greatly praising Cortés, saying he was the one who should be given the post of captain because, besides being courageous, he would know how to command and be feared and he would be very faithful in everything entrusted to him in matters of the fleet and everything else. Besides this, they said Cortés was Velázquez's godson because Velázquez was Cortés's sponsor when Cortés married doña Catalina Suarez.[9] In this way they persuaded Velázquez, who then chose Cortés as captain general, and the secretary Andrés Duero wrote up the orders skillfully, or, as the saying goes, in very good ink, giving Cortés plenty of power, as he wanted. When his selection was made public, some people were delighted and others disappointed.

Truly, Hernando Cortés was chosen to glorify our holy faith and serve His Majesty, as I will discuss later. Before going ahead, I want to talk about how the valiant and courageous Hernando Cortés was a nobleman distinguished by four noble lineages: the first, the Corteses, and so his father was named Martín Cortés; the second, through the Pizarros; the third, through the Monroys; the fourth, through the Altamiranos. As he was such a valiant, courageous, and successful captain, from here on I will not use any of these titles like "valiant," or "courageous" nor "Marquess del Valle," but only Hernando Cortés, because the very name Cortés was held in as much esteem in all the Indies and in Spain as was the name of Alexander in Macedonia and, among the Romans, Julius Caesar, Pompey, and Scipio and, among the Carthaginians, Hannibal, and in our Castile, Gonzalo Hernández,[10] the great captain. The valiant Cortés himself was happy that they

---

9. Normally, the person choosing the leader of an expedition and that leader in turn based their selections on familial relations, even extended ones, or on some other bond of association, for example having come from a particular region of Spain.

10. Spanish general instrumental in the siege and conquest of Granada; he also fought in the Italian wars between 1498 and 1511.

were not giving him those exalted titles, but only his name, and so I will call him from now on.

[XX] Well, since Hernando Cortés had now been chosen commander, he began to look for all kinds of weapons, such as *escopetas*,[11] gunpowder, and crossbows, and as much provisioning for arms as he could obtain, and he looked for barter items and other things necessary for the journey. He also began to refine and dress up his person much more than before, putting on his plumed helmet with his medal, a chain of gold, and a cloak of velvet set with some golden bowknots, that is, as a fierce and courageous captain. Of course, he had nothing to meet these expenses, because at that time he was very much in debt and poor, even though he had good Indians in encomienda and extracted gold from the mines. But he spent everything on his person and on finery for his wife, whom he had recently married, and on some guests from another place. People gathered round him because he was even-tempered and a man of good conversation, and twice he had been *alcalde*[12] in the town of San Juan de Baracoa, where he lived; in these lands, alcaldes are held in great esteem. Some merchant friends of his, Jaime Tría, Jerónimo Tría, and Pedro de Jerez, learned of his post as captain general, so they lent him four thousand pesos of gold and gave him credit for another four thousand in goods against his Indians, property, and pledges. He ordered two standards and flags to be made, the royal arms and a cross worked in gold on each side, with an inscription that said, "Brothers and Companions, let us follow the Sign of the Holy Cross, with True Faith, that with it We Might be Victorious." He ordered proclamations made and trumpets and drums sounded in the name of His Majesty and, in the king's royal name, Diego Velázquez, and in his own name as their captain general, to the effect that

---

11. An *escopeta* is a matchlock, smoothbore, muzzle-loading handgun that shot pellets; a very early predecessor to what became the shotgun.
12. The *alcalde* is both a municipal judge and a member of the municipal council.

anyone who wanted to go in his company to the newly discovered lands to conquer and settle them would receive shares of whatever gold, silver, and riches might be found, and, after they were pacified, encomiendas of Indians. For this Diego Velázquez had authority from His Majesty. Although this statement about authority from the king our lord was proclaimed, the chaplain Benito Martín, whom Diego Velázquez had sent to get it, had not yet returned from Castile with it.

Well, as this news became known throughout the island of Cuba, and Cortés also wrote to his friends in all the towns that they should join him on this voyage, some sold their property to get arms and horses, others made cassava bread and salt pork for the provisions and quilted cotton armor, and they provided themselves with what they needed as best they could. So we, more than three hundred fifty soldiers, gathered in Santiago de Cuba, where we left with the fleet. From the house of Diego Velázquez himself came his chief steward, Diego de Ordaz, sent by Velázquez to keep an eye on and busy himself with the fleet in case Cortés should plot against him, because Diego Velázquez was always afraid that Cortés would rebel, although he did not let him know that. A Francisco de Morla came, and an Escobar, whom we called "the Page," and an Heredia, Juan Ruano, Pedro Escudero, Martín Ramos de Lares, and many others who were friends and retainers of Diego Velázquez. Finally, I want to say here that I, too, came from the house of Diego Velázquez, because he was my kinsman.

Cortés was very attentive in readying the fleet, and he moved most quickly in everything, because malice and jealousy reigned among Velázquez's kinsmen. They were insulted that he neither trusted nor listened to them and that he gave the post of captain to Cortés because of Cortés's marriage, even though he had been Cortés's great enemy only a few days before. So they went around grumbling about their relative Diego Velázquez and even about Cortés, and in every way they could they tried to set Velázquez against Cortés so that Velázquez would revoke the power Cortés had been given to head the expedition. Cortés had been warned, so he was constantly in the governor's company, showing himself to be the governor's great servant and continually telling the governor that he would make him, God willing, a very illustrious lord, and rich, in a short time. In addition to this, Andrés de Duero kept warning Cortés that he should quickly embark himself and his soldiers because Diego Velázquez's relatives were changing Velázquez's mind with their pestering and persistent begging. Once Cortés understood that, he ordered his wife to send immediately, for loading on the ships, everything he needed by way of provisions and any gifts that women usually make their husbands for such a long voyage. He had already ordered a proclamation alerting the shipmasters, pilots, and all the soldiers that they were going to embark that night and that no one should stay ashore. When he saw that they were embarked, he went to take his leave of Diego Velázquez, accompanied by those great friends of his, many other gentlemen, and all the most noble citizens of that town. After many promises and embraces from Cortés to the governor and from the governor to him, Cortés took his leave. Early the next day, having heard mass, we went to the ships, and Diego Velázquez himself went with us. Again they embraced with an exchange of courtesies. We set sail, and with favorable weather we arrived at the port of Trinidad. As we went ashore, all the inhabitants of that town came out to receive us and entertained us kindly.

In Trinidad Cortés recruited additional men and ordered the purchase of arms and provisions. He also attracted individuals from the town of Santispíritus. In the meantime, Diego Velázquez had changed his mind regarding Cortés because of arguments his relatives had made and sent word to his brother-in-law, the alcalde mayor *of Trinidad, not to let the fleet pass and to take Cortés prisoner. Cortés convinced the relatives of Diego Velázquez to ignore Velázquez and to come into his, Cortés's, service. Then he left for Havana and made final preparations for the voyage. On the tenth day of February 1519, the fleet proceeded to the island of Cozumel.*

[XXVI] After three days in Cozumel, Cortés ordered us to muster so he would know how many soldiers there were. By his count, we had five hundred eight, not counting the sea captains, pilots, and sailors, who were about one hundred; sixteen horses and mares, all fit for jousting and charging; eleven large and small ships with one, like a brigantine,[13] that Ginés Nortes brought loaded; thirty-two crossbowmen and thirteen *escopeteros*; ten brass cannons, four falconets,[14] and a great deal of gunpowder and balls. I do not remember the number of crossbowmen very well, but that is not relevant to the story. After the muster, he ordered Mesa, the artilleryman, Bartolomé de Usagre, Arbenga, and a Catalan, all artillerymen, to keep the guns clean and in good repair and the cannons, balls and gunpowder ready for use. As captain of the artillery he put Francisco de Orozco, who had been a soldier in Italy. Also, he ordered two crossbowmen, Juan Benítez and Pedro de Guzmán, experts at preparing crossbows, to see that all the crossbows had two or three bow nuts and as many strings and forestrings, always taking care to store them, to have planes and spoke shaves, and to practice shooting at targets.[15] He also ordered that the horses be very much at the ready. I do not now know why I waste so much ink on recording the preparation of arms and all the rest, because Cortés truly took great care in everything.

---

13. A *brigantine* was a light, normally seagoing vessel equipped both for sailing and rowing, associated with Mediterranean cultures.

14. The *falconet* was a light cannon, normally on wheels, that shot round balls of approximately one pound.

15. The crossbow nut is the trigger mechanism on which the drawn string of the spanned crossbow is caught in preparation for loosing the bolt, that is, the projectile shot by the crossbow. The notches on nuts wore down with use and the strings either frayed or broke, requiring replacement.

Chapter 3

Jerónimo de Aguilar, the Lost Spaniard

[XXVII] As Cortés was careful in everything, he sent for Martín Ramos, a Biscayan, and me and asked us what we thought about the "Castilan, Castilan" that the Indians of Campeche had said to us when we came with Francisco Hernández de Córdoba. We described what we had seen and heard. Cortés said that he had thought many times about it and wondered if, by chance, some Spaniards were in that land. He said, "It seems to me we should ask those caciques of Cozumel if they have any news of them." Through Melchorejo from Cape Catoche, who now understood a little bit of the Castilian language and knew that of Cozumel very well, Cortés asked all the chieftains, and all of them said that they knew of certain Spaniards, and they described them; that they were in the interior, a two suns' walk; that some caciques were holding them as slaves; and that in Cozumel some Indian merchants had spoken with them a few days previously. All of us rejoiced at that news. Cortés told them to go immediately to the Spaniards with letters, which they call *amales* in their language. He gave shirts to the caciques and the Indians who were going with the letters, and he spoke affectionately to them and told them that when they returned he would give them more beads. The caciques told Cortés he should send ransom for the masters holding the Spaniards as slaves so they would let them come. Thus it was done, and the messengers were given all types of beads. Then he ordered two of the smaller ships—one of which was little larger than a brigantine—to be prepared with twenty crossbowmen and escopeteros, and he appointed Diego de Ordaz captain. He ordered the larger ship to stay off the coast of Cape Catoche for a week, and in the meantime they would go and return with the response to the letters, and the small ship would come back to give the response to Cortés about what they were doing, for

Cape Catoche is about four leagues[16] away and visible from Cozumel. In the letter, Cortés wrote, "Gentlemen and Brothers: I've learned here, in Cozumel, that you are in the power of a cacique, in custody, and I beg you, as a service, to come immediately here to Cozumel, and for this I'm sending a ship with soldiers, in case you have need of them, and ransom to give to those Indians you are staying with. The ship will wait a week for you. Come with all speed. You'll be well looked after by me and rewarded. I'm staying on this island with five hundred soldiers and eleven ships. God willing, I'm going in with them to a town called Tabasco or Potonchan."

They embarked in the ships with the letters and the two Indian merchants from Cozumel who carried them, and in three hours they crossed the small strait and dropped off the messengers. In two days the messengers gave the letters and ransom to a Spaniard whose name we learned at that time was Jerónimo de Aguilar, which I will call him from now on. When he had read the letters and received the ransom of beads, he was delighted and took it to his master, the cacique, so that he would give him permission to leave, which the cacique did, and Aguilar was able to go where he wanted. He walked to another town five leagues from there, where his companion Gonzalo Guerrero was, and as he read him the letters, Gonzalo Guerrero replied, "Brother Aguilar, I'm married, I have three children and here they regard me as a cacique when there are wars. Go with God, for I've tattooed my face and pierced my ears. What would those Spaniards say of me should they see me like this! See how attractive these children of mine are. Upon your life, let me have some of those green beads to give to them, and I'll say that my brothers sent them from my land." Then Gonzalo's Indian wife spoke with Aguilar very angrily in her language, saying, "Look how this slave comes to summon my husband.

---

16. A *league* is a measure of distance equivalent to the distance a person, or a horse, can walk in an hour's time, usually taken as equivalent to three and one-half English miles or five and one-half kilometers.

Go away and do not discuss this any further." Aguilar spoke again to Gonzalo, reminding him that he was Christian, that he should not lose his soul for an Indian woman, and if he was doing this for his wife and children, then he should bring them with him if he did not want to leave them. No matter what Aguilar said or how he admonished him, Guerrero would not come. It seems that Gonzalo Guerrero was a seaman, a native of Palos. When Jerónimo de Aguilar saw that Gonzalo Guerrero was not going to come, he went right away with the two Indian messengers to where the ship had been waiting for them, but when he got there, the ship had already left because the week the ship was to wait, and even one more day, had already passed. Because Aguilar had not come, Ordaz returned to Cozumel without bringing any news. When Aguilar saw that the ship was not there, he was very sad and returned to his master, to the town where he had been living.

Although Cortés was very angry with Ordaz for having left without having found the Spaniards or having news of them, he nonetheless set sail with the fleet for the Yucatan. The ship carrying all the cassava foundered, however, and had to return to Cozumel after having its cargo of foodstuffs taken off. The entire fleet returned with it, and Cortés and his men spent four days on that island repairing and reloading the ship.

[XXIX] When the Spaniard held by the Indians knew for certain we had returned to Cozumel with the ships, he rejoiced greatly, gave thanks to God, and very quickly embarked in a canoe with the two Indians who had brought him the letters and ransom. Because he paid well for the canoe with the green ransom beads we had sent him, he quickly found one and hired it with six Indian oarsmen. They rowed with such speed that they crossed the gulf between the two shores, some four leagues, in a short while, without running into strong sea winds. When they arrived on the coast of Cozumel and were still disembarking, some soldiers hunting the native pigs on that island told Cortés that a large canoe had come there, near the town, from Cape Catoche. Cortés ordered Andrés de Tapia and two other soldiers to go to see, for it was something new for Indians to come close to us in large canoes with no fear whatsoever. And they went immediately. As soon as the Indians who came in the canoe that carried Aguilar saw the Spaniards, they were fearful and wanted to re-embark and put out to sea. But Aguilar said to them in their language that they should not be afraid, that these were his brothers. Andrés de Tapia, when he saw they were Indians—because Aguilar looked like an Indian, no more no less—immediately sent a Spaniard to tell Cortés that seven Indians from Cozumel had arrived in a canoe. After they had come ashore, the Spaniard, mumbling badly and pronouncing poorly, said, "God and Saint Mary and Seville." Tapia went immediately to embrace him, and another of the soldiers went with great haste to ask Cortés for a reward for the good news about how the person who had come in the canoe was a Spaniard, and we all rejoiced to hear that. Then Tapia came with the Spaniard to where Cortés was, and before they arrived, some soldiers asked Tapia, "What has come of the Spaniard?" Even though the Spaniard was walking next to him, they mistook him for an Indian because he was dark anyway, and his hair was clipped like an Indian slave, he carried an oar over his shoulder, wearing one old native sandal, the other tied to his belt, a wretched old indigenous cloak, and a loincloth in worse shape with which he covered his private parts, and, tied up in the cloak was a bulky object that was a very old Book of Hours. Seeing them like that, Cortés was puzzled like the rest of the soldiers and asked Tapia what had come of the Spaniard, and when the Spaniard understood Cortés, he squatted down like the Indians do and said, "I am the Spaniard." Cortés immediately ordered that he be given things to wear, shirt and doublet, Valencian trousers, a hood, rope-soled sandals, for he had no other clothes, and he asked him about his life, what his name was, and when he had come to that land. Aguilar told him, although not articulately, that his name was Jerónimo de Aguilar, that he was a native of Ecija, that he was a member of one of the minor orders. He said he had become lost eight years earlier when he and fifteen other men and two women were going from the Darién[17] to the island of Santo Domingo with one Enciso y Valdivia, because there had been some differences and disputes. He said they were carrying ten thousand gold pesos and legal proceedings of some against the others, and that their ship entered the Alacranes,[18] which it could not navigate, so he, his companions, and the two women put themselves in the ship's boat, believing they could make the island of Cuba or Jamaica, but the currents were very strong and cast them on this land. He said that the Calachiones[19] of the region divided them up among themselves, sacrificing many of his companions to the idols while others died of illness, and a short time ago the women died of work because they were made to do the grinding. As for him, they had him ready for sacrifice, but one night he fled and went to that cacique with whom he was living (I do not remember any more the name he gave us then). Of all of them, only he and one Gonzalo Guerrero stayed.

Cortés told him he would be well cared for and rewarded, and he asked him about the land and towns. Aguilar said that because he was a slave, he knew nothing except how to serve, carrying wood and water and digging in the maize fields; he had not traveled more than four leagues, and during that one trip, while carrying a load, he fell ill from it. However, he understood that there are many towns. Then Cortés asked him about Gonzalo Guerrero, and Aguilar said that Guerrero was married, that he had three children, that he had tattooed his face and pierced his ears and lower lip, that he was a seaman from Palos, and that the Indians regarded him as courageous. He also said that a little over a year ago, a captain with

---

17. Sailing in 1511 from the Darién colony in Panama, transporting twenty thousand ducats of gold, Enciso y Valdivia ran aground on shoals named Las Viboras near Jamaica; the nineteen survivors of the wreck drifted westward in a small boat for about two weeks before landing on the Yucatan coast. Eight died of starvation during the two weeks, and those who made it to shore were captured by the local natives and were either enslaved or sacrificed.

18. The Alacranes Reef is in the Yucatan, north of the city of Merida.

19. *Calachione* is a term for a rank equivalent to cacique, captain, or chief.

three ships came to Cape Catoche (it seems to be when we came on the expedition with Francisco Hernández de Córdoba), and Guerrero was the one who came up with the idea that they should attack us, which they did, and that he came there with a cacique from a large town. When Cortés heard this, he said, "In truth, I'd like to get my hands on him because he'll never be up to any good." When the caciques of Cozumel saw how Aguilar spoke their language, they fed him very well, and Aguilar advised them always to have respect and reverence for the holy image of Our Lady and the cross, and they would come to understand that, because of this, much good would come to them. On the advice of Aguilar, the caciques asked for a letter of protection from Cortés so that if other Spaniards came to that port, the Indians would be well treated and the Spaniards would not harm them. Cortés gave them the letter at once. After taking leave with many flatteries and promises, we set sail for the Río Grijalva.

Once the fleet arrived at the Río Grijalva, Cortés and his men met more than twelve thousand warriors, whom they managed to defeat and claim the land for the Spanish Crown. The next morning Cortés discovered that Melchorejo had left the camp and fled in the night in a canoe to join the attacking Indians. On the Day of Our Lady of March, Cortés and his men encountered the full strength of the Indian warriors near the town of Cintla. "They came at us like mad dogs, in large squadrons that covered all the savannas, and they surrounded us on all sides and cast so many arrows, spears, and stones that, at the first assault, they wounded more than seventy of our men, and with the lances, hand to hand, they did us great harm." However, because the land was flat there, the Spaniards were able to maneuver so as to break up the Indian fighting squadrons and defeat them. "As it was the Day of Our Lady of March, a town that was settled some time later was named Santa María de la Victoria, both for the Day of Our Lady and for the victory." This was the first of the wars Cortés and his men fought in New Spain. Cortés made peace overtures to the caciques and they promised to come speak about it on the following day.

Chapter 4

Doña Marina, Interpreter

[XXXVI] The next morning, the fifteenth of March, 1519, many caciques and chieftains from that town of Tabasco and other towns came, showing all of us much respect, and they brought a present of gold, including four diadems, several small lizards, something like two small dogs, ear pieces, five ducks, two images of Indian faces, two golden soles like the ones on their own sandals, and other things of little value, whose worth I no longer remember. They also brought cloaks of the kind they make, very coarse, because those who know something of that province will already have heard that the ones they have in that country are of very little value. This present was nothing compared with the twenty women, and among them a particularly excellent woman who came to be called doña Marina after becoming Christian. Cortés received that present with pleasure, and he withdrew to talk with all the caciques and Aguilar the interpreter. He told them he was very grateful for what they brought, but he had one request: They should immediately order all their men, women, and children to settle that town, and he would like to see it settled within two days; if they did this, he would know there would be true peace. The caciques immediately sent for all the men, and, with their children and women, the town was settled in two days. The other thing he ordered was that they give up their idols and sacrifices, and they replied that they would do so. We made known to them through Aguilar, as best Cortés could, things touching our holy faith, how we were Christians and worshipped one sole, true God, and Cortés showed them a most venerable image of Our Lady with her precious son in her arms, and he told them that we worship that holy image because she is in heaven and she is Mother of Our Lord God. The caciques said that the great *tecleciguata*, which is what they call the great women in those lands, seemed very good and that they would like to have her in their town. Cortés said that, yes, he would give it to them, and he ordered them to make a proper altar, well constructed, which they immediately did. The next morning, he ordered two of our finish carpenters, Alonso Yáñez and Álvaro López, to make a very tall cross, and after ordering all this, he asked the caciques why they were attacking us when we had asked for peace three times. They answered that they had already asked and received pardon for it. The cacique said that his brother, the cacique of Chanpoton, had advised it so that he would not be regarded as cowardly. He had already been reproached and dishonored because he did not attack us when the other captain came with four ships, and it seems he meant Juan de Grijalva. Further, he said that the Indian we brought as an interpreter and who had fled one night advised him to attack us day and night. Cortés then ordered them to bring Melchorejo to him no matter what the circumstances, and they told Cortés that when Melchorejo saw that the battle was not going well for them, he fled, and even though they had looked for him, they did not know where he was. We learned later that they sacrificed him because his advice cost them so much. Cortés also asked them from where they brought the gold and those little jewels. They replied that they came from where the sun set, and they said "Culua"[20] and "Mexico," but because we knew neither what Mexico nor Culua was, we ignored it.

With this, the discussion stopped until the next day when we put on the altar the holy image of Our Lady and the cross, which we all worshipped, and fray Bartolomé de Olmedo said mass. All the caciques and chieftains were present, and that town was named Santa María de la Victoria, and the town of Tabasco has that name today. The same friar, with our interpreter Aguilar, preached many good things about our holy faith to the twenty

---

20. Bernal Díaz consistently uses "Culua" to designate *Colhua*, a term associated with Colhuacan, Tenochtitlan's parent state from where its royal line first came. *Colhua* means "one with grandfathers," with a long line of forbearers, specifically the old Toltecs.

Indian women they had given us and told them not to believe in their idols, that they were evil and not gods, nor should they sacrifice to the idols anymore because the idols deceived them, but instead they should worship Our Lord Jesus Christ. They were then baptized, and the name doña Marina was given to that Indian woman they had given us there, and she was truly a great cacica, daughter of great caciques and mistress over vassals, which clearly showed in her person. Further on I will talk about how and in what way she was brought there. I do not remember well the names of all the other women, nor is it relevant to name them. But these were the first Christian women in New Spain, and Cortés gave each captain his own. This doña Marina, because she was of good appearance, curious about things and uninhibited, he gave to Alonso Hernández Puerto Carrero,[21] who was a very fine gentleman, cousin of the Count of Medellín; when he left for Castile, doña Marina was with Cortés and he had a son by her, who was named don Martín Cortés.

All the caciques gave Cortés thanks, and there they declared themselves vassals of our great emperor. These were the first vassals in New Spain who pledged obedience to His Majesty.

Cortés then ordered that the next day, Palm Sunday, very early in the morning, they should come to the altar with their children and women to worship the holy image of Our Lady and the cross. He also ordered that six Indian carpenters should come then and go with our carpenters into the town of Cintla, where it pleased Our Lord God to give us victory in the past battle, as I have mentioned. He told them to cut a cross in the wood of a large tree that was called a ceiba, and they made the cross so that it would last a long time, because the cross will always be distinguished by bark that renews itself. When this was done, Cortés ordered them to prepare all the canoes they had to help us embark, because we wanted to set sail immediately on that

21. Bernal Díaz uses a number of variations on Alonso Hernández Puerto Carrero's last name, including Puertocarrero and PuertoCarrero; all designate the same person.

holy day. We set sail the next morning with fortunate navigation, and we followed the course to San Juan de Ulúa, always staying close to land.

[XXXVII] Before dealing with the great Montezuma and his great Mexico and Mexicans, I want to talk about doña Marina, how from childhood she was a great lady and cacica over towns and vassals. Here is her story: Her father and mother were lords and caciques of a town, Painala, eight leagues from the town of Guazacualco, and other towns were subject to it. Her father died when she was a very small child, and her mother married another young cacique with whom she had a son and, it seemed, they loved him very much, and the father and mother agreed that he should become cacique after their deaths. To avoid any obstacles, one night they gave the child, doña Marina, to some Indians from Xicalango so she would not be seen. At that same time, the child of one of their Indian slaves died, and they announced that the one who had died was the heiress doña Marina. The people of Xicalango gave doña Marina to the people of Tabasco, and the Tabascans gave her to Cortés. I met her mother and the son of this old woman, doña Marina's half brother, who was now a man and commanded the town jointly with his mother, because the old woman's last husband was dead. After becoming Christian, the old woman was named Marta and the son Lázaro. I know this very well because in 1523, after the conquest of Mexico and other provinces, and when Cristóbal de Olid had rebelled in Honduras, Cortés went there and passed through Guazacualco. We were with him on that entire journey as was the greater part of the citizens of the town. As doña Marina was such an excellent woman and good interpreter in all the wars of New Spain, Tlaxcala, and Mexico, Cortés always had her with him. During that journey a gentleman named Juan Jaramillo married her in the town of Orizaba.

In the town of Guazacualco, Cortés sent for all the caciques in that province in order to address them about the holy doctrine and about their good treatment, and doña Marina's mother and half brother, Lázaro, came with other caciques. Some days earlier doña Marina told me that she came from that province and was the mistress over vassals, and the captain Cortés knew it well, as did Aguilar the interpreter. When the mother and her son, the brother, came, they recognized one another, and clearly doña Marina was her daughter because she looked very much like her. They were afraid of her, believing that she had sent for them to find and kill them, and they cried. When doña Marina saw this, she consoled them and said they should not be afraid, that when they gave her to the people from Xicalango, they did not know what they were doing, and she forgave them, gave them many golden jewels and clothes, and said they could return to their town. She said that God had done her a great favor in getting her to give up idol worship and become a Christian, to have a son by her master and lord Cortés, and to be married to a gentleman like her husband Juan Jaramillo. Even were they to make her cacica of all the provinces in New Spain, she said she would not want to be that, but would rather serve her husband and Cortés than anything else in the world. I know this with absolute certainty.

Doña Marina knew the language of Guazacualco, which is the language of Mexico, and she also knew that of Tabasco, and Jerónimo de Aguilar also knew the language of Yucatan and Tabasco, which is the same; they understood each other well, and Aguilar translated everything into Castilian for Cortés. It was a great beginning for our conquest, and thus things turned out for us, praise God, very fortunately. I wanted to talk about this, because without doña Marina we could not have understood the language of New Spain and Mexico.

Chapter 5

First Encounters with Montezuma's People, San Juan de Ulúa

[XXXVIII] On Holy Thursday, 1519, we arrived with the entire fleet at the port of San Juan de Ulúa, and as the pilot Alaminos knew it well from when we came with Juan de Grijalva, he immediately ordered us to anchor in a place where the ships would be secure from the north wind, and they put their royal standards and weather vanes on the flagship. About a half hour after we had anchored, two very large canoes, which they call *pirogues*, arrived. In them were many Mexican Indians, and when they saw the standards and the large ship, they knew that was where they had to go to speak to the captain. They went directly to the ship, went aboard, and asked which was the *tatuan*, which means "ruler." Doña Marina understood because she knew the language very well, so she pointed to Cortés. The Indians paid their respects to Cortés, as was their custom, and they said to him that he was very welcome, that a servant of the great Montezuma, their lord, sent them to find out who we were, what we were seeking, and that if we needed something for ourselves and the ships to tell them and they would provide it. Cortés answered through the two interpreters, Aguilar and doña Marina, that he was very grateful, and he then ordered that they be given something to eat, wine to drink, and some blue beads. When they had drunk, he told them we had come to see them and to trade, we would be no bother to them at all, and they should approve of our arrival in that land. The messengers went back delighted. The next day, Good Friday, we disembarked our horses and artillery in some hills and dunes of sand that were there, very high, because there was no flat land, only sandy beaches. The cannons were pointed as seemed best to Mesa the artilleryman, and we made an altar where mass was then said. Huts and bowers were made for Cortés and the captains, and some three hundred soldiers transported wood, from which we made our huts, and the horses were put where they would be safe; this is how we passed that Good Friday. The next day, Saturday, the eve of Easter, many Indians arrived, sent by a chieftain, a governor under Montezuma, whose name was Pitalpitoque,[22] whom we called Obandillo. They brought axes and worked on the huts of the captain Cortés and the others nearby, and they put large coarse cloths on top of them to keep out the sun, for it was the Lenten season and very hot. They brought hens, maize bread, and plums, which were in season, and it seems to me they brought some gold jewels then, all of which they presented to Cortés, and they said that the next day a governor would come to bring more provisions. Cortés thanked them very much for it, and he ordered that they be given certain things as barter, with which they were delighted.

The next day, Easter, the Holy Feast of the Resurrection, the governor about whom they had spoken, Tendile,[23] a man of business, arrived and brought with him Pitalpitoque, who was also very illustrious among them. With them were many Indians with presents and hens and vegetables, and Tendile ordered them to remove themselves some distance away to a promontory. With much humility they bowed to Cortés and then to all of us soldiers who were closest. Cortés welcomed them through the interpreters, embraced them, told them to wait, and said he would speak to them later. In the meantime, he ordered that an altar be made, the best that could be done at that time, and fray Bartolomé de Olmedo, who was a great singer, sang the mass, the father Juan Díaz assisted, and the two governors and other chieftains of their company were at the mass. After mass, Cortés, certain captains, and the two Indian servants of the great Montezuma ate, and when the tables were taken away, Cortés with the two interpreters and those caciques withdrew, and he told them we were Christians and vassals of the greatest lord in the world, the emperor don Carlos, who has many great lords as vassals and servants, and that

---

22. Cuitlalpitoc.
23. Teudilli.

we came to these lands by his order, because for many years don Carlos has known of them and of the great lord who rules them, and he wanted to have that great lord as a friend and tell him many things in his royal name; Cortés also said that after the great lord knew and understood these things, he would be pleased, and that he would like also in good friendship to trade with him and his vassals, and he would like to know where his lordship rules so that they might meet. Tendile replied somewhat haughtily, "You have just now arrived and you already want to speak to him. Receive this present now that we give you in the name of our lord, and then you will tell me what might suit you." He then pulled many beautifully worked, rich pieces of gold from a large *petaca*[24] that is like a basket, and he sent for ten loads of white cotton cloth and feathers, things amazing to see, other things that I do not remember, and a lot of food, which included hens, fruit, and roasted fish. Cortés received it graciously and with smiles, and he gave them twisted beads and other small beads from Castile and asked that they order the people in their towns to come trade with us because he had brought many beads to exchange for gold. They said they would do as he ordered. We learned later that Tendile and Pitalpitoque were governors of some provinces called Cotastan,[25] Tustepeque, Guazpaltepeque, Tatalteco, and other towns they had recently subjugated. Then Cortés ordered that a chair with a back richly carved with inlays be brought, some pearls that were carefully worked and covered in some musk-imbued cotton to make them smell good, and a string of twisted diamond-cut beads as well as a crimson cap with a gold medal of St. George on horseback killing a dragon with his sword. He told Tendile to send that chair right away so that the lord Montezuma, whose name we already knew, could sit on it when Cortés came to see and speak with him, and that he should put that cap on his head. He also said that the king our lord ordered him to give Montezuma that stone and everything else as a sign of friendship because he knows

---

24. A *petaca* is a type of basket covered with leather or animal hide.
25. Cotaxtla.

he is a great lord; and he asked that a time and place be set when he could go to see Montezuma. Tendile accepted the gift and said that his lord Montezuma was such a great lord that he would be pleased to know our great king and that he would take him that present quickly and would return with a response.

Tendile, it seems, brought with him great painters, for there are such in Mexico, and he ordered them to paint from life the face, expression, body, and features of Cortés and all the captains and soldiers, as well as the ships and sails, horses, doña Marina, and Aguilar, even the two hounds, the cannons and balls, and our whole army, and he carried the paintings to his lord. Cortés then ordered the artillerymen to have the cannons well loaded with a good load of powder so that when they were fired, there would be a huge noise. He ordered Pedro de Alvarado and all the horsemen to prepare themselves with small bells on their horses' breastplates, so Montezuma's servants could see them charge, and Cortés also went on horseback and said, "It would be good if we could gallop in these sand dunes, but they will see that we even get stuck in sand on foot. Let us go to the beach after the tide goes out and gallop two by two." He gave charge of all the horsemen to Pedro de Alvarado, whose sorrel mare was a great runner and turner. All this was done in front of those two ambassadors and, so that they might see the guns go off, Cortés pretended that he wanted to speak again with many of the chieftains, and then they fired the cannons. As the weather was calm then, the stones resounded throughout the forest with great noise, and the governors and all the Indians were terrified by such unfamiliar things, and they ordered their painters to paint all of it so their lord Montezuma might see it.

It seems that a soldier had a half-gilded but rusty helmet. Tendile, who was the more curious of the two Indians, saw it and said he would like to examine it, that it looked like one that had been left to them by their ancestors in the lineage from which they came, and they had put that one on their god Huichilobos,[26]

---

26. Huichilobos, now referred to as Huitzilopochtli, is the tribal deity of the Mexica, the god of war and associated with the sun.

so their lord Montezuma would be pleased to see this one. They immediately gave the helmet to him, and Cortés told them that because he wanted to know whether the gold of this land was the kind we extract from the rivers in our land, they should send him that helmet filled with grains of gold for us to send to our great emperor. After all this, Tendile took his leave of Cortés and all of us, and after many promises Cortés offered him, Tendile took his leave and said he would return in all due haste with his response. With Tendile gone, we came to understand that, besides being an Indian of great importance, he was the fastest runner his master Montezuma had. He went quickly and told the entire story to his lord, showing him all the painted sketches he had brought and the present Cortés had sent him. It is said that when the great Montezuma saw it, he was amazed, and, on the other hand, he was very happy, and when he saw the helmet and the one his Huichilobos had, he was sure that we were those people his ancestors said would come to rule over this land.

[XXXIX] When Tendile left with the present the captain Cortés had given him for his lord Montezuma, the other governor, Pitalpitoque, stayed in our camp. He stayed in some huts a distance from us, where they brought Indian women to prepare bread from their maize, hens, fruit, and fish, and from that they provided Cortés and the captains who ate with him, but for us, the soldiers, nothing, unless we gathered shellfish or went to fish. At that time many Indians came from the towns I mentioned, whose governors were those servants of the great Montezuma, and some of them brought gold, jewels of little value, and hens to exchange for our trade goods, which were green beads, rhinestones, and other jewels, and we fed ourselves with these, because most soldiers had trade goods, as we had learned during Grijalva's expedition that it was good to carry beads. Six or seven days passed like this. Then Tendile came one morning with more than a hundred Indians loaded with goods. With them came a great Mexican cacique who looked like the captain Cortés in his face, features, and body; the great Montezuma had deliberately sent him because, according to what they said, when Tendile brought a picture of Cortés's face, all the chieftains with Montezuma said that a chieftain named Quintalbor looked like Cortés. So Montezuma called that great cacique to go with Tendile, and, as he looked like Cortés, we called him that in the camp, this Cortés here, that Cortés there. Let us return to his arrival and what they did. As he arrived where our captain was, he kissed the ground, and with clay braziers filled with incense they perfumed Cortés and all the rest of us soldiers who were close by. Cortés showed them much affection and seated them next to him.

That chieftain who came with that present was, along with Tendile, charged with speaking. As I have said, his name was Quintalbor. After welcoming us to that land and saying many other things, he ordered the present they carried to be brought out on top of some sleeping mats they called *petates* and other cotton cloths to be spread over them. The first present was a wheel in the shape of a sun the size of a wagon wheel, of very fine gold and with all types of painting, a great work to see, worth, as they said after they had weighed it, more than ten thousand pesos; another larger wheel of brilliant silver representing the moon with other figures on it, and it was of great weight, worth a great deal; and he brought the helmet filled with small grains of gold as they take it from the mines, which was worth three thousand pesos. That gold in the helmet was worth even more to us than if they had brought twenty thousand pesos because we knew then for certain that there were good mines. In addition, he brought twenty golden ducks, particularly excellent work, very lifelike, some gold in the likeness of the kind of dogs they kept, many golden pieces of jaguars, mountain lions, and monkeys; ten collars of excellent workmanship and other pendants; and twelve arrows, a bow with its string, and two staffs of the kind justices carry, five palm spans in length; all this was of very fine molded gold. Then he ordered brought forward crests of gold and rich green feathers and other crests of silver and fans of the same material; then golden deer made from molds, and there were so many things and it was so many years ago that I cannot remember them all. Then he ordered brought there more than thirty loads of cotton cloth, of such excellence and with so many types of embroidery, with feathers of so many colors, that I do not want to write anything more about it because I will not know how to describe it. After he had presented it all, that great cacique, Quintalbor, and Tendile, said to Cortés that he should accept that present with the great goodwill with which their lord sent it, and that he should share it with the *teules*[27] and men he brings with him. Cortés accepted it with pleasure. Those ambassadors said to Cortés that they wanted to tell him what their lord sent them to say, and the first thing they said to him was that their lord rejoiced that such strong men, as they have said we are, have come to his land because he knew about the incident at Tabasco. He also said Montezuma would very much like to see our great emperor, for he is a great lord, because even from such distant lands as we came, the emperor knew of Montezuma, and he will send him a present of valuable stones, and, while we were there in that port, if he might serve us in some way, he would do so with great goodwill. As for the meetings, he said we should not be concerned about them for there was no reason to have them, and he gave many objections to them.

Cortés, looking delighted, again said thank you to them, and with many friendly words and promises, he gave each governor two shirts of Holland cloth and blue rhinestones and other little things, and he requested them to return as his ambassador to Mexico to say to their lord, the great Montezuma, that because we had crossed so many seas and come from such far lands only to see him and to speak to him in person, that if he, Cortés, were to return not having seen Montezuma, our great king and lord would not receive him well, and that wherever Montezuma might be, Cortés wanted to come to see him and do whatever he orders. The governors said they would tell Montezuma that, but the meetings Cortés says he wants are out of the question. To Montezuma, Cortés sent with those messengers, from our poor

---

27. *Teul* is a term used generally to signify a god or an idol. Bernal Díaz uses it primarily to designate the former.

resources, a cup of Florentine glass, etched and gilded with many groves of trees and hunting scenes, three shirts of Holland cloth, and other things, and he entrusted his response to them. The two governors left, and Pitalpitoque stayed in the camp, and it appears that Montezuma's other servants told him he should have food brought from the nearby towns.

[XL] Pitalpitoque, who had stayed in order to bring food, slackened off so much that he brought nothing to the camp, so we had very little food because the cassava became bitter from mold and rot and dirty from cockroaches. If we did not go to gather shellfish, we did not eat, and the Indians who used to bring gold and hens to trade no longer came as they had at the beginning, and those who did come were reserved and fearful. We were waiting hour by hour for the messengers who went to Mexico. Just then Tendile returned with many Indians, and after having paid their customary respects, perfuming Cortés and all of us with incense, he delivered ten loads of very fine and precious feathered cloaks and four *chalchiuis*,[28] green stones of very great value, worth more among them than emeralds are among us, and they are green. He also presented some pieces of gold, which they said were worth by themselves, apart from the chalchiuis, three thousand pesos. Then came Tendile and Pitalpitoque, but the other great cacique, Quintalbor, did not return, having fallen ill on the road, and those two governors withdrew with Cortés, doña Marina, and Aguilar, and they told Cortés that their lord Montezuma received the present with pleasure but, as for the visits, they should speak no more about it. They said he sent those valuable stones, the chalchiuis, for the great emperor because they are so valuable that each one of them is worth an entire load of gold, that he held them in the greatest esteem and that Cortés should not send any more messengers to Mexico.

---

28. Usually *chalchihuites*, a word seemingly derived from indigenous languages meaning "green stone" or, possibly, "jade," but often used to designate any precious stone.

Chapter 6

The Totonacs, Cortés's First Allies

[XLI] One day, another soldier and I, standing guard on the sandbanks, saw five Indians coming along the beach, and so as not to make an uproar for nothing in the camp, we let them come up to us. With smiling faces they paid their respects in their way, and using hand signals, they told us we should take them to the camp. I told my companion that he should stay at his post and I would go with them, for at that time my feet did not weigh me down as they do now that I am old. When they came to where Cortés was, they showed him great respect and said to him, "*Lope luzio*, lope luzio," which in the Totonac language means, "Lord, and great lord." These men had large holes in their lower lips, in which were some stone disks painted blue, others with thin leaves of gold and, in the ears, very large holes in which were other disks with gold and stones, and they dressed and spoke very differently from the Mexicans who were usually with us. When doña Marina and Aguilar, the interpreters, heard that *Lope luze*, they did not understand it. Doña Marina asked in the language of Mexico if there were among them nahuatlatos, which are interpreters of the Mexican language, and two of the five replied, that, yes, they understood it, and they said we were welcome, that their lord sent them to find out who we were and that he would be pleased to serve men who were so courageous, because it seems they already knew about the incidents in Tabasco and Potonchan. They said more, that they would have come to see us before if not for fear of the people of Culua, who usually were there with us. Culua means Mexicans, which is as if we might say Cordobans or Sevillians, and they said they found out that three days ago the Mexicans had fled to their lands. From one discussion to another, Cortés learned that Montezuma had enemies and opponents, which pleased him, and with gifts and friendly words, he took his leave of those five messengers and told them to tell their lord he would come to see them very soon. From then on, we called the Indians from there the *lopes luzios*.

Let us move on to talk about the fact that there were always a lot of mosquitoes in those sandy beaches, both the long-legged ones and the small ones they call *xexenes*, which are worse than the large ones, and we could not sleep because of them; there were no provisions, the cassava was beginning to run out and become very moldy and dirty from the cockroaches, and some of the soldiers, especially the servants and friends of Diego Velázquez who used to have Indians on the island of Cuba, were longing to return to their homes. When Cortés saw how things were, he ordered us to go to Quiahuiztlan, a fortified town, where the ships would be sheltered by a great rock. As we were setting about the task of leaving, friends, kinsmen, and servants of Diego Velázquez asked Cortés why he wanted to make that voyage without provisions, saying there was no possibility of going on because more than thirty-five soldiers had died in our camp from wounds from the Tabasco incident and from ailments and hunger, that the country was large and the settlements full of people, and that the Indians would attack one day or another. They said it would be better for us to return to Cuba and to render account to Diego Velázquez of the gold traded, which was significant in quantity, and about Montezuma's great presents, the sun and silver moon, the helmet with bits of gold from mines, and all the jewels and cloth I mentioned. Cortés answered them that it was not good advice to return without seeing everything, that until now we have not been able to complain of fortune, that we should give thanks to God who has helped us in everything, and, as for those who have died, it usually happens in times of war and hardships, and it will be good to know what there is in the land, so in the meantime, unless he was much mistaken, we could eat maize and provisions that the Indians of neighboring towns had. With this response, the faction of Diego Velázquez was somewhat calmed down, but not much, and they still formed small groups, and there was talk in the camp about returning to Cuba.

As a response to this talk, Cortés agreed with the men most closely associated with him to create, found, and settle a town, which they named Villa Rica de la Veracruz. Although the physical town was not yet built, they appointed its municipal officers: alcaldes, Alonso Hernández Puertocarrero and Francisco de Montejo; captain of expeditions, Pedro de Alvarado; maestre de campo,[29] Cristóbal de Olid; aguacil mayor,[30] Juan de Escalante; treasurer, Juan de Mejía; standard-bearer, "to somebody Corral"; and constable of the camp, Ochoa, a Basque, and Alonso Romero. "The regidores[31] I will not record because naming a few of them is useless, but I will say that the pillory was put in the plaza and a gallows outside the town."

The most important appointment went to Cortés, who was named justicia mayor[32] and captain general. To him was conceded a fifth of whatever gold the expedition acquired, after having taken out the royal fifth.[33] In searching out a secure place to settle, Cortés and his men determined to go to the fortified native town Quiahuiztlan, where the ships would be protected by the rock and port opposite the town. The road to Quiahuiztlan passed through Cempoala, the most important of the Totonac-speaking towns. When they drew close to the town, "twenty Indian chieftains came out to greet us on behalf of their cacique, and they brought some native red pinecones, very fragrant, which they gave with great affection to Cortés and the horsemen; they told Cortés that their lord was waiting for us in

---

29. *Maestre de campo* was a rank of high order in the militia, designating someone who commanded a large number of men.

30. *Aguacil mayor* is roughly chief constable, a position combining judicial, military, civil, and police powers that might or might not be held by a person with legal training.

31. A *regidor* was a member of a municipal council.

32. The *justicia mayor* was the chief administrator of justice in the domain of his jurisdiction, with broad responsibility and authority for appointing other administrators of justice and judges. Once the title is confirmed by the regent the individual retains it for life, even if he is relieved of his responsibilities.

33. With the formal establishment of the town and the naming of its officers, Cortés and those who supported him laid the ground for declaring their independence from Diego Velázquez.

his lodgings, but because he was very fat and heavy, he could not come out to receive us." The town they entered "was so lush that it seemed like a garden and so populated with men and women that we praised God greatly that we had discovered such lands."

The fat cacique came out to receive us in the plaza, and I will call him that because he was very fat. He made a great bow to Cortés and perfumed him with incense as is their custom, and Cortés embraced him. They lodged us there in some very good and large buildings, where we all fit. They gave us something to eat and brought some baskets of plums, which were plentiful because they were in season, and bread of maize. As we had arrived hungry and we had not seen so much food as this, we named that town Villaviciosa,[34] and I will call it Seville. Cortés ordered that no soldier should annoy the townspeople nor leave that plaza, and when the fat cacique got word that we had eaten, he sent a message to Cortés that he would like to come to see him. He came with a good many Indian chieftains, all of them wearing large gold lip rings and rich cloaks. Cortés also went out from the building to meet him. With a very great show of affection and friendly words, he embraced him again. Then the fat cacique ordered brought a present of jewels, gold, and cloaks he had readied, and although it was not much and was of little value, he said to Cortés, "Lope luzio, lope luzio, accept this with goodwill," and if he had more, he would have given it to him. I have already said that in the Totonac language they mean, "Lord and great lord" when they say lope luzio, etc. Cortés said to the fat cacique, through doña Marina and Aguilar, that he would pay him in good works, that whatever he needed they should tell Cortés, and he would do it for them because we are vassals of so great a lord, the emperor don Carlos, who commands many kingdoms and principalities and sent us to right wrongs, punish the wicked, and command them not to sacrifice more souls. He explained many other things concerning our holy faith.

When the fat cacique heard that, sighing, he complained vigorously of the great Montezuma and his governors, saying that just a

---

34. Literally, "lush or luxuriant town."

short time ago, Montezuma had subjugated him and carried away all his golden jewels, and he has them so oppressed that they dare not do anything but what he orders because he is lord of great cities and lands, vassals, and armies of war. Because Cortés realized that at present he could not deal with their complaints, he said he would do something to see that those wrongs were righted, but, because he was going to see his *acales*, the word for "ships" in the Indian language, and set up his residence and headquarters in the town of Quiahuiztlan, he could not look into their complaints until he had established his headquarters. The fat cacique gave a considered answer. The next morning we left Cempoala, and they had readied, to bear loads, more than four hundred Indians, called *tamemes* in those parts, who carry two *arrobas*[35] on their shoulders as far as five leagues. When we saw so many bearers we were delighted, because those of us who did not have Indians from Cuba always carried our packs on our shoulders, and only about five or six of them came in the fleet. Doña Marina and Aguilar told us that when these lands are at peace, the caciques are obliged, without waiting to be asked, to offer tamemes to carry loads. From then on, wherever we went we asked for Indians to carry the loads.

[XLVI] The next day at ten, we arrived at the fortified town of Quiahuiztlan, which was among large rocks and very high hills, and if there were resistance, it would be difficult to take. Proceeding in good order and believing there might be war, the artillery went ahead and all of us went up into that stronghold in such a way that, if something were to happen, we were prepared for it. At that time, Alonso de Ávila was captain. As he was arrogant and had a bad disposition, he gave a soldier named Hernando Alonso de Villanueva a blow to his arm with his lance because he was not proceeding in good order, which maimed him, and afterward he was called Hernando Alonso de Villanueva "the Lame."[36] They will say that I always digress to tell old stories. Let us leave it and say that, going through half that town we found no Indians whatsoever with whom

---

35. An *arroba* is a measure of weight equal to about twenty-five pounds.
36. "*El Manquillo.*"

to speak, which surprised us. They had fled from fear that same day when they saw us climbing up to their houses. We saw, standing at the highest point of the stronghold in a plaza next to which they had the *cus*[37] and large houses of their idols, fifteen Indians with fine cloaks, each with a clay brazier holding some of their incense. They came to where Cortés was and, with incense, perfumed him and those of us soldiers near him, and with deep bows, they told Cortés that he should pardon them for not having come out to see us, that we were very welcome and should rest. They said they had stayed away until they could see what we were because they feared us and the horses, but they would order the rest of the Indians to return that night to the town. Cortés showed them great affection and told them many things about our holy faith, as we customarily did wherever we went. He told them that we were vassals of our emperor don Carlos, and he gave them some green beads and other little things from Castile. They then brought hens and maize bread.

In the midst of these discussions, they came to tell Cortés that the fat cacique from Cempoala was coming in a litter on the shoulders of many Indian chieftains. When the cacique arrived, he spoke with Cortés, together with the cacique and other chieftains of that town, complaining about Montezuma. He talked about Montezuma's great powers and spoke with such tears and sighs that Cortés and those of us who were present took pity. In addition to telling how Montezuma had subjugated them, he said that each year they demanded many of their sons and daughters for sacrifice and others to serve in their houses and fields. He had many other complaints, so many that I do not remember them anymore. He also

---

37. *Cu* (and its plural, *cus*) is the Spanish adaptation of the Mayan word *ku,* pronounced with a glottalized *k,* which is not a sound normal to Spanish speech. The term designates a building or temple, normally quite high, set aside for religious practice. In general, one may think of the term as the rough equivalent of another term Bernal Díaz uses in relation to such structures, *adoratorio,* with which he often pairs *cu.* According to one authority, one pronounces the singular *cu* as *coo,* the sound a dove or pigeon makes, whereas one pronounces the plural, *cus,* as *quays* or *cways.*

said that Montezuma's tax collectors took their wives and daughters from them, if they were beautiful, and raped them. They did the same thing throughout the entire land of the Totonac language, more than thirty towns. Cortés consoled them as much as he could through our interpreters, saying he would help them in every way he could and would put an end to those thefts and wrongs and that the emperor our lord had sent him to these parts for that purpose. They should not have any worries at all, he said, for they would soon see what we would do about it. They took some comfort from these words, but their hearts were not put to rest because of their great fear of the Mexicans. In the midst of these discussions, some Indians from the same town came in great haste to tell all the caciques speaking with Cortés that five Mexicans, Montezuma's tax collectors, were coming, and when the caciques heard this, their faces went pale and they trembled with fear. They left Cortés alone and went to receive the Mexicans. They promptly decorated a hall with branches, prepared something to eat, and made a lot of chocolate for them, that being their best drink. When the five Indians entered the town, they came to where we were, because that is where the house of the cacique and our lodgings were, and they passed with such self-assurance and arrogance that they went ahead without speaking to Cortés or any of us. They wore rich embroidered cloaks and loincloths of the same kind (which is the way people wore trousers at that time), and their sleek hair was gathered up as though tied on top of the head, and each had some flowers, smelling them, and other Indians, like servants, carried flyswatters for them. Each had a staff with a hook in his hand, accompanied by many chieftains of other towns of the Totonac language, who did not leave them until taking them to their lodgings and, with great ceremony, giving them something to eat. After they had eaten, they had the fat cacique and the rest of the chieftains summoned and reproached them for having lodged us in their towns, and they asked them what business they had now seeing and speaking to us; their lord Montezuma would not be pleased with that because they should not have sheltered us nor given us gold jewels without his permission. They threatened the fat cacique and other chieftains, saying that they had to supply twenty Indian men and women to appease the gods for the crime they had committed. As this was going on, Cortés asked doña Marina and Jerónimo de Aguilar, our interpreters, why the caciques were agitated when those Indians came and who they were. Doña Marina, who understood very well, told him what had happened. Cortés immediately summoned the fat cacique and all the other chieftains and asked them who those Indians were that they were making such a feast for them. They answered that those Indians were the tax collectors of the great Montezuma, who had come to find out why they had received us without permission of their lord. They were now demanding twenty Indian men and women to sacrifice to their god Huichilobos so that he would give them victory against us because, they said, Montezuma says he wants to take us to be his slaves. Cortés consoled them and said they should not be afraid, that he was there with all of us and would punish the Mexicans.

[XLVII] When Cortés understood what the caciques were saying, he told them he had already said that the king, our lord, had ordered him to punish evildoers and not to permit sacrifices or robberies, and because those tax collectors came with such a demand, he ordered them immediately bound and kept as prisoners. When the caciques heard this, they were frightened by such boldness, ordering that the great Montezuma's messengers be mistreated. They were afraid and did not dare do it. Cortés insisted that they immediately put the tax collectors in shackles, and they did so in such a way that they put them on long poles with collars, as is their custom, so they could not get away from them. One of the tax collectors did not allow himself to be tied, and they beat him. Cortés also ordered all the caciques to give no more tribute or obedience to Montezuma and to announce this in all the towns of their allies and friends. He also ordered that, if there were more such tax collectors in other towns, they should let him know, and he would send for them. That news spread throughout the province because the fat cacique immediately sent messengers to make it known, and the chieftains who had come in the company of those tax collectors also announced it, each immediately breaking away to go to his town to give notice as soon as they saw the Mexicans taken prisoner. Because such marvelous and important things were happening, they said that human men would not have dared to do this, but teules, which is what they called the idols they worshipped. For this reason, from that time on, they called us teules, which is, as I have said, either gods or demons, and when I say teules in this account, where our people are mentioned, you know that it is said of us.

Let us return to talking about the prisoners, whom they wanted to sacrifice, on the advice of all the caciques, so that none of them could inform Mexico. When Cortés heard about it, he ordered them not to kill the prisoners, saying he wanted to keep them, and he put some of our soldiers to watch them. At midnight Cortés sent for those soldiers who were guarding the prisoners and said, "See that you free the two who seem to be the quickest of mind, and do it in such a way that the Indians of these towns do not detect it," and he ordered them to bring the two Indians to his lodging. When the Indians were before him, he asked them through our interpreters why they were prisoners and from what land they came, pretending he did not know who they were. They replied that the caciques of Cempoala and that town, with the assistance of their followers and ours, had seized them. Cortés replied that he knew nothing of this, and it grieved him, and he ordered that they be given something to eat. He said many friendly things to them and told them to go immediately to tell their lord Montezuma that we all were his great friends and servants, that he had taken off their shackles so nothing else bad would happen to them, that he had the caciques who had taken them prisoner scolded, and that any service of his they might need, he would most willingly provide. They should also say he would order that their three companion Indians, who were being held in fetters, be freed and protected, and that they should go very quickly so they would not be seized again and killed. The two prisoners replied that they were in his debt, but they were afraid they would fall back into the hands of the Totonacs because they had, of necessity, to pass through their lands. Cortés then ordered six seamen to carry the Indians that night in a small boat to about four leagues from there, letting them out in a safe place beyond the boundaries of Cempoala.

When dawn came and the caciques of that town and the fat cacique found two prisoners missing, they wanted very much in earnest to sacrifice the other three had Cortés not taken them from their custody. Cortés pretended to be angry because the other two had fled, and he ordered a chain brought from the ship, bound the other three with it and ordered them to be carried to the ships, saying he wanted to guard them himself because such little attention to security had been shown with respect to the others. When they had taken the Indians to the ships, he ordered that their chains be removed and, with kind words, he told them he would send them right away to Mexico. Then, all the caciques of Cempoala, of that town and the others of the Totonac language who were there together, asked Cortés what would become of them, for certainly the powers of Mexico, of the great Montezuma, would come after them, and they would not be able to avoid being killed and destroyed. Cortés, looking cheerful, said that he and his brothers would defend them, and we would kill anyone who bothered them. Then all those towns and caciques promised they would be with us in everything we commanded them to do, and they would assemble their forces against Montezuma and all his allies. Here they pledged obedience to His Majesty before Diego de Godoy, the notary, and they sent to tell the rest of the towns of that province everything that had happened. Because they now gave no tribute at all and the tax collectors did not appear, there was no limit to their happiness over having been freed from that domination.

[XLVIII] Having established an alliance and friendship with more than thirty mountain towns called the Totonacs, which at that time rebelled against the great Montezuma, pledged obedience to His Majesty and said they would serve us, we very quickly decided, with that support, to found the Villa Rica de la Veracruz on some plains half a league from the fortress-like town called Quiahuiztlan, with a street layout, a church, town square, dockyard, and everything suitable to a town; and we built a fortress, hurrying as fast as we could from starting the foundations to finishing it high enough to cover with timber, making recesses, round towers, and outer defensive walls. Cortés was the first to carry earth and stones on his shoulders and dig the foundations, and all the captains and soldiers constantly worked at it, laboring to finish it quickly, some on the foundations, others in making the mud walls, others in carrying water, others in the lime kilns making bricks and tiles, and some searching for food. Others worked on the wood, blacksmiths on the nails, because we had two blacksmiths, and in this way all of us, from the highest to the lowest, kept at it continually, including the Indians who helped us, so the church and houses and most of the fortress were finished quickly.

In the midst of this, it seems that the great Montezuma received word in Mexico about how they had imprisoned his tax collectors and stopped obeying him and how the Totonac towns had rebelled. He was furious at Cortés and all of us, and he ordered a large army of warriors to come to attack the towns that had rebelled and not leave a single person in them alive, and he prepared to come against us with a great force of captaincies. At that instant, the two Indian prisoners freed by Cortés arrived. When Montezuma heard that Cortés had let the prisoners go and sent them to Mexico and received the promises Cortés had sent him, Our Lord God soothed his anger, and he decided to send to inquire about us and what we wanted. For this purpose, he sent two youths who were nephews of his, great caciques, in the charge of four old men. With them he sent a gift of gold and cloaks and a message of thanks to Cortés for freeing his servants. On the other hand, he sent a complaint that, with our help, those towns had dared to commit such treason against him, stopped giving him tribute, and renounced their obedience to him. He also said that now, because he was certain we are the ones his ancestors said would come to his lands, and that we must be of his lineage, he did not immediately send to destroy the traitors because we were in their houses. With passing time, however, they would not be able to boast of those treasons.

Cortés accepted the gold and clothes, which were worth more than two thousand pesos. He embraced them and said by way of apology that he and all of us were very much friends of their lord Montezuma, and for that reason he was watching over his three tax collectors. He immediately ordered them brought from the ships and delivered them well dressed and well treated. Cortés also lodged a major complaint with Montezuma, describing how his governor, Pitalpitoque, left the camp one night without saying anything to them. He said that was not acceptable, and he believes and feels certain that the lord Montezuma would not have ordered him to commit such a villainous act. For that reason, he said, we came to those towns where we were, and we have received honor from them. He asked Montezuma, as a kindness, to forgive them for the disrespect they showed. As for their refusing him tribute, they cannot serve two lords, and in the days we have been there, they have served us in the name of our king and lord. Cortés also said that he and all of us, his brothers, would soon go to see and serve Montezuma, and once we were there, we would attend to everything Montezuma might command. After these and many other discussions, he ordered that blue rhinestones and green beads be given to those youths, who were great caciques, and to the four old men in charge of them, men of importance. He honored them, and there before them, because there were large meadows, Cortés ordered Pedro de Alvarado, whose sorrel mare was very responsive to the reins and a good charger, and other horsemen to gallop and skirmish, which the visitors were delighted to see. Taking their leave, very content with Cortés and all of us, they went to their Mexico.

At that time Cortés's horse died, and he bought or they gave him another named el Arriero,[38] a dark chestnut, which belonged to Ortiz the musician and Bartolomé García the miner. It was one of the best horses that came in the fleet. Let us stop talking about this, and I will describe how those towns of the mountains,

---

38. This term normally designated someone in charge of beasts of burden, but the term could also be "the Carrier."

our friends, and the town of Cempoala had previously been very fearful of the Mexicans, believing that the great Montezuma was going to send his large armies of warriors to destroy them, but when they saw those relatives of the great Montezuma, who came with the presents I mentioned, offer themselves as servants to Cortés and all of us, they were astonished. Some of the caciques said to others that we certainly were teules because Montezuma was afraid of us, for he sent us gold as presents. If earlier we had a great reputation for being strong and courageous, from then on it was much more.

Cortés established peace between Cingapacinga and Cempoala, which had been traditional enemies but now began a friendship "that none of them ever broke." Other Totonac towns also gave their loyalty to the Spanish Crown. Cortés also ordered that the idols of the Cempoalans be cast down and broken, replacing them "with an altar and the holy image of Our Lady and the holy cross." Alonso Hernández Puertocarrero and Francisco de Montejo were commissioned as representatives to go to Castile with the gold they had accumulated and to carry a letter to Emperor Charles V, the Holy Roman Emperor who was also King Carlos of Spain. In the letter they summarized what had occurred to that point, asking the emperor "to favor them in everything rather than the favorites of don Juan Rodríguez de Fonseca, bishop of Burgos and archbishop of Rosano,[39] who was disposed to grant the lands to someone like Diego Velázquez." They also requested that Hernando Cortés be named governor of the newly discovered territories. When Diego Velázquez heard of the shipment of gold being sent

---

39. Juan Rodríguez de Fonseca, bishop of Burgos and archbishop of Rosano (1451–1524) was one of the most powerful and effective of the Spanish Crown's bureaucrats. He organized the *Casa de la Contractacíon* (House of Trade), which was responsible for collecting the royal fifth, and established the Royal and Supreme Council of the Indies from a subcommittee of the Casa, which came to oversee all Spanish activities of financial importance in the Americas and Asia.

to Spain, he filed a formal complaint with the Royal Audiencia[40]
and began to assemble a large fleet under the command of Pánfilo
de Narváez to capture or kill Cortés and his men. Following a
heated disagreement and discussion with those members of his
expedition who remained loyal to Diego Velázquez and desired
to return to Cuba, and discovering a plot among those persons
against himself, Cortés ordered that all their ships be grounded
and scuttled, thereby precluding the possibility of defections.
This done, Cortés and his men turned their attention to going to
Mexico, leaving a party of men headed by Juan de Escalante as
captain of the port and town of Villa Rica de la Veracruz.

Chapter 7

The Tlaxcalans: Hard-Won Allies

[LXI] Once we had fully considered the departure for Mexico,
we sought advice on the road we should take, and the chieftains
of Cempoala decided that the best and most advantageous way
was through the province of Tlaxcala, because the people there
were their friends and mortal enemies of the Mexicans. They
had forty chieftains, all warriors, ready to go with us, and they
helped us a great deal on that journey; they also gave us two
hundred tamemes to carry the artillery. But we poor soldiers
did not need tamemes, because at that time we had nothing to
carry but our arms—lances, escopetas, crossbows, shields, and
all other types of arms—and we slept and marched with them,
and for footwear we had hemp sandals, and, as I have said, we

---

40. A royal audiencia derived its authority from the Council of the Indies and was responsible for its administrative functions, including a
judicial one, in a given territory of the Spanish empire.

were always very ready to fight. We left Cempoala in the middle of August 1519, always in very good order with scouts and certain very fast soldiers in front.

> *The march took the Spaniards through a number of towns and up into the mountains where "a wind came off the snowy mountains that were to one side, which made us shiver with cold." In all the towns Cortés talked about the Catholic faith and decried the worship of idols and the practice of human sacrifice. As Cortés and his party made their way toward Tlaxcala, they sent ahead two chieftains of Cempoala with a letter announcing their arrival and a red felt hat of Flanders, "which was the fashion then." As soon as the two messengers arrived with the letter and the hat, the Tlaxcalans ordered them seized without waiting to hear more.*

[LXVII] Trusting in our good fortune, commending ourselves to God, we left the next day for Tlaxcala. As we were going on our way, our two messengers who had been taken prisoner appeared, and it seems that, since the Indians who were in charge of guarding them were taken up by war, they became careless, and they escaped from their shackles. They became so frightened by what they had seen and heard that they could hardly speak of it, because, according to what they said, when they were prisoners, the Tlaxcalans had threatened them, saying: "Now we are going to kill those you call teules and eat their flesh, and we will see if they are as strong and brave as you proclaim, and we will also eat your flesh, because you come in treachery and with lies from that traitor Montezuma." No matter how much the messengers insisted that we were against the Mexicans and we considered all the Tlaxcalans as brothers, they did not get anywhere with their arguments. When Cortés and all of us heard those arrogant words, and as the Tlaxcalans were prepared for war, although it gave us something to think about, we all said: "Well, if that's how it is, forward, so be it." We commended ourselves to God and continued on, our flag unfurled, carried by our standard-bearer Corral, because the Indians of the small town where we slept told us that for certain the Tlaxcalans would come out on the road to keep us from entering, and the people of Cempoala also told us this. As we went along in this way, we were talking about how the horsemen should charge and return at slack rein with their lances slanting, and three by three so they might support one another; when they broke through the squadrons, they should hold their lances at face level, but they should not stop to give lance thrusts so that the Indians would not get their hands on the lance. Should that happen, should they grab hold of a lance, the horseman would hold on to it with all his strength, bracing it under his arm, and putting spurs to his horse, and with the strength of the horse, he would get it loose or drag the Indian along behind him.

They will ask today why so much concern when we had not yet seen enemy warriors attacking us. To this I reply by saying what Cortés said: "Look, gentlemen companions; you see that we are few. We have always to be as ready and cautious as if not only did we see the enemy coming to fight, but we should imagine that we were already engaged in battle. As it happens many times that they get their hands on the lance, we must be careful in such a case as this and in other things that pertain to war. I've understood well that in fighting we don't need warnings, because I've learned that however well I should say it, you will perform with much greater spirit without them."

In this way we went about two leagues, and we found a very strong fortress built of stone and some kind of mortar so hard that it was necessary to break it apart with iron pickaxes, and made in such a way for defense and offense that it was extremely difficult to take. We stopped to look at it, and Cortés asked the Zocotlan Indians for what purpose that fortress was made in this way. They said that because there was continuous warfare between their lord Montezuma and the Tlaxcalans, the Tlaxcalans had made it strong to defend their towns, because already we were in their land. We rested awhile, and this information and the fortress gave us much to think about. Cortés said: "Gentlemen, let us follow our banner, which is the sign of the holy cross, and with it we will be victorious."

And all of us to a person replied that, trusting in our fortune we should go, that God is the true strength.

We began to march in the order I have said. Not very far along, our scouts saw some thirty Indians who were lookouts, with two-handed swords, shields, lances, and feather plumes. The swords are pieces of flint that cut much better than razors, made in a way that they could not be broken nor the blades pulled from their handles, and are as long as broadswords;[41] and the Indians wore their emblems and plumes. When our scouts saw them, they came to warn us. Cortés ordered them to go after the Indians and to try to take some of them without wounding them. Then he sent five other horsemen so that they would be able to assist if there should be an ambush. With our entire army we went at a quick pace and in good order, because the friends we brought with us told us that for sure there would be a great number of warriors waiting in ambush. When the thirty Indians on the lookout saw that the horsemen were coming toward them and motioning to them with their hands, they did not wait until the horsemen reached them and took some of them; but they defended themselves very well, and with their war clubs and lances they struck the horses. When our people, their horses wounded, saw the Indians fight so wildly, they tried to do what they were obliged to do and killed five of them. In the midst of this, a squadron of more than three thousand Tlaxcalans waiting in ambush came on suddenly and with great fury, and they began to shoot arrows at our horsemen who were now all together, showered arrows and fire-hardened spears on them, and worked marvels with their two-handed swords. In that instant we arrived with our artillery, escopetas, and crossbows. Little by little the Indians began to turn away, although they stayed a good while fighting in good order.

---

41. The foregoing is Bernal Díaz's description of a macana, translated as "war club" from this point on. *Macana* is a Taino term the Spaniards brought with them from the West Indies, whereas the Nahuatl term for this weapon was *macuahuitl*.

Aztec warriors wielding macanas (macahuitl), which are oak swords or clubs fitted with rows of obsidian blades. Aztec warriors used these weapons to slash, inflicting long bleeding wounds, or sever, as when they decapitated a mare Cortés's party brought. *Florentine Codex.*

In that skirmish, four of our men were wounded, and it seems to me that a few days later one of them died of his wounds. As it was late, the Tlaxcalans withdrew and we did not pursue them; they left about seventeen dead, not counting the many wounded. Where those skirmishes took place, the ground was level, and there were many houses with maize fields and stands of maguey plants, from which they make their wine. We slept near a stream, and because there was no oil, we treated our wounds with grease from a fat Indian we had killed there who was opened. We had a very good dinner of some small dogs they raised because all the homes were empty and they carried off their goods, and although they carried the little dogs off with them, at night the dogs returned to the houses and there we captured them, and they made very good eating. We were very alert the entire night, with sentries, good patrols, scouts, and the horses saddled and bridled for fear the Tlaxcalans might attack us.

[LXIII/LXIV] The next day Cortés and his men set out and came upon two squadrons of warriors numbering about six thousand. His attempts at negotiation failed, so shouting "Santiago, and at them," he led his men into battle. Although the Spaniards killed and wounded many of the Indians with their guns, more than forty thousand warriors were waiting in ambush with their captain Xicotenga;[42] their devices were white and red because those were Xicotenga's colors. Cortés and his men were overwhelmed by the huge numbers, but "the great mercy of God helped and protected [them]."

While we were in the midst of these bitter fights among those great warriors and their fearful broadswords, it seems that many of the strongest of them decided to join together to get their hands on a horse. They launched an attack and grabbed hold of a very good mare, well trained in sport and charging, and the horseman who was on her, a good rider named Pedro de Morón. As he and three other horsemen charged, breaking through the squadrons of enemies, because those were their orders so they could assist one another, the Tlaxcalans grabbed hold of his lance so that he could not withdraw it and others gave him slashes with their broadswords and wounded him badly. Then they slashed the mare, cutting her neck all around, leaving it hanging by the skin; and she was left dead there. If his fellow horsemen had not promptly helped Pedro de Morón, they would have killed him too. Well, maybe we could have helped him with the entire squadron. I say again that, for fear they might destroy us all, we could not go from one spot to another, that we had enough to do to defend ourselves

---

42. Xicotencatl, and in this instance Xicotencatl el mozo (the younger).

so they would not defeat us, and we were very much in danger. However, we rushed to where the mare was and managed to save Morón and take him away from the Tlaxcalans who were already carrying him away half-dead. We cut the girths of the mare so we would not leave the saddle behind, and there, in that rescue, they wounded ten of our men. It seems to me that our soldiers then killed four Indian captains, for we were marching together closely and did them much damage with our swords, because when that happened, they began to withdraw and took the mare, which they cut into pieces to show in all the towns of Tlaxcala. We learned later that they had offered to their idols the horseshoes, the hat from Flanders, and the two letters we sent them asking for peace. The mare they killed belonged to Juan Sedeño, but because at that time Sedeño had three wounds from the day before, he gave it to Morón who was a very good rider. Morón died then of the wounds two days later, because I do not remember seeing him anymore.

Later in the battle Cortés's men killed many Indians, including eight important captains, so the Indians retreated. The next day Cortés tried again to negotiate through prisoners his men had taken. "Xicotenga's response was that we should go to his town where his father was, where they will make peace by filling themselves with our flesh and honoring their gods with our hearts and blood." Xicotenga followed this response with an attack involving fifty thousand men led by some of the great Tlaxcalan chiefs, including Xicotenga's father (also called Xicotenga), Maseescaci, and Chichimecatecle. According to Bernal Díaz, "because we are men and fear death, many of us, even the majority of us, confessed to the Mercedarian father and the secular priest Juan Díaz, who were hearing confessions the whole night; and we commended ourselves to God, that he might protect us from being defeated." Because of divisions among the leaders of the Indians, and great coordination among Cortés's artillery, escopetas, and crossbows, as well as the effectiveness of the cannons, "and above all the great mercy of God, which gave us courage to sustain ourselves," Cortés and his men held off the attack.

[LXVI] After the battle I have described and taking in it the three Indian chieftains, our captain Cortés sent them along with the two others in our camp, who had gone other times as messengers, and he ordered them to tell the caciques of Tlaxcala that we begged them to come immediately to make peace and give us passage through their land to Mexico, as we had sent other times to say, and that if they did not come now, we would kill all their people, but because we cared very much for them and wanted to have them as brothers, we would not bother them if they did not give us cause to do so. He spoke many kind words to them to make them our friends. Very willingly, those messengers immediately went to the head town of Tlaxcala and gave the message to all the caciques named by me before, whom they found gathered together, with many other elders and *papas*, and they were very sad, as much for the poor outcome of the war as for the death of the captains who were their relatives or sons and who died in the battles, and it is said they did not willingly listen. They decided they would summon all the diviners and papas and others who drew lots, called *tacalnaguas*, who are like witches, and they told them to look through their prophesies, bewitchments, and lots to see what kind of people we were and if, by continually attacking us day and night, they could defeat us; also they wanted to know whether we were teules as the men of Cempoala said, and what things we ate, and they should look into all of this very carefully. When the diviners, witches, and many papas came together and made their prophesies and threw their lots, all the things they usually do, it seems that, in the lots, they found that we were men of flesh and bone, that we ate hens, dogs, bread, and fruit when we had it, that we did not eat the flesh of Indians nor the hearts of those we killed, for, as it seems, the Indian friends we brought from Cempoala made them believe we were teules, that we ate Indian hearts, that the cannons threw flashes of lightning like those that fall from the sky, that the hound was a tiger or lion, and that the horses could catch the Indians when we wanted to kill them; and they told them many other childish things. The worst of all that the papas and diviners told them was that by day we could not be defeated but by night, because at nightfall our strength left us; and the witches told them more, that we were strong and courageous, and that we had all these powers during the day until the sun set, but at nightfall we had no power at all. When the caciques heard that, and they took it as true, they sent to tell their captain general, Xicotenga, so that he would then quickly come one night with great forces to attack us. He, when he learned this, gathered about ten thousand Indians, the bravest they had, and he came to our camp. From three sides, they began to shoot arrows and cast single-pointed spears from straps, and from the fourth side, the men with swords, war clubs, and broadswords attacked suddenly, certain that they would carry some of us off to sacrifice.

Our Lord God caused better, for as secretly as they came, they found us very much ready, because as soon as our scouts and lookouts heard their great din, they came at breakneck speed to give the alarm; and as we were so accustomed to sleeping wearing our sandals and armor, the horses saddled and bridled, and every type of weapon at the ready, we resisted them with escopetas, crossbows, and sword thrusts. They quickly turned their backs. As the field was flat and the moon was out, the horsemen followed them a little way, where in the morning we found about twenty of them lying dead and wounded. So they returned with great loss and very regretful for having come at night. I have even heard that because what the papas, fortune-tellers, and witches told them did not turn out well, they sacrificed two of them.

That night they killed one of our Indian friends from Cempoala and wounded two soldiers and a horse, and we captured four of them. When we found ourselves free of that sudden skirmish, we gave thanks to God, buried the friend from Cempoala, treated the wounds and the horse, and we slept in the camp through what was left of the night with great precaution, just as we usually did. When day broke and we saw how all of us had two and three wounds, very tired, others sick and bandaged with rags, Xicotenga always pursuing us, and now we were missing more than forty-five soldiers who had died in the battles or from illnesses and chills, another twelve sick, our captain Cortés also with fevers, and even the Mercedarian father; with the hardship and weight of the armor we always wore on our backs and other misfortunes with chills and lack of salt, which we did not eat and could not find, and, more than this, we were taken up with thinking about what end we would meet in these wars and, were they to end there, what would become of us, where would we go, for we considered the idea of entering Mexico a joke because of their great armies, and we said among ourselves that if the Tlaxcalans, whom our friends from Cempoala had made us believe were peaceful people, had reduced us to such a condition, what would happen when we found ourselves at war with the great powers of Montezuma? Besides this, we did not know about those who were settled in Villa Rica, nor they of us.

Let us talk about how doña Marina, even though she was a native woman, had such manly strength and courage that, even though she heard each day that they wanted to kill us and eat our flesh with chilies and had seen us surrounded in the recent battles and saw that now we were all wounded and sick, we never saw weakness in her, but much greater strength than a woman's. Doña Marina and Jerónimo de Aguilar spoke to the messengers we were now sending and told them that the Tlaxcalans should immediately come to make peace, that if they did not come within two days we would go to kill them and destroy their lands, and we would go to seek them in their city. With these bold words, they went to the head town where Xicotenga the elder[43] and Maseescaci were.

[LXVII] When the messengers we had sent to negotiate peace arrived at Tlaxcala, they found the two most principal caciques, Maseescaci and Xicotenga the elder, father of the captain general also named Xicotenga, in consultation. After they heard the message, they were hesitant for a short while and did not speak, but it pleased God to inspire them to make peace with us. They

---

43. Xicotencatl, *el viejo* or *el ciego* ("the elder" or "the blind"); also, later, don Lorenzo de Vargas.

sent for all the rest of the caciques and captains in their towns and those of a province next to them, called Guaxocingo,[44] who were their friends and confederates. When they were all together in that town, which was the head town, Maseescaci and the old Xicotenga, who were very wise, made a speech, something like this as we later learned, although not these exact words: "Our friends and brothers: You have already seen how many times those teules who are in the country expecting attacks have sent us messengers asking for peace, and they say they are coming to help us and have us as brothers, and likewise you have seen how often they have taken many of our vassals prisoner, and they have not harmed them, and they release them quickly. You see well how we have attacked them three times with all our forces, both by day and by night, but we have not conquered them, and they have killed many of our men, sons, relatives, and captains in the assault we have made on them. Now again they return asking for peace, and the people of Cempoala who come in their company say they are opponents of Montezuma and his Mexicans, and they say they have ordered the towns of the Totonac sierra and Cempoala not to give him tribute. You will certainly remember that the Mexicans have made war on us every year for more than a hundred years, and you see well that we are as if penned up in our lands, and we do not dare go out to look for salt, so we do not have any to eat, nor even cotton, and we wear few cotton cloaks, for if some of us go out or have gone out to look for it, few return with their lives, because those treacherous Mexicans and their allies kill them and make them slaves. Now our tacalnaguas and diviners and papas have told us what they think of these teules, and it is that they are brave and strong. It seems to me that we should try to make friends with them, and if they are not men but teules, in one way or another let us keep full company with them. Four of our chieftains should go immediately and bring them good things to eat, and let us show them love and peace so that they support us and defend us from our enemies, and let us bring them here with us,

---

44. Huejotzingo.

and let us give them women so we might have relatives from their descendants, for, according to what the ambassadors they sent to negotiate peace say, they bring women with them."

When all the caciques and chieftains heard this speech, it seemed good to them, and they said it was the right thing, that they should immediately go to make peace, that someone should be sent to let the captain Xicotenga and the rest of the captains with him know they should come home immediately without making any more war, and tell them that we have already made peace; right away they sent messengers about it.

The captain Xicotenga the younger would not listen to the four chieftains and showed great anger and spoke to them with abusive words; he was against peace. He said he had already killed many teules and the mare, that he wanted to attack us another night and finish conquering and killing us. When his father Xicotenga the elder and Maseescaci and the rest of the caciques heard this response, they were so angry they immediately sent to order the captains and the entire army not to go with Xicotenga to make war on us nor obey anything he ordered, unless it was to make peace; nonetheless, he did not obey. When they saw the disobedience of their captains, they at once sent the same four chieftains they had sent another time to come to our camp and bring provisions and negotiate peace in the name of all Tlaxcala and Guaxocingo; but the four old men, for fear of Xicotenga the younger, did not come at that time.

[LXIX] Meanwhile, in the camp, groups of men began discussing the great dangers they faced everyday in the wars with the Tlaxcalans.

Those who spoke and took part in it most were those who had left their homes and allotments of Indians on the island of Cuba. Up to seven of them, whom I do not want to name here, to save their reputation, met and went to the hut and lodging of Cortés. One of them, who spoke for all, because he expressed himself well and had a good sense of what he was to propose, said, as though counseling Cortés, that he should consider how we were faring, badly wounded, thin, and beaten down, and the great hardships we experienced by night with watches, lookouts, patrols, and scouts and fighting both by day and by night, and that by their count, since leaving Cuba, more than fifty-five companions had been lost, and we knew nothing of those whom we had left settled in Villa Rica; that, although God had given us victory in battles and skirmishes since we came from Cuba and had been in that province and had sustained us with his great mercy, we should not tempt him so many times, and that it might turn out worse than Pedro Carbonero;[45] that he had put us in a place no one had expected, and one day or another, we would be sacrificed to idols, which it please God not to permit; that it would be good to return to our town and the fortress we had built, and we could stay among the towns of the Totonacs, our friends, until we built a ship that could take a message to Diego Velázquez and to other parts and islands to ask them for help and aid; and that now it would be good to have the ships we scuttled, or we might have left at least two of them for a necessity, if it might occur; and that without informing them of this, nor of anything else, on the advice of some people who do not know how to consider matters of fortune, he ordered all of them scuttled, and may it please God that he and those who have given him such advice not have to repent of it; that we were no longer able to endure the burden, much less the immense additional grief; and that we were going along worse than beasts, because after the beasts have done their daily work, they have their packs taken off and are given something to eat and rested, but that we, day and night, always were going along loaded with arms and wearing our sandals.

And they said more: That if he looked in all the histories, those of the Romans, of Alexander, or of the best-known captains the world has had, they would not have dared to wreck the ships, as

---

45. Pedro Carbonero, a mythic Spanish hero, conducted raids into the strongholds of the Muslims with little regard for his own life or the lives of his men. He died conducting such raids.

he had done, and with so few people invade such large populations with so many warriors, so that it appears he will be the author of his own death and all of ours, but he should wish to save his life and ours; and that we should return right away to Villa Rica, for that land was peaceful; that they had not said this until then because they had not found time for it because of the many warriors we faced every day from all sides, and although they had not yet returned again, they believed they certainly would return, for Xicotenga, with his great power, had not come after us for the past three days, so he must be gathering men, and we must not wait for another battle like the past ones; and they said other things about the matter.

Cortés, although they spoke to him somewhat arrogantly, given that they were proceeding as if they were giving advice, answered them very gently and said that he was well aware of many of the things they had said, and that from what he had seen and believed, in all the world there were no Spaniards stronger, nor having fought with such spirit, nor having endured such excessive hardships as we, but that had we not gone with arms always on our backs and endured watches and patrols and cold, we would already have been lost, and that it was to save our lives that we had to accept those hardships and others greater. He also said: "Why is it, gentlemen, that we talk about deeds of bravery, when truly Our Lord is pleased to help us? When I think about us surrounded by so many captaincies of enemies and seeing them use their broadswords and coming so close to us, it now horrifies me, especially when they killed the mare with a single slash, how lost and defeated we were, and then I recognized your very great spirit more than ever. Since God delivered us from such great danger, I have hoped he would continue to do so in the future." He said more: "For in all such dangers, you saw no idleness in me, for I was there with you." He was right in saying it, because certainly in all those battles, he was at the front. "I wanted, gentlemen, to remind you, that, as Our Lord has been pleased to protect us, we must have hope that it will be the same in the future, for ever since we entered into this land, we preached in all those towns the holy doctrine as best we were able and tried to destroy their idols. Since we now see that neither the captain Xicotenga nor his captaincies appear, and they don't dare return out of fear because we must have done them much harm in recent battles, and they're not able now to gather their men, having already been defeated three times, I trust in God and his advocate, St. Peter, who intercedes for us, that the war of that province has ended." He said further that the scuttling of the ships was very well advised and that if he had not called some of them to counsel with him as he had others, it was because of what he experienced on the sandy beach, which he did not want to remind them of now; that the counsel and advice they were giving him now were the same as what they gave him then; that they consider that there are many gentlemen in the camp who would be very much against what they are now asking and counseling, and it would be better that we should always guide all matters toward God and carry them out in his holy service. "As to what you gentlemen say, that never did any of the most renowned Roman captains undertake such great feats as we, you're right, and in the future, with God's help, they'll say in the histories that will record this much more than they say about the ancients, for, as I've said, everything we do is in the service of God and our great emperor don Carlos. Under his righteous justice and Christianity, we'll be aided by the mercy of God Our Lord, and he'll sustain us so that we go from good to better. So, gentlemen, it's certainly not a good thing to take a step backward, for if these people and those we leave behind in peace were to see us turn back, the stones would rise against us, and as now they regard us as gods or idols and call us such, they'd consider us cowardly and weak. As for what you say about staying among the friendly Totonacs, our allies, if they should see us turn back without going to Mexico, they'd rise against us, and the reason would be that, because we stopped them from giving tribute to Montezuma, he'd send his Mexican forces against them to make them pay tribute again, and he'd attack them over it, and he might even order them to attack us, and they, in order not to be destroyed, because they very much fear the Mexicans, would do it. So, where we thought we had friends, there would be enemies. When the great Montezuma learned that we had turned back, what would he say? How would he regard our words and what we said in our messages? That it was all mockery or childish games. So, gentlemen, if one way is bad and the other worse, it's better to stay where we are, where the ground is very flat and all well populated, and this our camp well supplied, sometimes hens and other times dogs. Thanks be to God we are not lacking in things to eat, if we had salt, which is the greatest lack we have at present, and clothes to protect us from the cold. As to what you say, gentlemen, that since we left the island of Cuba, fifty-five soldiers have died from wounds, hunger, cold, illness, and hardship and that we are few and all very wounded and sick, God gives us the strength of many, because it's an acknowledged fact that wars use up men and horses and that sometimes we eat well, but we didn't come here to rest but to fight when the occasion presented itself. Therefore, I ask you, gentlemen, please, since you are gentlemen and people who, instead of this, should be encouraging those you see showing weakness, that from now on, you stop thinking about the island of Cuba and what you left there and try to do what you've always done as good soldiers, for after God, who is our help and aid, we have to depend on our own strong arms."

When Cortés had given this response, those soldiers repeated their same conversation and said that everything he said was all very well, but that when we left the town we had settled, our intention was, and still is now, to go to Mexico, for it has great fame as so strong a city with such a multitude of warriors. The people of Cempoala said that those Tlaxcalans were peaceful and did not have a reputation like those of Mexico, but we have been so at risk for our lives that if they should battle us again another day, we are now too exhausted to hold fast; and even if they did not attack us, the journey to Mexico seemed to them a terrible thing, and he should be careful what he said and ordered. Cortés answered them somewhat angrily that it was better to die as good men, as the Psalms say, than to live dishonored. Besides what Cortés told them, all the rest of us soldiers who had elected him captain and advised him about scuttling the ships said loudly that he should not worry about people standing around in groups nor listen to such talk, but, with the help of God, with good concerted action, we would be ready to do what is necessary. So all the discussion stopped. It is true that they grumbled about Cortés and cursed him, and even those of us who had advised him and those from Cempoala who brought us this way, and they said other ugly things; but in such times, they were tolerated. In the end, everyone obeyed very well.

I will stop speaking about this, and I will talk about how the old caciques of the head town of Tlaxcala sent messengers again, another time, to their captain general, Xicotenga, to say that without fail he should come right away in peace to see us and bring us things to eat, because all the caciques and principal chieftains of that land and of Guaxocingo had ordered it; and they also sent to order the captains who were in his company not to obey him in anything at all if he did not go to negotiate in peace. This they sent to tell him three times, because they knew for certain he would not obey them; rather Xicotenga had resolved that one night he was going to attack our camp again, because for doing so he had gathered twenty thousand men, and as he was arrogant and very stubborn, now as in the other times, he would not obey.

[LXX] As Xicotenga had a very bad disposition and was obstinate and arrogant, he decided to send us forty Indians with food—hens, bread, and fruit—and four women, old, wretched-looking Indian women, much copal and many parrot feathers. From the appearance of the Indians who brought these things, we believed they came in peace, but when they arrived at our camp, they perfumed Cortés without doing him the reverence usual among them, and they said: "The captain Xicotenga sent you this so that you can eat. If you are fierce teules as the people of Cempoala say, and if you want sacrifices, take these four women to sacrifice and you can eat their flesh and their hearts. Because we do not know how you do your sacrifices, we have not sacrificed them now in front of you. But if you are men, eat these hens, bread, and fruit, and if you are gentle teules, here we have brought you copal and parrot feathers; make your sacrifice with that." Cortés answered, with our interpreters, that he had already sent to them to say he desired peace and he had not come to make war. Rather, he had come to beg them and show them on behalf of Our Lord Jesus Christ, the one in whom we believe and whom we worship, and of the emperor don Carlos, whose vassals we are, that they should neither kill nor sacrifice anyone as they usually do; that we are all men of flesh and bone, like them, and not teules, but Christians; that it is not our custom to kill anyone, but that if we wanted to kill, all the times they attacked us day and night gave us many occasions for committing cruelties; and that he gave them thanks for the food they brought there, and he said they should not be foolish as they had been but should come in peace.

It seems that those Indians Xicotenga sent with the food were spies who were to look at our huts, horses, and artillery and see how many of us were in each hut, our comings and goings, everything there was in our camp. They stayed all day and night, and some went with messages to Xicotenga and others arrived. The friends we brought from Cempoala watched and got the idea, for it was not customary for our enemies to be in the camp day and night with no purpose and that it was certain they were spies. They were even more suspicious because when we went to the little town of Zunpancingo, two old men of that town told the Cempoalans that Xicotenga was prepared with many warriors to attack our camp by night in such a way that they would not be detected. The Cempoalans at that time took it as a hoax or bravado, and because they did not know for certain they had not said anything to Cortés. But doña Marina immediately learned of it and told Cortés. To learn the truth, Cortés ordered that two of the Tlaxcalans who seemed to be men of goodwill be taken aside, and they confessed that they were spies; and two others were taken and they also said that they were Xicotenga's spies and gave the whole reason why they had come. Cortés ordered them to be set free, and again another two were taken, who said no more no less than the others, and they also said that their captain Xicotenga was waiting for their report in order to attack us that night with all his captaincies. When Cortés learned this, he made it known throughout the whole camp so that we would be very alert, believing they would come as they had planned.

Then he ordered seventeen of those Indian spies seized, and he had the hands of some of them cut off and the thumbs of others, and he sent them to their lord Xicotenga. He said he had carried out that punishment for their audacity in coming that way, and Xicotenga and his men could come whenever they wanted, day or night, that we would be waiting for him there two days, and that if within the two days he did not come, we would go looking for him in his camp; that we would already have gone to attack them and kill them except that we liked them very much, and that they should not be foolish but should come in peace. They say that it was at that moment when Xicotenga was about to set out from his camp with all his forces to attack us at night as he had planned, those Indians with the hands and thumbs cut off got there. When he saw his spies coming in that way, he was astonished and asked the reason for it, and they told him everything that had happened. From then on, he lost his spirit and arrogance, and in addition to this, one captain with whom in past battles he had had a partisan conflict had already left his camp with all his men.

[LXXI] While we were in our camp not knowing whether the Indians were going to come in peace, as we very much desired, and we were occupied with cleaning our arms and making bolts for the crossbows, each one doing what was necessary for making war, one of our scouts came at great speed saying that by the main road from Tlaxcala, many Indian men and women were coming with loads, and they were coming straight down the road toward our camp; the other scout, his companion, who was on horseback, was watching to see where they went. Soon, the other companion on horseback came and said that the Indians were coming directly to where we were and that from time to time they were making short stops. Cortés and all of us were delighted with that news because we believed it was about peace, as it was. Cortés ordered that there not be any show of alarm or emotion and that we should be hidden in our huts. Then, from among all those people who were coming with the loads, four chieftains came forward who had authority to negotiate peace, as they had been ordered by the old caciques. Making signs of peace, which was to bow their heads, they came directly to the hut and lodging of Cortés, put a hand on the soil, kissed the ground, gave three bows, burnt their copal, and said that all the caciques of Tlaxcala, their vassals and allies, friends and confederates, were coming to put themselves under the friendship and peace of Cortés and all his brothers, the teules, who were with him; that he should pardon them for not having come out peacefully and for the attacks they had made on us, because they believed and were certain we were friends of Montezuma and his Mexicans, who have been their mortal enemies since ancient times, because they saw that many of his vassals who pay tribute to him came with us and in our company, and they believed that they were trying to enter their land with deceit and treachery, as was their custom, to steal their children and women, and for this reason they did not believe the messengers we had sent to them; more than this, they said that the first Indians who came out to attack us as we entered into their lands did not do so by their command and counsel, but by that of the Chontales[46] and Otomis, who were wild people and without reason, and when they saw we were so few, they believed they could capture us and carry us as prisoners to their lords and win thanks from them; that now they come to ask pardon for their boldness, and they brought those provisions and would bring more every day; that we should receive it with the friendliness with which it was sent; and that within two days, the captain Xicotenga would come with other caciques and give a fuller account of the goodwill all of Tlaxcala has for our friendship. After they had finished this speech, they bowed their heads, put their hands on the earth, and kissed the ground.

[LXXII] As Our Lord God, through his great mercy, was pleased to give us victory in those battles of Tlaxcala, our fame

---

46. *Chontales* refers generally to groups indigenous to southern Mexico and modern-day Central America.

flew through all those territories, and it reached the ears of the great Montezuma in the great city of Mexico; if before they considered us teules, which are their idols, from here on we had an even greater reputation among them as strong warriors. It shocked people all over the land that with there being so few of us and the Tlaxcalans having such great forces, we conquered them, and now they had sent to ask peace from us. So Montezuma, great lord of Mexico, whether as a very benevolent person or because he feared our coming to his city, sent five chieftains of great importance to Tlaxcala and to our camp to welcome us and to say that he took much pleasure in the great victory we had against so many squadrons of opponents. He sent a present, worth about a thousand gold pesos in very rich jewelry, very carefully worked, and twenty loads of fine cotton cloth. He sent to say he would like to be a vassal of our great emperor and it pleased him that we were already close to his city because of the goodwill he had for Cortés and all the teules, his brothers. He said that Cortés should see how much tribute he wanted each year for our great emperor, that he would give it in gold, silver, cloth, and chalchiui stones, provided we not go to Mexico. This was not because he did not welcome us with very goodwill, but because the land was barren and rough, and, if he saw our hardships, it would make him very sad, and, perhaps, he could not remedy them as well as he would like. Cortés replied to him that he was very grateful for the goodwill he showed, the present he sent, and the offer to give tribute to His Majesty. He begged the messengers not to leave before going to the head town of Tlaxcala, for he would send them off from there so they might see how the war was turning out. He did not want to give his response at once because the day before he had purged himself with some chamomiles from the island of Cuba, which are very good for anyone who knows how to take them.

[LXXIII] While Cortés was talking with Montezuma's ambassadors and wanted to rest because he was ill from fever and purging from the day before, they came to tell him that the captain Xicotenga was coming with many caciques and captains and that they were all clothed in white and red cloaks. Half of each cloak was white and the other red, which was their device and livery. Xicotenga was coming very much in peace, and about fifty chieftains accompanied him. When Xicotenga arrived at Cortés's lodging, he showed Cortés very great respect in his bows and ordered much copal to be burned. Cortés, with great affection, indicated that Xicotenga should sit next to him. Xicotenga told him that he came on behalf of his father, of Maseescaci and all the caciques and governing body of Tlaxcala, to beg him to grant them our friendship; that he came to pledge obedience to our king and lord and to ask pardon for having taken up arms and attacked us; that if they did so, it was because of not knowing who we were, for they were sure we had come on behalf of their enemy Montezuma, and, as many times the Mexicans tend to use craftiness and guile to enter their lands and rob them and plunder, they believed that this is what they were doing now; and that for this reason they endeavored to defend their people and native country and were obliged to fight; that they were very poor, with no gold, silver, precious stones, cotton cloths, or even salt to eat, because Montezuma does not let them go out to look for it; that if their ancestors had had some gold and valuable stones, they had given them to Montezuma when they occasionally made peace and truces so the Mexicans would not destroy them, but this was in times long past. Because at present they had nothing to give, he should pardon them; their poverty is the reason for it and not lack of goodwill.

He complained a great deal about Montezuma and his allies, all of whom were against them and attacked them, although they had defended themselves very well. Now they wanted to do the same with us but could not; even though they had gathered three times with all their warriors, we were invincible. When they recognized this about us, they wanted to be our friends and vassals of the great lord, the emperor don Carlos, because they were certain that in our company they, their women and children would be protected and defended, and they would not always be in fear of sudden assault by the treacherous Mexicans. He made many other promises concerning themselves and their city.

This Xicotenga was tall, broad shouldered, and well built, and his face was long, somewhat pitted, and broad; he was about thirty-five years old and stately in appearance. Cortés thanked him very politely, using friendly words, and said he would accept them as vassals of our king and lord and as our friends. Then Xicotenga begged us to come to his city, because all the caciques, elders, and papas were waiting for us with great joy. Cortés replied that he would come quickly and that he would have gone immediately except that he was busy negotiating with the great Montezuma, but once he had sent off Montezuma's messengers, he would come.

The Mexican ambassadors were present at all these conversations and promises, and the peace caused them great concern because they understood well that no good whatsoever would come to them because of it. When Xicotenga had taken his leave, the ambassadors of Montezuma asked Cortés, half laughing, if he believed any of those promises they had made on behalf of all Tlaxcala; that it was all a trick; that we should not believe them; that they were the words of traitors, deceitful; that they said them so that after they had us in their city, in a place where they could safely take us, they would attack and kill us; that we should remember how many times they had come to kill us with all their forces, and as they could not, and they lost many dead and wounded, they now wanted to avenge themselves by asking for a fake peace. Cortés answered them with a very brave expression, saying he did not care in the least whether they should have had such thoughts as the Mexicans had said, and even if everything they said was true, he would take satisfaction in punishing them by taking their lives, and that this would be true whether they attacked by day or by night, in the fields or in the city, that it was all the same to him, and the reason he is determined to go there is to see if it is true. Seeing his determination, the ambassadors begged him to stay in our camp for six days, because they wanted to send to their lord Montezuma two of their companions, who would return with a response within that time. Cortés promised to do so, first, because as I have said, he had a fever, and also, even though he appeared not to heed the things those ambassadors said to him, he understood that, if they were true, he had to take them into account until he saw greater certainty of peace.

Because at that time the Tlaxcalans had come in peace, and all along the road by which we came from our Villa Rica de la Veracruz the people were our friends and allies, Cortés wrote to Juan de Escalante, whom he had left in the town to finish building the fort and as captain of some sixty old and sick soldiers who stayed there. In these letters he informed them of the great mercies Our Lord Jesus Christ had shown us in our victories in the battles and skirmishes since we had entered the province of Tlaxcala, where now the Indians had come for peace, and he asked all of them to give thanks to God for it and to see that they always favor the Totonac towns, our friends. Cortés also asked Juan de Escalante to send right away by courier two jugs of wine he had left buried in a certain marked part of his lodging as well as wafer hosts from those they had brought from the island of Cuba, because we had already finished the ones we brought on this expedition. It is said that in the town they took great pleasure in those letters, and Escalante wrote about what had happened there. Everything came very quickly. At that time, we erected a magnificent, tall cross in our camp, and Cortés ordered the Indians of Cingapacinga and those in the houses near our camp to plaster a place for it with lime and have it beautifully decorated.

Let us return to our new friends, the caciques of Tlaxcala, who, when they saw we were not going to their town, came to our camp with hens and prickly pear fruits, then in season, and each one brought provisions he had in his house and gave it to us with goodwill, without wanting anything at all in return, always begging Cortés to come soon with them to their city. Because we were waiting six days for the Mexicans, as Cortés had promised, he held them off with gentle words. When the time the Mexicans had set had passed, six chieftains, men held in great esteem, came from Mexico and brought an exquisite present sent by the great Montezuma, which was more than three thousand gold pesos worth of rich jewels of various styles and two hundred pieces of cloth, very fine cloaks, covered with feathers and other fancy work. When they presented it, they said to Cortés that their lord Montezuma rejoiced in our good fortune, but he begged him most earnestly on no account to go with the Tlaxcalans to their town, nor to trust them, that they wanted to bring him there to rob him of his gold and cloth because they are so poor that even a good cloak of cotton cloth is beyond them, and that knowing that Montezuma considers us as friends and is sending us the gold, jewels, and cloaks, they would try even harder to rob us. Cortés happily received that present and said he was grateful and would repay the lord Montezuma with good deeds, that if he sensed that the Tlaxcalans had in their thoughts what Montezuma sent to warn them, he would pay them for it by taking all their lives; but he said he knew with certainty they would not attempt such vile deeds and that he still wanted to go to see what they might do. In the midst of these exchanges many other messengers came from Tlaxcala, telling Cortés that all the old caciques from the head town of the whole province were coming close to our huts to see Cortés and all of us, to bring us to their city. When Cortés learned this, he begged the Mexican ambassadors to wait three days for the messages to their lord, because he had at present to discuss and attend to the past war and the peace they were now negotiating; and they said they would wait.

The old caciques of all Tlaxcala, fearful of Cortés's negotiations with the Mexicans, came to his camp to talk him into coming immediately to their city.

Before going any further, I would like to say that in all the towns through which we passed and in others where they knew about us, they called Cortés "Malinche," and from here on, I will call him this, Malinche, in all the conversations we might have with any Indians in this province as well as the city of Mexico, and I will not call him Cortés except where appropriate. The reason Cortés was given this name is that, as doña Marina our interpreter was always in his company, especially when ambassadors arrived or in discussions with caciques, and she spoke to them in the Mexican language, they called Cortés "Marina's captain," and for short they called him Malinche. I also want to say that, from the time we entered the land of Tlaxcala until we went to their city, twenty-four days had passed; so we entered the city on September 23, 1519.

[LXXV] Even though we were in a land where we saw clearly that the people were of goodwill and very peaceful, we did not forget about being well prepared, as was usual with us. It seems that a captain of ours, to whom fell the watch when scouts, look-outs, and sentries were to be posted, said to Cortés, "It seems, sir, that they're very peaceful; we don't have need of so many guards nor to be as cautious as we usually are." Cortés said: "Look, gen-tlemen, I, too, can see well what you've said, but it's good prac-tice that we be on the alert, and although they may be very good people, we mustn't have faith in their peacefulness, but act as if they were going to attack and we see them coming against us, for many captains have been defeated because of overconfidence and carelessness. We, especially, must be very alert as we're so few and because the great Montezuma sent to warn us, even though it might be false and not true." Let us stop talking about such exchanges and the order we kept on our watches and guards and return to talking about how Xicotenga the elder and Maseescaci, who were great caciques, became annoyed with Cortés and said through our interpreters: "Malinche, either you consider us ene-mies, or you show in actions that you do not have confidence in us and in the peace you have given us and we you, and we say this because we see how you keep watch and came along the roads on the alert as you did when you were coming against our squadrons. This we believe you do, Malinche, because of the falsehoods and evil things the Mexicans have secretly told you to put you on bad terms with us. Be sure you do not believe them, for now you are here and we will give you everything you want, even ourselves and our children, and we will die for you; for that reason you can ask for hostages at your will." Cortés and all of us were astonished at the pleasantness and kindness with which they said this. Cortés

answered that is what he had believed and had no need of hostages, but that seeing their goodwill was enough; as for being on
the alert, we always did so as a matter of custom, and he should
not take it badly; for all the promises they gave us, he was grateful
and would repay them in the time to come. With these conversations over, other chieftains came with large provisions of hens,
maize bread, prickly pear fruit, and other types of vegetables that
the land provided, and they supplied the camp very fully. In the
twenty days we were there, there was always more than enough;
and we entered this city, as I said, on the 23rd of September, 1519.

[LXXVI] The next morning Cortés ordered that an altar be
put up so that mass could be said, because we now had wine and
wafer hosts. The secular priest Juan Díaz said mass because the
Mercedarian father was feverish and very weak, and Maseescaci,
the elder Xicotenga, and other caciques were present.

It seems that all the caciques had agreed among themselves to
give us, from among their daughters and nieces, the most beautiful maidens to marry. The elder Xicotenga said: "Malinche, so you
might know more clearly the good we want for you and that we
desire to please you in everything, we want to give our daughters
to be your wives and have children because we want to have you
as brothers, for you are so good, strong, and courageous. I have
a very beautiful daughter, and she has not been married; I want
her for you." Likewise, Maseescaci and all the rest of the caciques
said they would bring their daughters and that we should accept
them as wives, and they said many other words and made other
promises, and all day both Maseescaci and Xicotenga stayed close
to Cortés. As he was blind from age, Xicotenga, with his hand,
felt Cortés on his head, beard, and face and ran his hands over all
his body. Cortés replied to them regarding the women that he and
all of us were very grateful and that we would repay them in good
deeds as time went on. The Mercedarian father was present there,
and Cortés said to him: "Father, it seems to me that this will be
a good time to try to get these caciques to give up their idols and
not to sacrifice; they'll do whatever we order them because of the
fear they have of the Mexicans." The friar said: "Sir, that's all very

well, but let's leave it until they bring the daughters, and then we'll have an occasion to talk about it. You'll say that you don't want to accept the women until they promise not to sacrifice any longer; if that works, good; if not, we'll do what we're obliged to do." So it was left for the next day.

[LXXVII] The next day the same old caciques came and brought five beautiful young Indian maidens with them, and for Indians they were very good-looking and nicely adorned, and for each Indian woman they brought another Indian girl as her servant, and all were daughters of caciques. Xicotenga said to Cortés: "Malinche, this is my daughter; she has not been married and is a maiden, take her for yourself." He gave her to him by the hand and said he should give the others to the captains. Cortés thanked him, and with a pleasant expression said that he accepted them and took them as their own, but at present they should stay with their parents. The same caciques asked why we did not take them now. Cortés replied, "Because I want first to do what is ordered by Our Lord God, in whom we believe and whom we worship, and what the king our lord sent us to do"—which was to have them remove their idols and see that they no longer sacrifice or kill people, nor do the other evil and filthy things they have the custom of doing—"and believe in what we believe, which is one true God alone."

With pleas, we ordered them immediately to clear out a newly built cu nearby, take away some idols, plaster it, and clean it in order to put a cross and an image of Our Lady there, which they did right away. In it mass was said, those cacicas were baptized, and the name of doña Luisa was given to the blind Xicotenga's daughter. Cortés took her by the hand and gave her to Pedro de Alvarado, and he said to Xicotenga that the one to whom he gave her was his brother and his captain and that he should give it his approval because she would be very well treated by him; and Xicotenga was content. The daughter or niece of Maseescaci was given the name doña Elvira, and she was very beautiful, and it seems to me that Cortés gave her to Juan Velázquez de León; the rest were given baptismal names, all with doña, and Cortés gave them to

Gonzalo de Sandoval, Cristóbal de Olid, and Alonso de Ávila. When this was done, Cortés told them why two crosses were put up, and it was because their idols feared them and that wherever we set up a camp or slept, we put them in the roads, and they were very content with all this.

Chapter 8

The Incident at Cholula

[LXXIX] Our captain, realizing we had been resting seventeen days in Tlaxcala and were hearing about the great riches of Montezuma and his thriving city, resolved to consult all of us captains and soldiers who he felt had a strong will to go forward, and it was decided that our departure would be very soon. There were many dissenting discussions about this course in the camp because some soldiers said it was frightening for us to enter so strong a city, we being so few in number, and they talked about the great forces of Montezuma. Cortés replied that it was too late now to do anything else because our goal and battle cry had always been to see Montezuma, so counsel otherwise was now useless. Those in opposition, seeing that he said this with such determination, and sensing that many of us soldiers supported Cortés very willingly by shouting, "Go right on ahead!" dropped their opposition. The ones involved in this talk of opposition were the ones who had property in Cuba, but I and the other poor soldiers had always offered our souls to God, who created them, and our bodies to wounds and hardships, even to death in the service of Our Lord God and His Majesty.

We spoke about the road we should take to Mexico, because Montezuma's ambassadors who were with us, who were going as guides, said that the best and most level road was through the city of Cholula, where we would be well taken care of because they were vassals of the great Montezuma, and to all of us it seemed good advice to go by that city; however, when the caciques of Tlaxcala learned that we were going to go where the Mexicans were directing us, they were very sad and again said that in any case we should go by Guaxocingo where their relatives and our friends were and not by Cholula, for in Cholula Montezuma always kept his double-dealings hidden. However much they talked to and counseled us not to enter that city, our captain, with our very fully discussed advice, was still resolved to go through Cholula. For one thing, everyone said it was a large town with many towers and high, large cus, set down on a beautiful plain that truly looked from afar at that time like our Valladolid in Old Castile. For another reason, it was an area near large settlements, and we would have many provisions and have our friends the Tlaxcalans close at hand. Our intention was to stay there until we saw how we could go to Mexico without having a war, because the great power of the Mexicans was to be feared; unless Our Lord God first extended us his divine hand and mercy, with which he always helped us and gave us strength, we could not enter Mexico.

After many discussions and resolutions, our road was through Cholula. Cortés then ordered that messengers go to ask the people of Cholula why, being so close, they did not come to visit and pay us the respect due us as messengers of such a great king and lord as the one who sent us to notify them of their salvation. He asked that all the caciques and papas of that city come immediately to see us and pledge their loyalty to our king and lord; if not, he would consider them to have bad intentions. While he was saying this and other things appropriate for a message to them about this matter, they came to let Cortés know that the great Montezuma was sending four ambassadors with presents of gold; never, from what we had seen, did he send a message without a present of gold and cloth, because they consider it an insult to send messages if they do not send presents with them.

[LXXXI] I have already said how our captain sent messengers to Cholula so they would come to see us at Tlaxcala. The caciques of that city, when they learned what Cortés ordered them to do, thought it best to send four Indians of little standing to make excuses for them and to say that because they were ill they could not come; they did not bring provisions or anything else, but dryly gave that response. When those messengers arrived, the caciques of Tlaxcala were present, and they said to our captain that the Cholulans sent those Indians to make a mockery of him and all of us, for they were *maceguales*, people of low status. So Cortés immediately sent them back with four Indians of Cempoala, warning the Cholulans that chieftains should come within three days, for Cholula was only five leagues from there, and that if they did not come he would consider them rebels. He said that when they came, he would tell them things that would be well advised for the salvation of their souls and good principles for their way of life, and we would have them as friends and brothers as are the Tlaxcalans, their neighbors, but that if they resolved otherwise and did not want our friendship, we would not for that reason try to displease and annoy them. When the caciques heard that message, they replied that they were not coming to Tlaxcala because the Tlaxcalans were their enemies, and they knew that the Tlaxcalans had said many bad things about them and their lord Montezuma. They said that we should come to their city and leave the boundaries of Tlaxcala, and that if they did not act as they should, we could consider them exactly as we had sent to say they were. When our captain saw that the excuse they gave was very just, we decided to go there. When the caciques of Tlaxcala saw that we were so determined to leave for Cholula, they said to Cortés: "So you want to believe the Mexicans and not us, who are your friends. We have already told you many times to watch out for the people of Cholula and the power of Mexico. So that you can have better support from us, we have readied ten thousand warriors who will go in your company." Cortés thanked them very much, but consulting with all of us decided it would not be good to bring so many warriors to a land where we wanted to find friends, but it would be good to take a thousand, and he asked them for that many and said that the rest should stay in their homes.

> *[LXXXII] When Cortés and his men set out on the road for Cholula, they were welcomed by messengers, chieftains, sent by the caciques of Cholula. Bernal Díaz observed that "most of them wore cotton cloths made like Moorish tunics, like those the Zapotecan Indians wear." The chieftains objected to the armed Tlaxcalans coming to their city. Cortés felt they were right to object, so he sent Pedro de Alvarado and Cristóbal de Olid to ask the Tlaxcalans to stay outside the city. Cortés then asked the chieftains to pledge loyalty to the king, and they did so, "but not before a notary."* [47]

[LXXXIII] The Cholulans had received us very ceremoniously and certainly with goodwill, except that as was found out afterward, Montezuma sent to order his ambassadors who were with us to arrange with the Cholulans that, together with a squadron of twenty thousand men Montezuma had sent, they should be ready, when the Mexicans entered the city, for all of them to attack us night or day, seize us, and carry those of us they could, bound, to Mexico. He sent them great promises, much jewelry and clothing, and a golden drum, and he told the papas of that city they were to take twenty of us to make sacrifices to their idols. With everything arranged, and when the warriors Montezuma sent were in some huts and thickets about a half league from Cholula and others already inside, in the houses, all of them ready with their arms, defenses put up on the rooftops, pits and barricades in the streets so the horses could not run, and some houses already filled with long poles, leather collars, and ropes with which they were to bind and carry us to Mexico, Our Lord God did better, so that everything turned out the opposite on them.

---

47. The significance of this phrase is that although the pledge of loyalty might be morally binding, it was not, strictly speaking, legally binding.

Let us leave this now and return to talking about how, when they lodged us, they fed us very well the first two days, but although they seemed peaceful, we continued always to be very much at the ready because of our good custom of doing so. On the third day, they neither gave us anything to eat nor did any cacique or papa appear, and if any Indians came to see us, they were at a distance and did not come to us but were laughing as though mocking us. When our captain saw that, he told doña Marina and Aguilar, our interpreters, to tell the ambassadors of the great Montezuma who were there to order the caciques to bring some food, but what they brought was water and wood; and some old men who brought it said there was no more maize. That same day, other ambassadors from Montezuma came and joined those who were with us, and they said to Cortés very shamelessly that their lord sent them to say that we should not go to his city because he had nothing to give us to eat and that they wanted to return right away to Mexico with a response. When Cortés understood that, and he thought poorly of their speech, he said very blandly to the ambassadors that he was surprised a great lord like Montezuma would have so many changes of mind, and he begged them not to go to Mexico because the next day he wanted to leave to see Montezuma and do whatever he might order, and it seems to me that he gave them some strings of beads. The ambassadors said that, yes, they would stay.

This done, our captain ordered us to come together, and he said to us: "I see there is something very wrong with these people; let's be very much on the alert in case some mischief is going on with them." Then he sent for the principal cacique, and I do not remember his name now, to come or send some other chieftains; the cacique replied that he was ill and could not come. When our captain heard that, he ordered us to bring to his lodgings two of the many papas from the great cu near our lodgings, using persuasive arguments. We brought two of them without doing them disrespect, and Cortés ordered that each one of them be given a chalchiui, which are very much valued among them, like emeralds, and he asked them with kindly words why the cacique and chieftains and all the rest of the papas were afraid, that he had sent for them and they did not want to come. It seems that one of those papas was very important among them, something like a bishop, for he had charge or command over all the rest of the cus of that city, and they held him in great respect. He said that they, the papas, had no fear of us; that if the cacique and chieftains did not want to come, he would go himself to summon them, and that when he spoke to them, he believed they would do as he wanted and come. Then Cortés said that he should go ahead but that his companion should wait there until he returned. That papa went and summoned the cacique and chieftains, and soon they came with him to Cortés's lodging. He asked them through our interpreters why they were afraid and why they had not given us anything to eat; that if they were having difficulties with our being in their city, the next morning we would leave for Mexico to see and speak to the lord Montezuma; that they should have tamemes ready to carry the baggage and *tepuzques*, which are the cannons, and also that they should bring food right away. The cacique was so fearful he hardly managed to speak and said they would go look for the food, but that their lord Montezuma had sent to order them not to give us food, nor did he want us to go on from there.

In the midst of these discussions, three people from Cempoala, our friends, came in and secretly said to Cortés that they had found, close to where we were lodged, holes dug in the streets covered over with wood and earth on top, which, if one did not look carefully, could not be seen, that they removed the earth from on top of one hole and it was filled with very sharp stakes to kill the horses if they charged, that the rooftops were filled with stones and adobe brick defenses, and that they were certainly not for a good purpose, because they also found barricades of thick wood in another street. At that moment there arrived eight of the Tlaxcalan Indians we had left outside the city, who did not enter Cholula, and they said to Cortés: "Be careful, Malinche, for there is something wrong in this city; we know that this night they have sacrificed to their idol, the one for war, seven people, five of them children, so that it will give them victory against you, and also we have seen that they are removing all the baggage and women and children." When Cortés heard that, he immediately sent the Tlaxcalans to their captains to let them know to be ready if we sent for them. He spoke again to the cacique and papas and chieftains of Cholula, saying they should not be afraid nor be upset, and they should think about the loyalty they had pledged and they should not break it, that if they did he would punish them for it. He reminded them that we had already said we wanted to set out in the morning and he had need of two thousand warriors from that city to go with us, like the Tlaxcalans had given us, because they will be necessary on the roads. They told him, yes, they would provide them and asked permission to go then to get them ready. They left very content because they believed that, with the warriors they were going to give us and with Montezuma's captaincies in the thickets and huts, we could not escape death or capture because the horses would not be able to charge, and because of certain defenses and barricades, which they now advised those in the garrison to make in such a way that there would be only a narrow lane, through which we could not pass. They warned the Mexicans that the next day we were going to leave and they should all be very much prepared, because they would give us two thousand warriors and, when we were going along off our guard, between the two forces they would make their captures there, and they could bind us; they were certain of this because they had made sacrifices to their war idols and had been promised victory.

Let us stop speaking about this, which they thought was a certainty, and return to our captain, who wanted to know in detail everything about the agreement and what was happening. He told doña Marina to take more chalchiuis to the two papas who had spoken first, for they were not afraid, and to tell them with kindly words that Malinche wanted to talk to them again, and that she should bring them with her. Doña Marina went and spoke to them in that way she knew so well how to do, and with the gifts they came with her right away. Cortés told them they should speak the truth about what they knew, for they were priests of the idols and chieftains who should not lie; he told them that what they said would not be revealed in any way whatsoever because the next day we were going to leave, and he would give them a great deal of cloth. They said the truth was that their lord Montezuma knew we were coming to that city, and each day he was of many minds; he could not definitely decide what to do. Sometimes he ordered them to do us much honor and guide us to his city if we went there, and other times he sent to say that it was not his will that we go to Mexico. They said that now recently his Tezcatepuca and his Huichilobos, for whom they had great devotion, had counseled him that they should kill us there in Cholula or carry us bound to Mexico, that the day before he had sent twenty thousand warriors, half of them already here inside the city and the other half nearby in some ravines. They said they had already been informed we were going to go tomorrow and about the barricades they had ordered erected, the two thousand warriors that were to be given to us, and how they had already made an agreement that twenty of us were to be sacrificed to the idols of Cholula. Cortés ordered that these papas be given very highly decorated cloaks and begged them not to talk about all of this, for if they revealed it, we would kill them on our return from Mexico. He told them we wanted to go early in the morning and that they should have all the caciques come then so that he might speak to them.

That night Cortés took counsel about what we should do, because he had with him extraordinary men with good advice; but as such things often go, some said it would be best to change the route and go by Guaxocingo; others said we should try to make peace in whatever way we could, and we should return to Tlaxcala; others of us gave an opinion that if we allowed those treacheries to pass without punishment, then wherever we went others would treat us worse, and because we were there in that great town with plenty of provisions, we should attack them, because they would feel it more in their homes than in the country, and we should get the Tlaxcalans ready right away so that they might join in; and to everyone this last advice seemed right. This is how it happened: Because Cortés had said we were going to leave the next day, we should make as though we were packing up our things, which were little enough, and in some large, high-walled courtyards there where we were lodged, we should attack the Indian warriors, for that is what they deserved. As for the ambassadors of Montezuma, we should conceal what we were doing and tell them that the evil Cholulans had wanted to do something treacherous and cast the blame for it on their lord Montezuma and on them, as his ambassadors, but we did not believe he ordered any such thing. We begged them to stay in their lodging and not have any more conversation with the people of that city so that they would give us no reason to think they were joining in these treacheries, and so they might go with us to Mexico as guides. They replied that neither they nor their lord Montezuma knew anything at all about what we were telling them, and although they did not like it, we put guards over them so they would not leave without permission and so Montezuma would not know we knew he was the one who ordered it to be done.

That night we were very much ready and fully armed, the horses saddled and bridled, with many sentries and patrols, but this is what we were always accustomed to do, because we were very certain that all the captaincies, Mexican as well as Cholulan, would attack us that night.

An old Indian woman, wife of a cacique, because she knew the agreement and trap they had set up, came secretly to doña Marina, our interpreter. She had seen that doña Marina was young, good-looking, and rich, so she spoke to her and counseled her to come with her to her house if she wanted to escape with her life, because it was certain that night or the next day they were going to kill all of us; the great Montezuma had already ordered and arranged that, between the combined forces of that city and the Mexicans, none of us would stay alive except those to be carried to Mexico. Because she knew this and from the compassion she had for doña Marina, she said she had come to tell her that she should gather all her belongings and come with her to her house, and that there she would marry her to her son, brother of another young man who accompanied the old woman. When doña Marina heard this, and in everything she was very sharp-witted, she said to the old woman: "Oh Mother, how much I thank you for what you have told me! I would go with you now except that I have no one here whom I can trust to carry my clothes and golden jewels, which are many. For your life, Mother, wait here a little while, you and your son, and tonight we will go, but now you see that these teules are on watch and will hear us." The old woman believed what doña Marina said to her and stayed there talking with her, and doña Marina asked her how they were going to kill us and how and when and where the arrangement was made. The old woman told her neither more nor less than what the two papas had said. Doña Marina replied: "Well, that affair being so secret, how did you come to know about it?" She said her husband had told her about it; he was a captain of one of the parties of that city and, because he is a captain, he was now with the warriors in his charge, arranging for them to join with the squadrons of the great Montezuma in the ravines, and she believed they would be together waiting for us when we left, and there they would kill all of us. She had known of the plan for three days, because her husband had received a gilded drum from Mexico, and Montezuma had also sent rich cloaks and golden jewels to the other three captains so they would carry us bound to their lord Montezuma. When she heard it, doña Marina deceived the old woman and said: "Oh, how I rejoice in knowing that your son, to whom you want to marry me, is an important person. We have been talking a great deal; I do not want them to notice us. For that reason, Mother, stay here; I will begin to bring my possessions, because I will not be able to remove them all, and you and your son, my brother, will take care of them, and then we will be able to go!" The old woman believed it all. The old woman sat down to rest with her son. Doña Marina went immediately to the captain and told him everything that happened with the Indian woman, whom Cortés immediately ordered to be brought before him. He questioned her about the treasons and agreements; and she told him no more and no less than the papas. He posted a guard over her so she would not leave.

When dawn broke, it was something to see the haste with which the caciques and papas brought in the warriors, bursting with laughter and delighted, as if they had already caught us in their trap and nets! They brought more Indian warriors than we had asked for, and they did not fit in the courtyards, even as large as they are, and still today, in memory of the past, they are not destroyed. As early as it was in the morning when the Cholulans came with the warriors, we were already very prepared for what had to be done. The soldiers with swords and shields were posted at the gate of the great courtyard so as not to let any of the armed Indians leave, and our captain was on horseback accompanied by many soldiers as his guard. When he saw how early the caciques and papas and warriors had come, he said: "How much these traitors want to see us in the ravines so they can gorge themselves on our flesh; but Our Lord will do better for us!" He asked for the two papas who had given away the secret, and they told him the papas were at the gate of the courtyard with the other caciques who were about to come in. Cortés ordered Aguilar, our interpreter, to tell them to go to their homes, that we did not have any need of them now; he did this because they had done us a good deed and should not receive harm for it, so in this way they would not be killed by us. As Cortés was on horseback and doña Marina near him, he asked the caciques why they wanted to kill us the night before when we had done them no harm and whether we had done or said something to make them deal in treasons, other than warn them about the things that we told people in all the towns through which we had come, namely, that they should not be evil, nor sacrifice men, nor worship their idols, nor eat the flesh of their neighbors, that they should not practice sodomy, and that they should have a good way of life, and things touching on our holy faith, all this without compelling them in anything. Why, then, did they now recently prepare many long and stout poles and collars and better ropes in a house near the great cu, and why for three days have they made barricades and holes in the streets and defense works on the rooftops, and why have they taken their children and women and goods from the city? He said their ill will had been very obvious, and they could not conceal their treacheries; they had not even given us anything to eat, and as a mockery they brought water and wood and said there was no maize. He said he knew well that they had many captaincies of warriors in some ravines near there, with many other warriors who had joined them this night to do the treachery they had arranged, believing that we were going to go by that route to Mexico. So as payment for our coming to have them as brothers and tell them what Our Lord God and the king order, they wanted to kill us and eat our flesh and had already prepared the pots with salt and *ají*[48] and tomatoes. If they wanted to do this, it would have been better to attack us in the fields like brave and good warriors, as their neighbors the Tlaxcalans had done. He knew for very certain everything they had planned in that city and even that they promised their idol, advocate of war, that they were going to sacrifice twenty of us before the idol, and that three nights ago, they sacrificed seven Indians so the idol would give them victory, which it promised, but as the idol is evil and false, it neither has nor had power against us, and all this wickedness and treachery that they arranged and put into place would now fall back onto them.

Doña Marina said all this to them and made them understand it very well. When the papas, caciques, and captains heard it, they said that all of it was true, just as he said it, but that they were not to blame for it, because Montezuma's ambassadors had arranged it by order of their lord. Then Cortés told them that the royal laws mandate that such treasons as those cannot go unpunished, and that they must die for their crime. Then he ordered an escopeta to be fired, which was the signal we had

---

48. The term *ají* comes from the Antilles, used at first for the Mexican chili. In Peru the local chilies are called ají to this day. Bernal Díaz wavers between the Antillean word and the Nahuatl word, which would finally win out in Mexico.

prepared for that purpose, and they were given a blow they will remember forever because we killed many of them, so the promises of their false idols did them no good. Not two hours passed before our friends the Tlaxcalans, whom we had left in the field, arrived, and they fought very fiercely in the streets, where the Cholulans had many captaincies and were defending the streets so we would not enter, but they were soon routed. The Tlaxcalans went through the city plundering and taking captives, and we could not stop them. The next day, other captaincies came from other Tlaxcalan towns, and they did great damage, because they were on very bad terms with the people of Cholula. When Cortés and the rest of us saw that, out of pity we stopped the Tlaxcalans from doing more harm. Cortés ordered Cristóbal de Olid to bring him all the captains of Tlaxcala so he could speak with them, and they did not delay in coming. He ordered them to gather all their men and stay in the field, and they did so, and only the Cempoalans stayed with us.

Just then, certain papas and caciques of Cholula—but from other districts of the town, who were not part of the treachery according to what they said, and as it is such a large city, it had separate factions and parties—begged Cortés and all of us to pardon the offense of the treacheries that had been planned against us, for the traitors had paid with their lives. Then came the two papas, our friends, who had disclosed the secret to us as well as the wife of the captain, the old woman who wanted to be doña Marina's mother-in-law, and they all begged Cortés for pardon. When they said that to him, Cortés feigned great anger and ordered the ambassadors of Montezuma, who were detained in our company, to be called, and he said that, although that whole city deserved to be razed, out of respect for their lord Montezuma, whose vassals they were, he would pardon them, but that from now on they must be good, and that should what happened in the past occur another time, they would die for it. Then he had the caciques of Tlaxcala who were in the field summoned, and he told them to return the men and women whom they had captured, that the damage they had done was enough. Although the Tlaxcalans did not want to return their prisoners, and they said the Cholulans deserved much more harm because of the treacheries they had constantly received from that city, at Cortés's order they returned many people, but they were very rich from this time, with gold, cloaks, cotton, salt, and slaves. Besides this, Cortés made them friends with the people of Cholula, and from what I have since seen and understood, they never broke that friendship. He also ordered all the Cholulan papas and caciques to bring the people back and to hold *tianguez*[49] and markets, and they should not be afraid, for no trouble would come to them. They replied that, within five days, they would have the whole city repopulated, because at that time most of the people who lived there had gone into hiding. They also said it was necessary for Cortés to name a cacique for them, because the one who formerly ruled them was among those who died in the courtyard. Cortés then asked to whom the caciqueship properly came, and they said it was his brother, whom he immediately appointed as governor until something different should be ordered.

The event at Cholula had several consequences. First, the Spaniards' reputation for bravery was enhanced and spread throughout the land. Second, Montezuma sought advice from Huichilobos as to how to deal with the Spaniards, sacrificing a number of Indians to propitiate the god. Montezuma further strove to negotiate with Cortés in hope of deflecting his intention to come to Mexico. But in the end, Cortés and his men determined to continue on to that city. Although they were accompanied on that journey by one thousand Tlaxcalan warriors, the Cempoalans who had been with them to that point decided from fear of the Mexicans to return to their homes. Expressing the Spaniards' resolve, Bernal Díaz writes, "as we are men and feared death, we never stopped thinking about it; and as that land is very heavily populated, we were always making short marches and commending ourselves to

---

49. *Tianguez* is the term for an Indian market, generally quite extensive.

God and his blessed mother, Our Lady, and discussing how and in what way we might enter the city, and we held the great hope in our hearts that, because Our Lord Jesus Christ had protected us from all past dangers, he would also protect us from the power of Mexico."

Chapter 9

The Great Montezuma

[LXXXVII] We went to spend the night in a town called Ixtapal-atengo, where half the houses are in the water and the other half on solid ground, where there is a little mountain, and now there is a roadside inn, and there we had a good supper. Let us return to the great Montezuma, who, when his messengers arrived and he heard the response Cortés sent him,[50] immediately decided to send one of his nephews, Cacamatzin, lord of Texcoco,[51] with great pomp to welcome Cortés and all of us. As we always customarily posted watches and scouts, one of our scouts came to advise us that a great number of Mexicans were coming peacefully by the road, and it appeared they were coming dressed in rich cloaks. When this happened, it was very early in the morning, and we wanted to set out, but Cortés told us to stay in our lodging until we could see what was happening. At that moment came four chieftains who bowed low to Cortés, and they told him that near there Cacamatzin, great lord of Texcoco, nephew of the great Montezuma, was coming, and he requested as a favor that we

---

50. Cortés, responding to one last attempt by Montezuma to keep the Spaniards from entering Mexico, sent messengers to Montezuma to tell him that he and his companions were resolved to come, that their king and emperor expected them to do so, and that they were on the road.
51. Bernal Díaz also uses both "Tezcuco" and "Tezcoco."

wait until he arrived. Soon Cacamatzin arrived with the greatest pomp and grandeur we had ever seen in any Mexican lord, for he came in a very rich litter, worked in green feathers, much silver, and other rich clusters of precious stones set in ornamental raised tree designs worked in the finest gold. Eight chieftains carried the litter on their shoulders, all of them, according to what they said, were lords of towns. When they had come near the lodging where Cortés was, they helped Cacamatzin from the litter, swept the ground for him and removed the straw where he was going to pass, and when they came before our captain they made the greatest bows and Cacamatzin said to him: "Malinche, we have come here, I and these lords, to serve you and give you everything you might need for yourself and your companions and to lead you to your homes, which is our city, for so our lord the great Montezuma has ordered us, and he asks that you pardon him for not coming himself; he did not come because he is ill, not for lack of very goodwill that he has for you."

When our captain and all of us beheld such grandeur and majesty as those caciques showed, especially the nephew of Montezuma, we were greatly impressed and discussed among ourselves what, if that cacique brings such lavishness, the great Montezuma would do. When Cacamatzin had delivered his speech, Cortés embraced him and showered him and all the rest of the chieftains with many friendly words. He gave him three stones called margaritas, which sparkle with many colors from within, and to the other chieftains he gave blue rhinestones, and he thanked them and asked when he could repay the lord Montezuma for the favors he does for us every day. The discussions over, we set out right away, and as those caciques I have talked about brought many people with them, and as many other people came out to see us from the neighboring towns, all the roads were filled.

The next morning we arrived at a broad causeway, and we headed for Iztapalapa. When we saw so many cities and towns built in the water, and other great towns on dry land, and that causeway so straight and level as it went to Mexico, we were amazed. We said it looked like the enchanted things they tell of in the book of Amadís[52] because of the great towers and cus and buildings that are in the water, all built of stonemasonry. Some of our soldiers even asked if what we saw was not a dream, and it is not to be wondered at that I write here in this way, because there is so much to ponder that I do not know how to describe it, seeing things never heard of nor even dreamed of as we were seeing: when we arrived near Iztapalapa, seeing the grandeur of the other caciques who came out to receive us, Coadlavaca,[53] the lord of that town, and the lord of Coyoacan,[54] both very close relatives of Montezuma; when we entered that town of Iztapalapa, the appearance of the palace where we were lodged, how large and well built it was, of very fine stonework, and the wood from cedar and other fine-smelling trees, with great courtyards and rooms, things wonderful to see, covered with decorated cotton awnings. After having looked carefully at all that, we went to the orchard and garden, which was such a wonderful thing to see and to pass through that I never grew tired of experiencing the variety of trees and the scent each one had, the terraces full of roses and flowers, the many fruit trees and native rose gardens, a pond of fresh water, and something else worth seeing: that, through an opening they had made, large canoes could enter the garden from the lake without landing, everything very whitened and bright with all kinds of stone and pictures on it that gave much to ponder, and birds of many kinds and species that came into the pond. I say again that I was there looking at it, and I believed that never in the world had lands like these been discovered, because at that time there was no Peru, nor any idea of it. Now all this is fallen down, ruined; there is nothing.

---

52. *Amadís of Gaul* was the tale of a knight-errant popular in Spain during the fifteenth and sixteenth centuries.

53. Bernal Díaz uses three names—"Coadlavaca," "Cuedlavaca," and "Coadlavac"—for the leader now commonly known and referred to as Cuitlahuac.

54. Also Cuyuacan.

N

1. Causeway to Iztapalapa and Coyoacan
2. Causeway to Tacuba / Tlacopan
3. Causeway to Tepayaca
4. Ceremonial Center of Tenochtitlan and Palaces of Montezuma
5. Tlatelolco and Great Marketplace

Tenochtitlan 1519

0 mile ½

Tenochtitlan 1519. This schematic drawing is of Tenochtitlan at the time the Spaniards first sighted it. The image shows the three major causeways leading to the city from Iztapalapa and Coyoacan to the south, Tacuba to the west, and Tepayaca to the north. The causeways were wide enough to accommodate ten horses abreast according to Bernal Díaz. A series of canals, used to move water from one part of the surrounding lake to another and for canoe and pirogue transportation through the city, ran under the causeways, which were bridged over them. The bridges could be taken up when necessary for the defense of the city.

[LXXXVIII] The next morning, we left Iztapalapa, accompanied by those great caciques I mentioned earlier; we went forward along our causeway, which is eight paces in width and goes so straight to the city of Mexico that it seems to me it does not twist in the slightest. Although it is very broad, it was so completely crowded with people that there was not room for all of them, some of them entering Mexico, others coming out, and the Indians who were coming to see us, and we could not pass by all those many who came, and the towers and cus were filled with people as were canoes from all parts of the lake. It was not surprising, because they had never seen horses nor men like us. Seeing such wonderful things, we did not know what to say or whether what appeared before us was real. On one side, on the land, were great cities, and in the lake many more, and we saw it all filled with canoes, and on the causeway many bridges at intervals, and in front of us was the great city of Mexico; and we, we did not number even four hundred soldiers, and we remembered very well the many warnings that had been given us, that we should be careful about entering Mexico, that they were going to kill us as soon as they had us inside. Let the curious readers consider whether what I am writing here has in it much to ponder; what men have there been in the world who would have had such daring?

But let us go on. We were going along our causeway. When we arrived where another small causeway separates off and goes to Coyoacan, another city with something like towers that were their *adoratorios*, many chieftains and caciques came wearing very rich cloaks with a style of liveries differentiating some caciques from others, and the causeways were full of them. The great Montezuma sent those caciques ahead to receive us, so when they arrived before Cortés, they said in their language that we were very welcome, and as a sign of peace they touched the ground with their hand and kissed the earth with the same hand. There we stopped for a good while, and from there Cacamatzin, lord of Texcoco, the lord of Iztapalapa, the lord of Tacuba, and the lord of Coyoacan went forward to meet the great Montezuma, who was arriving in a rich litter accompanied by other great lords and caciques who had vassals.

When we came near Mexico, where there were other small towers, the great Montezuma stepped out of the litter, and the great caciques supported him by the arm under a wonderfully rich canopy the color of green feathers with great gold handwork, much silver, many pearls and chalchiui stones, hanging from a kind of embroidered edge; there was much to look at in it. The great Montezuma was very richly attired after his manner, and he was wearing footwear like sandals, for this is what they call what they wear on their feet, the soles of gold and, on the upper part, clusters of very precious stones. The four lords who supported his arms wore a rich type of clothing after their manner, which seems to have been kept ready for them on the road so that they might enter with their lord, for they were not wearing those cloaks when they came to receive us. Besides those four lords, four other great caciques came, who supported the canopy over their heads, and many other lords, who went before the great Montezuma sweeping the ground on which he would tread, and they spread cloths so that he would not step on the earth. None of those lords, not even in thought, looked at him in the face but kept their eyes lowered in great respect, except those four relatives and nephews of his who supported his arms. When Cortés was told and he saw and understood that the great Montezuma was coming, he dismounted from his horse, and when he was close to Montezuma, they showed each other great respect. Montezuma welcomed him, and our Cortés replied with doña Marina that he hoped he was in very good health; and it seems to me that Cortés, through doña Marina, who was next to Cortés, offered Montezuma his right hand; Montezuma did not take it, but he gave his own hand to Cortés. Then Cortés brought out a necklace he had in hand, made of some glass stones called margaritas, which sparkled with many colors from within, and it came strung on some cords of gold with musk so that it would give off a good scent. He put it around the neck of the great Montezuma, and when he had done so, he was going to embrace him, but those great lords who were with Montezuma held his arm to keep Cortés from doing it, because they consider that contempt.

Then Cortés through the interpreter doña Marina told him that his heart now rejoiced having seen so great a prince, that he took it as a great kindness that he had come in person to receive him and the favors he continually does for him. Then Montezuma said to him other very polite words and ordered two of his nephews who supported his arms, the lord of Texcoco and the lord of Coyoacan, to show us to our lodgings, and Montezuma with his two other relatives, Coadlavaca and the lord of Tacuba, who accompanied him, returned to the city, and those great companies of caciques and chieftains who had accompanied him also returned with him. As they turned back with their lord, we were watching how they all went with their eyes fixed on the ground, not looking at him, keeping close to the wall and accompanying him with great respect. In that way, we had room to enter by the streets of Mexico without so much difficulty.

I want to talk about the multitude of men, women, and boys in the streets, on the rooftops and in canoes in those canals, who came to look at us. It was something to note, for now that I am writing, everything comes before my eyes as if it were yesterday when this happened. Considering the matter, it is a great favor Our Lord Jesus Christ did us in giving us the grace and courage to dare enter such a city and for having saved me from many dangers of death, as you will see further on. I give him much thanks for it and for giving me time enough to write about it, although not as fully as is suitable and as the subject requires. Let us leave the words, for deeds are the real testimony for what I say here and elsewhere. Let us return to our entry into Mexico. They took us to lodge in a large house with lodgings for all of us, which had belonged to the father of the great Montezuma, Axayaca,[55] where, at that time, Montezuma had his great adoratorio of idols and a very secret chamber of golden figures and jewels, which was the treasure he had inherited from his father Axayaca, and he never touched it. Also they took us to lodge in that house because, as they called us teules and regarded us as such, we should be among

---

55. Axayacatl.

the idols or teules they kept there. Be it for one reason or be it for another, there is where they took us, where they had great courtrooms and halls covered with canopies of native cloth for our captain and rush mats with small canopies for each one of us. There are no better beds, however great the lord might be, because they do not use them; and all those palaces, very bright, whitened, swept, and decorated with branches.

When we arrived and entered into a large courtyard, the great Montezuma, who was waiting there for our captain, took him at once by the hand and led him into the lodging and hall where he was to stay, which he had very richly adorned for him after their manner, and he had ready a very rich necklace of gold in the shape of crustaceans, a very marvelous work, and Montezuma himself put it around the neck of our captain Cortés, and the great honor he did Cortés gave his captains much to be amazed at. After Montezuma had put the necklace on him, Cortés thanked him through our interpreters, and Montezuma said: "Malinche, you are in your home, you and your brothers; rest." Then he went to his palace, which was not very far away, and we divided our lodgings by captaincies, our artillery aimed in a suitable direction, and the order we were to keep very carefully discussed and we, both those on horseback and soldiers, were to be very much on the alert. They had a sumptuous meal ready for us, according to their use and custom, which we ate at once. This was our fortunate and bold entry into the great city Tenochtitlan, Mexico, on the eighth day of November in the year of Our Savior Jesus Christ 1519. Thanks to Our Lord Jesus Christ for all of it, and if I have not expressed other things that I should have said, may you all pardon me, for I do not know better how to express it even now.

[LXXXIX] When the great Montezuma had eaten and he learned that our captain and all of us had done the same some time ago, he came with the greatest pomp to our lodging with numerous chieftains, all his relatives. When they told Cortés Montezuma was coming, he went out to the middle of the hall to receive him, and Montezuma took him by the hand; they brought some seats made according to their usage, very rich and worked with many designs in gold. Montezuma told our captain to be seated, and both of them sat down, each on his own seat. Then Montezuma began a very good speech, saying he was delighted to have in his home and kingdom such courageous gentlemen as were the captain Cortés and all of us. He said that two years ago, he had news of another captain who came to Chanpoton, and also last year they brought him news of another captain who came with four ships. He said he had always desired to see them, and now that he had us with him, he would serve us and give us of everything he had, that truly it must be certain we are the men his ancestors, many years past, had said would come from where the sun rose to rule over these lands; we must certainly be the ones because we had fought so bravely in the affairs of Potonchan, Tabasco, and with the Tlaxcalans; they had brought him lifelike pictures of all the battles.

Cortés answered him through our interpreters, who were always with him, especially doña Marina, and said to him that neither he nor all of us knew how to repay him for the great favors we received every day. He said it certainly was true that we came from where the sun rises, and we are vassals and servants of a great lord called the emperor don Carlos, who has many and great princes subject to him. Having news of Montezuma and of what a great lord he is, our emperor sent us to these parts to see him and to beg that he and all his vassals become Christians as is our emperor and all of us, so that their souls will be saved. Later on, he said, he will explain to him further how and in what way this would be done, how we worship only one true God, who he is, and he will hear many other good things, as had his ambassadors Tendile, Pitalpitoque, and Quintalbor when we were on the sandy beaches.

[XCI] The great Montezuma was about forty years old, of goodly stature and well proportioned, slender and not fleshy, not very dark in color, but the appropriate shade for an Indian. He did not wear his hair very long, but long enough to cover his ears, his beard small and sparse, dark, well shaped, his face somewhat long and cheerful, nice looking eyes, and in his demeanor his looks could show affection on the one hand, and, when necessary, sternness. He was very neat and clean; he bathed once every day in the afternoon. He had many women as concubines, daughters of lords, because he had two great cacicas as his legitimate wives, and when he lay with them, it was so much in private that no one managed to find out about it except some of those who served him. He was free of sodomy. The cloaks and other clothing he put on one day he would not put on again for three or four days. In other halls close to his own, he had more than two hundred chieftains in his guard, and not all of these could speak with him, but a very few, and when they went to speak to him, they had to take off their rich cloaks and put on others of little value, but they had to be clean, and they had to enter barefoot, with their eyes downward, fixed on the ground, and not look him in the face. They made three bows before they reached him, at that time saying, "Lord, my lord, my great lord," before they came up to him. When they made the report for which they had come, he dismissed them with few words. In taking their leave, they did not turn their backs to him, but kept their faces and eyes lowered toward the ground and toward where he was, not turning their backs until they left the hall.

I noticed another thing: When other great lords came from far-off lands regarding disputes or business, when they reached the lodgings of the great Montezuma, they had to come barefoot and with poor cloaks, and they could not enter directly into the palace but had to walk around a little on one side of the palace door, because to enter directly and hastily was considered disrespectful.

As for eating, his cooks prepared him more than thirty different dishes, which they made according to their style and custom, and they put them over small earthen fire pots so they would not get cold, and for what the great Montezuma was going to eat, they prepared more than three hundred plates, and more than a thousand for the guard. When he was going to eat, Montezuma would sometimes go out with his chieftains and stewards, and they would point out to him which dish was best and from what birds and other things it was prepared, and as they advised him, so he would eat, but it was very few times that he went out to see it, and only as an amusement. I have heard said that they used to cook the flesh of boys of a very young age for him, but, as he had such a variety of dishes made of so many things, we did not notice if it was human flesh or other things, because daily they cooked hens, cocks with wattles, pheasants, native partridges, quail, tame and wild ducks, deer, native pork, reed birds, pigeons, hares and rabbits, and many sorts of birds and things that are bred in this country, and they are so numerous that I cannot finish naming them so quickly. So we paid no attention to it. But I know with certainty that after our captain reprimanded him for sacrificing and eating human flesh, he ordered that from then on, they should not prepare him such food.

Chapter 10

Montezuma Imprisoned

[XCII] As we had now been in Mexico four days, and neither the captain nor any of us had left the lodgings except to go to Montezuma's houses and gardens, Cortés said to us that it would be good to go to the large plaza and see the great adoratorio of their Huichilobos, that he wanted to send to tell the great Montezuma and ask for his approval. For that purpose, he sent as messenger Jerónimo de Aguilar and doña Marina, and with them one of our captain's small pages, Orteguilla, who now understood something of the language. When Montezuma learned this, he sent to say that we were welcome to go, but on the other hand, he feared we might do some dishonor to his idols, so he decided to go with us in person with many of his chieftains. He came out of his palace in his rich litter and went half the distance; near some adoratorios, he stepped out of his litter, because he considered it a great dishonor to his idols to go as far as their house and adoratorio in that way. Great chieftains took him by the arm with their arms; lords of vassals went before him carrying two staffs like scepters held on high, which was the sign that the great Montezuma was coming there. When he went in his litter, he carried a wand, half-gold and half-wood, held up like a staff of justice. Thus he went and ascended his great cu accompanied by many papas, and he began to perfume and perform other ceremonies to Huichilobos.

Let us leave Montezuma, who had already gone ahead as I have said, and return to Cortés and our captains and soldiers, who, as was customary, were armed night and day, and as Montezuma was used to seeing us armed when we went to see him, he did not look at it as anything new. I say this because our captain and all the rest who had horses went to Tlatelolco on horseback, and most of our soldiers went fully at the ready. Many caciques whom Montezuma had sent accompanied us.

When we arrived near the great cu, before we had climbed a single step, the great Montezuma sent from above, where he was making sacrifices, six papas and two chieftains to accompany our captain. They went to take him by the arms to help him, as they helped their lord Montezuma, ascend the stairs, which numbered one hundred fourteen, believing he would become tired, but Cortés would not let them come near him. After they had climbed to the top of the great cu, on a small plaza at the top, they had something like platforms and on them some large stones where they put the poor Indians to sacrifice, and there was a large image like a dragon and other evil figures and much blood that had been shed that day.

When we arrived, Montezuma came out of an adoratorio where his cursed idols were, which was at the summit of the great cu, and two papas came with him; showing much respect to Cortés and all of us, he said: "You will be tired, Lord Malinche, from climbing this our great temple." Cortés said to him through our interpreters, who were with us, that nothing made him or the rest of us tired. Then Montezuma took Cortés by the hand and told him to look at his great city and all the rest of the cities that were in the water and the many other towns around the same lake on the land; and he said that if Cortés had not had a good view of his great marketplace, from there he could see it much better. So we were looking at it, because that great and accursed temple was so high that it commanded the entire view, and from there we saw the three causeways that entered into Mexico, that of Iztapalapa, which was the one through which we entered four days before, that of Tacuba, through which we fled the night of our great defeat when Coadlavaca, the new lord, drove us from the city, as I will discuss later on, and that of Tepeaquilla.[56] We saw the fresh water that came from Chapultepec, which supplied the city, and on those three causeways the bridges that were built at certain intervals, through which the water from the lake flowed from one side to the other; and we saw on that great lake such a multitude of canoes, some bringing provisions and others merchandise and others cargo. We saw that in that whole great city and all the other cities built in the water, one could not pass from one house to another except by some wooden drawbridges or canoes; and we saw in those cities cus and adoratorios like towers and fortresses, all gleaming white, which was a wonderful thing to see, and the houses with flat roofs, and on the causeways other small towers and adoratorios, which were like fortresses. After having looked carefully and considered everything we had seen, we turned to look at the great marketplace and the multitude of people in it, some buying and others selling, and the murmur and hum of the voices and words spoken there carried more than a league. Among us were soldiers who had been in many parts of the world, in Constantinople and in all of Italy and Rome, and they said that a marketplace so well laid out, with such order and size and full of so many people, they had never seen before.

Let us leave this and return to our captain, who said to fray Bartolomé de Olmedo, who was there: "It seems to me, Father, that it'll be good if we sound out Montezuma as to whether he'd

---

56. Tepeaquilla refers to Tepeyacac (later Tepeac), which later became the site of the chapel, now the basilica of Guadalupe.

let us build our church here." The father said that it would be
good if successful, but it seemed to him it was not appropriate
to speak about it at that time, that he could not see Montezuma
agreeing to such a thing. Then our Cortés said to Montezuma
through doña Marina, the interpreter: "Your grace is a very great
lord and worthy of much more. We have rejoiced at seeing your
cities. What we ask as a favor, since we are here in this temple of
yours, is that you show us your gods and teules." Montezuma said
that first he would speak with his chief papas. Then when he had
spoken to them, he said we should enter a small tower and apart-
ment like a hall, where there were two objects like altars with very
rich planking on the top of the roof, and at each altar two figures,
like giants, with very tall bodies and very fat. The first, which was
on the right hand, they said was the figure of Huichilobos, their
god of war, and he had a very wide face and countenance with
deformed and terrifying eyes. The whole of his body was covered
with precious stonework, gold, pearls, and seed pearls, held on
with glue they make in this country from some sort of root, and
all the body and head was covered with it, the body encircled by
great snakes made of gold and clusters of stones, and in one hand
he held a bow and in the other some arrows. Another small idol,
which they said was his page, was there next to him holding a
short lance and a shield, very rich with gold and precious stonework. Huichilobos had around his neck some faces of Indians and
other things like their hearts, the latter of gold, some of them of
silver, with many blue precious stones. There were some fire pans
with incense, which is their copal, and in them were burning three
hearts from Indians who had been sacrificed that day; they had
made the sacrifice with smoke and copal. All the walls of that adoratorio were bathed and black with crusts of blood, and likewise
the floor, and it all had a terrible smell. Then we saw on the other
side, on the left hand, the other great figure, the same height as
Huichilobos, and he had a face like a bear, eyes that shone made
of their mirrors, which they call *tezcal*, and the body had rich
stones glued on it like Huichilobos, because, according to what
they said, the two were brothers, and this Tezcatepuca was the god

of the inferno, who had charge of the souls of the Mexicans; his body was encircled with some figures like small devils with tails like snakes, and on the walls so many crusts of blood and the floor all bathed in it that in the slaughterhouses of Castile there was not such a stench. They had offered it five hearts from the sacrifices of that day, and in the highest part of the cu was another recess, the wood very richly worked, and another figure like a half man, half lizard, all covered with rich stones and half-cloaked. They said that the body of this figure was full of all the seeds to be found in the whole world, and they said he was the god of sowing and fruit; I do not remember his name, and everything was covered with blood, walls as well as altar, and there was such a stench that we could hardly wait to get outside. They had there an exceedingly large drum, and when they beat it, its sound was so sad and, as they say, like an instrument of hell, and one could hear it more than two leagues from there; they said that the skins of that drum were from very large snakes.

In that small place they had many diabolical things to see, bugles and trumpets and knives, and many hearts of Indians they had burned and used to perfume those idols of theirs, and every-thing clotted with blood. There was so much of it that I curse it all; and as it smelled so much like a slaughterhouse, we could not wait to get away from such a bad stench and worse sight. Half laughing, our captain said to Montezuma through our interpreter: "Lord Montezuma: I do not see how such a great lord and wise man as your grace has not come to the conclusion that your idols are not gods, but evil things called devils. So that your grace might come to know this, and all your papas might see it clearly, do me a favor: Grant that on the top of this tower, we might put a cross, and in one part of these adoratorios where your Huichilobos and Tezcatepuca are, we will have a space apart where we might put an image of Our Lady (which image Montezuma had already seen), and you will see by the fear these idols have of it that they have you deceived." Montezuma replied half angrily, and the two papas with him showed signs of upset, and he said: "Lord Malinche, if I had believed that you were going to say such dishonorable things as you have, I would not have shown you my gods. We consider them to be very good, for they give us health, rain, good plantings, and victories and whatever we want; and we must worship them and sacrifice to them. What I beg of you is that you not say any more words dishonoring them." When our captain heard that and saw him so agitated, he did not talk about it anymore, but with a cheerful face said to him: "It is now time for your grace and us to go." Montezuma replied that it was good, but that before he left he had to pray and make a certain sacrifice to make up for the great *tatacul*, which means a great mistake, that he had committed in allowing us to ascend his great cu and see his gods and for the dishonor we did them in speaking badly of them. Cortés said to him: "Since that is the way it is, please pardon me." Then we went down the stairs, and as there were one hundred fourteen of them and some of our soldiers were suffering from sores,[57] their thighs hurt them as they went down. I will stop talking about their adoratorio and will say how the surroundings seemed to me and what they were like, and if I do not talk about them as accurately as I should, do not be surprised, because at that time I had other thoughts to attend to regarding what we had on our hands with respect to military matters and in what my captain ordered me, not in telling stories.

[XCIII] When our captain Cortés and the Mercedarian friar saw that Montezuma was unwilling to allow us to put a cross or build a church in the cu of Huichilobos, and because ever since we entered that city of Mexico, when mass was said we had to make an altar on tables and then take it apart again, we decided to ask the stewards of the great Montezuma for masons so that we could make a church in our lodgings; the stewards said they would tell Montezuma. Our captain also sent to tell him this through doña Marina and Aguilar and his page, Orteguilla, who already understood something of the language, and Montezuma soon gave his permission and ordered that we be given all supplies necessary. In

---

57. Bernal Díaz uses *bubas*, a term that here refers to sores associated with syphilis.

two days, we had our church built and the holy cross put before the lodgings, and there mass was said every day until the wine was gone. As Cortés, other captains and the friar were ill during the wars of Tlaxcala, they had made the wine we had for masses go too quickly; but after the wine was gone, we were still in the church on our knees each day praying before the altar and images, for one thing because we were obliged to do it as Christians and as a good habit, and for another so that Montezuma and all his captains should see us on our knees in front of the cross, especially when we prayed the Ave Maria, so they might be inclined to it.

When we were all in those lodgings, as we were of such character that we inquired into and wanted to know everything, while we were looking for where the best and most suitable place was for the altar, two of our soldiers, one of them was a finish carpenter named Alonso Yáñez, saw on a wall signs that there had been a door there which was closed up, very well plastered and burnished. As there was talk, and we had been told that Montezuma had the treasure of his father, Axayaca, in that lodging, we suspected it would be in that room, which had been closed and plastered over just a few days before. Yáñez told Juan Velázquez de León and Francisco de Lugo, who were captains, also relatives of mine, and Alonso Yáñez kept company with them as their servant, and those captains told Cortés, so the door was secretly opened. When it was open, Cortés with certain captains went inside first, and they saw such a number of jewels, plate and ingots of gold, and chalchiui stones and other great riches, they were beside themselves and did not know what to say about such wealth. Soon all the other captains and soldiers learned of it, and we very secretly went to see it; and when I saw it, I say that I was astonished, and as in that time I was young and had never in my life seen riches like those, I was sure that there could not be the like anywhere in the world. All our captains and soldiers decided that we would not even think of touching any of it, but that the stones should be put again in the doorway, and it should be closed and plastered as we had found it, and that we should not speak of it so that Montezuma should not hear about it until another time.

Let us leave this about the riches and say that, as we had such brave captains and soldiers and of such good counsel and judgment, and primarily as we were very certain Our Lord Jesus Christ put his divine hand on all our affairs, four of our captains took Cortés aside in the church together with twelve soldiers in whom he had confidence and confided, and I was one of them; we asked him to look at the net and trap we were in, the great strength of that city, the bridges and causeways, the words of warning they gave us in all the towns through which we had come that Huichilobos had advised Montezuma to let us enter his city and they would kill us there; we said he should understand that the hearts of men are very changeable, especially among the Indians, and he should not have confidence in the goodwill and kindness Montezuma was showing us, because from one hour to the next he would change when he felt like attacking, and if he should stop our food or water or raise any bridge, we would not be able to fend for ourselves; and we told him to look at the great number of Indian warriors Montezuma had as his guard, and what could we do to attack them or defend ourselves, because all the houses were in the water? How could our friends the Tlaxcalans enter to help us?

Since all this we were telling him was something to think about, he should right away seize Montezuma if we wanted to secure our lives, and that it should not wait another day. He should consider that all the gold Montezuma gave us and what we had seen in the treasury of his father, Axayaca, and all the food we were eating would turn into arsenic in our body, that neither day nor night could we rest nor sleep with this thought, and that if any of our soldiers told him anything other than this, they would be like senseless beasts drawn to the sweetness of the gold, not seeing death staring them in the face. When Cortés heard this, he said: "Don't believe, gentlemen, that I'm asleep or that I don't have the same concern; I'm sure you must have felt it in me; but, what power do we have to be so bold as to seize such a great lord in his own palace with his guards and warriors? What means can be found to try to put it into effect without his giving the alarm to his warriors and their attacking us immediately?"

Our captains, Juan Velázquez de León, Diego de Ordaz, Gonzalo de Sandoval, and Pedro de Alvarado, replied that, with the right words, we could draw him out from his hall and bring him to our lodgings and tell him he must be our prisoner, that if he became agitated or cried out, he would pay with his person, that if Cortés did not want to do this at once, he should give them permission and they would get it under way, that between the two great dangers in which we found ourselves, the thing that was best and most to the purpose was to take him and not wait for them to attack us, for if he began, what way out would we have? Also some of us soldiers told him it seemed to us that the stewards of Montezuma who served us provisions were insolent and did not bring us as much as in the first days. Also two Tlaxcalan Indians, our friends, said secretly to Jerónimo de Aguilar, our interpreter, that it did not seem that the Mexicans had goodwill toward us during the last two days. We were discussing for a good hour whether we should seize him or not and how we could do it. This last advice suited our captain. One way or another we were going to take him prisoner, but we left it for the next day. All that night we were praying to God to direct our plan to his holy service.

After these discussions, the next morning, two Tlaxcalan Indians came very secretly with some letters from Villa Rica. What they contained was that Juan de Escalante, who stayed there as chief constable, was killed, and six soldiers with him, in a battle the Mexicans waged against him, and they also killed his horse and many Totonac Indians he had in his company, and that all the towns of the sierra and Cempoala and its subject towns were stirred up and would not bring food nor serve in the fort. They did not know what to do, for earlier the Indians had considered them teules, but now that they had seen this rout, they had become savage, both the Totonacs and the Mexicans, and they considered the Spaniards as nothing, nor did they know how to remedy the situation. When we heard that news, God knows what sorrow we all had. It was the first rout we had in New Spain. Let the curious reader consider how adverse fortune comes with the turning of the wheel. Anyone who had seen us enter that city with such a solemn and triumphant reception, and had considered us rich with what Montezuma had given every day both to the captain and to us, and had seen the house described by me filled with gold and how they considered us teules, which are idols, and that we won all our battles—and now for such great misfortune to have come to us that they did not hold us in the same esteem as before, but considered us men who could be conquered, and to have felt how insolent they were to us! At the end of more discussion, it was agreed that that same day, one way or another, Montezuma would be seized or we would all die doing it. So that the readers may see this battle of Juan de Escalante and how they killed him, the six soldiers, the horse, and the Totonac friends he had with him, I want to describe it here before I talk about the seizing of Montezuma in order not to leave anything out, because it must be clearly understood.

[XCIV] As Bernal Díaz writes, "It happened this way": Juan de Escalante, captain and constable general of New Spain in Villa Rica, had been ordered by Cortés to assist the towns in the area with everything they might need. The garrison Montezuma kept near Tuzapan, one of many he had in all the provinces, demanded tribute of Indian men and women and provisions from some of these towns. The towns refused, and the Mexican captains threatened to destroy those towns and take the people off as captives, saying that Montezuma had ordered this. These Totonac friends came to Juan de Escalante and complained. The Mexicans ignored Juan de Escalante's order not to annoy or rob the towns, and he sent threatening messages. In the battle that ensued, the Totonacs, terrified by the large number of Mexican warriors, fled at the first engagement and left Juan de Escalante alone to fight the Mexicans.

In those skirmishes and attacks, the Mexicans carried off a soldier, whose name was Argüello, a native of León; he had a very large head with a black curly beard, and he was very sturdy in appearance, young and very strong. They wounded Escalante and six other soldiers very badly, and they killed his horse. He returned to Villa Rica, and within three days he and the other soldiers had died.

The Mexican captains, after having the battle with Juan de Escalante, sent to tell Montezuma about it and even presented him the head of Argüello, who seems to have died of his wounds on the road, for they had carried him off alive. We learned that Montezuma, when they showed the head to him, as it was robust and large and had a full curly beard, was terrified and fearful to look at it and ordered them not to offer it to any cu in Mexico but to other idols in other towns. Montezuma asked his captains how, because they were thousands of warriors, they did not conquer so few teules. They replied that neither their spears nor arrows nor good fighting was any use to them, that they could not make them retreat, because a great *tequecihuata*[58] of Castile appeared before them, and that lady frightened the Mexicans and said words to her teules that encouraged them. Then Montezuma believed that the great lady was Saint Mary, who we had told him was our advocate, whose image with her precious son in her arms we had earlier given to Montezuma. However, I did not see all this because I was in Mexico, but some conquistadors who were there said it, and please God that it should be so. Certainly all of us soldiers who came with Cortés believed it very much, and it is true that the divine compassion of Our Lady, the Virgin Mary, was always with us, for which I give her much thanks. I will now go on to talk about what happened regarding the seizure of Montezuma.

[XCV] As we had decided the day before to seize Montezuma, we spent the whole night in prayer, begging God that it would happen in such a way that it would redound to his holy service, and the next morning we agreed on how to do it. Cortés took with him five captains, who were Pedro de Alvarado, Gonzalo de Sandoval, Juan Velázquez de León, Francisco de Lugo, and Alonso de Ávila, and me, and our interpreters, doña Marina and Aguilar; he ordered all of us to be very much on the alert and the horsemen to have their horses saddled and bridled. As for our arms, there

---

58. *Tequecihuata* means "lady," referring here to the Virgin Mary.

is no need for me to call them to mind because always, day and
night, we were armed and wearing our sandals on our feet, which
at that time was our footwear, and whenever we went to speak
with Montezuma, he always saw us armed in that way; I say this
because when Cortés went with the five captains and all had their
arms with them, Montezuma did not take it as anything new, nor
did it disturb him. When all of us were ready, our captain sent
to Montezuma to let him know we were coming to his palace,
for we customarily did this, so he would not be disturbed seeing us suddenly arrive. Montezuma understood more or less that
Cortés would be coming angry about the affair at Almería,[59] but
he thought nothing of it and told him to come and he would be
welcome. When Cortés entered, after paying his usual respects,
he said to him through our interpreters: "Lord Montezuma, I am
astonished that you, such a valiant prince, having given yourself
out as our friend, should order your captains who are on the coast,
near Tuzapan, to take up arms against my Spaniards, to have the
audacity to rob the towns that are in the keeping and under the
protection of our king and lord, demanding Indian men and
women from them to sacrifice, and to kill a Spaniard, my brother,
and a horse." He did not speak of the captain nor the six soldiers
who died as soon as they arrived at Villa Rica, because Montezuma did not yet know of it nor did the Indian captains who had
attacked them. Cortés also told him: "And because you were such
a friend, I ordered my captains to serve and assist you in every
possible way, but your grace, on the contrary, has not done this
for us. Also in the matter of Cholula, your captains with a great
number of warriors had arranged at your orders to kill us. I over-
looked it at the time because of my great regard for you, but now
your vassals and captains have become insolent and have secret
discussions, stating that you want us killed. I do not want to start
a war or destroy this city for these reasons. Everything will be for-
given if right away silently and without making any disturbance,

---

59. The incident in which Juan de Escalante and the other soldiers were
killed.

you come with us to our lodgings; you will be served there and looked after very well, as if in your own house. But if you make a disturbance or call out, these captains of mine will immediately kill you; I brought them for no other purpose." When Montezuma heard this, he was terrified and stunned, and he replied that he had never ordered them to take up arms against us, that he would send immediately for his captains so that the truth would be known, and he would punish them. In that instant, he took from his arm and wrist the sign and seal of Huichilobos, which is what he did when he ordered something serious and important so that it would be carried out, and it would be carried out at once. As for going as a prisoner and leaving his palace against his will, he said he was not a person who could be ordered to do such a thing, and it was not his desire to go. Cortés replied with very good arguments, and Montezuma replied with better ones about why he should not have to leave his house, so that more than half an hour was spent in these discussions. When Juan Velázquez de León and the rest of the captains saw that time was being wasted over this matter and they were in a great hurry to have him removed from his house and taken prisoner, they spoke to Cortés somewhat agitated and said: "What are you doing with all these words? Either we take him prisoner, or we stab him. So, tell him again that if he cries out or makes a disturbance, we will kill him, because it is better that we now secure our lives or lose them."

As Juan Velázquez said this with a loud and somewhat terrifying voice, because that was his way of speaking, and Montezuma saw that our captains were angry, he asked doña Marina what they were saying with those loud words. Because doña Marina was very shrewd, she said to him: "Lord Montezuma, what I counsel you is that you go right away with them to their lodging without making any noise, for I know that they will pay you much honor as the great lord you are; otherwise you will be left dead here, but in their lodgings you will learn the truth." Then Montezuma said to Cortés: "Lord Malinche, granted that if that is the way you want it, I have a legitimate son and two legitimate daughters. Take them as hostages and do not insult me in this way. What will my chieftains say if they see me taken off as a prisoner?" Cortés told him again that he had to go with us personally, and there was nothing else to be done. After many arguments, he said he would go willingly. Then Cortés and our captains spoke many friendly words to him and requested as a favor that he not be angry and that he tell his captains and the men of his guard that he was going of his own will because he had had discussions with his idol Huichilobos and the papas who served him and it was better for his health and safety to be with us. Then, his rich litter was brought, in which he usually went out with all his captains accompanying him. He went to our lodging, where we put guards and watchmen over him. Cortés and all of us provided for him all the services and pleasures we could, as best we could, and we used no shackles at all on him.

Soon all the great Mexican chieftains and his nephews came to see and talk with him to learn the reason for his imprisonment and whether he ordered them to attack us. Montezuma told them he was content to be there with us for some days, by his own will not by force, that if he wanted something he would tell them, and that neither they nor the city should be alarmed, nor should they be worried about it, because his Huichilobos approved of his being there, and certain papas who knew about it told him this, for they had spoken with the idol about it. In this way, as I have told it, the capture of the great Montezuma took place. There, where he was staying, he had his service, his women, and his baths in which he bathed himself, and twenty great lords, counselors, and captains were always in his company, and he adjusted to being a prisoner without showing any emotion, and ambassadors from distant lands came there with their disputes, and they brought him his tribute, and he carried on his important business.

I will stop talking at present about this imprisonment, and let us talk about how the messengers whom Montezuma sent with his sign and seal to summon the captains who killed our soldiers brought them before him as prisoners. What he said to them I do not know, but he sent them to Cortés for judgment. Their testimony was taken in Montezuma's absence, and they confessed that what I have stated before was true, that their lord had ordered them to attack and collect tributes, and that if some teules should come to their defense, they should attack them or kill them too. When Cortés heard this testimony, he sent to inform Montezuma how they condemned him in this matter; Montezuma excused himself as best he could. Our captain sent to say that he believed the testimony, and although Montezuma deserved punishment according to the command of our king that the person who orders anyone to kill others, whether guilty or not, shall die for it, he was so fond of Montezuma and so wished him well, that even should he be guilty, before he would make Montezuma pay for it, Cortés would pay the penalty himself. Despite all this he sent to tell him, Montezuma was fearful. Without wasting any more arguments, Cortés sentenced those captains to death, ordering that they be burned in front of Montezuma's palace; so that there would be no problems until they were burned, he ordered fetters put on Montezuma himself. When they put the fetters on, Montezuma groaned, and if he was fearful before, he was much more so then.

After the burning was over, Cortés went with five of our captains to his lodging and personally took the fetters off. He spoke such kind words that Montezuma's anger soon went away, because our Cortés told him that, not only did he consider him a brother, but much more; that as he was lord and king of so many towns and provinces, if he could, as time went on, he, Cortés, would make Montezuma lord of more lands, those he has not been able to conquer, that did not obey him, and that if he wanted to go to his palace, he gave him permission to do so. Cortés said this through our interpreters, and while Cortés was saying it, it seemed that tears came to Montezuma's eyes. He replied with great courtesy that he was very thankful. But he understood well that everything Cortés said was just words, and that for now, perhaps it was better for him to be there as a prisoner, because, as his chieftains were many and his nephews and relatives came every day to say it would be good to attack us and remove him from prison, as soon as they saw him outside, they might persuade him to do just that. He did not want to see turmoil in his city, but if he did not do their will, perhaps they would want to raise up another lord, and he was removing those thoughts from their minds by saying that his god Huichilobos had sent to say that he should remain a prisoner. From what we understood, and it is very likely, Cortés had told Aguilar to tell Montezuma secretly that, although Malinche wanted to order him freed from prison, the rest of our captains and soldiers did not want that. When he heard it, Cortés threw his arms around him and embraced him and said: "It is not in vain, Lord Montezuma, that I care as much for you as I do for myself."

Then Montezuma asked Cortés for a Spanish page named Orteguilla who was serving him, who already knew the language and who was very useful both to Montezuma and to us because, through this page, Montezuma asked and learned much about things of Castile, and we about what his captains said to him, and truly the page was so attentive that Montezuma liked him very much. Let us stop speaking about how Montezuma was now quite pleased with the great flattery and services and with conversation he had with all of us; whenever we passed before him, even if it was Cortés, we took off our quilted caps or helmets, for we were always armed, and he was very polite to us and honored us all.

I will give the names of Montezuma's captains who had been condemned to be burned. The principal one was named Quetzalpopoca,[60] and the others were named, one of them Coate and the other Quiavit; I do not remember the name of the other, and it does not matter much knowing these names. When this punishment became known in all the provinces of New Spain, they were very fearful, and the towns of the coast where they had killed our soldiers returned again to serve the settlers who stayed in Villa Rica very well. The curious readers who are reading this must consider what great deeds we did then: wrecking our ships; daring to enter such a strong city, having had so many warnings that they would kill us once they had us inside; having the audacity to seize the great Montezuma, king of that land, in his own large city and his own palace, when he had such a great number of

---

60. Cuauhpopoca.

warriors in his guard; and then daring to burn his captains before his palace, putting him in fetters while justice was being done.

Many times, now that I am old, I stop to consider the heroic things we did in that time, and it seems to me that I see them there before me, and I say that we ourselves did not do our deeds, but they were all guided by God. For what men have there been in the world who, numbering four hundred soldiers (and we did not even reach that number) dared enter a city as strong as Mexico, which is larger than Venice and more than fifteen hundred leagues distant from our Castile, and seize so great a lord and execute his captains before him? There is much to ponder in this, but not dryly as I have told it.

Montezuma now called together the caciques of the whole land to pledge obedience to His Majesty, the emperor don Carlos, and "they pledged their obedience to His Majesty, and they showed much sadness, and Montezuma could not keep back the tears. We had such affection for him and he was so kind, that for us to see him weep softened our own eyes, and one soldier wept as much as Montezuma. Such was the affection we had for him."

During this period of Montezuma's captivity, with daily inter-action between the Spaniards and that great cacique, a bond of friendship arose, based on games of totoloques, *long conversations about the Christian faith, joking, the exchange of gifts and other such activities, and the Spaniards developed both respect for and understanding of Montezuma.*

Montezuma also told Cortés where he collected his gold and Cortés sent three separate groups to the three locations Montezuma named. All returned with gold and accounts of how it was collected.

Further, Montezuma gave his entire treasury from his father to Cortés for the emperor don Carlos. "Looking it over and tak-ing off all the ornamentation and things it was set in took three days; even three of Montezuma's goldsmiths came from a town called Escapuzalco to take it apart and undo it. I say there was so much, that after it was taken apart, there were three piles of

gold and by weight it was more than six hundred thousand pesos,
without the silver and many other riches, and I do not count in
this the ingots and plates of gold and the gold in grains from the
mines."

   With all the gold and jewels assembled, the royal fifth was
taken out, another fifth for Cortés, some for the costs Cortés had
incurred for the fleet on the island of Cuba, more for the expense
Diego Velázquez had for the scuttled ships, another portion for the
representatives who went to Castile, also for those who stayed in
Villa Rica, for the horse that died, for Juan Sedeño's mare killed
with a slash from a war club, for the Mercedarian priest and the
secular priest Juan Díaz, and the captains, and those who brought
horses, double shares, and escopeteros and crossbowmen the same.
"Very little remained for each share, and because it was so little,
many soldiers did not want to accept it, and Cortés was left with
it all, for at that time we could not do anything but be quiet,
because to ask for justice was useless."

Chapter 11

Diego Velázquez Seeks to Regain Control:
Pánfilo de Narváez

[CIX] Let us go back a little bit in our story, so that what I will
now say might be well understood. I have already said in the chapter that speaks of it[61] how Diego Velázquez, governor of Cuba,
knew that we had sent our representatives to His Majesty with all
the gold we had collected, the sun and the moon, many diverse
jewels, gold in grains taken from the mines, and many other
things of great value, but that we had not sent Velázquez anything

---

61. See Chapter 5.

at all. He also learned that don Juan Rodríguez de Fonseca, bishop of Burgos and archbishop of Rosano, who at that time was president of the Indies and commanded all very absolutely because His Majesty was in Flanders, had treated our representatives very badly. They say that this same bishop sent from Castile much assistance to Diego Velázquez and advice and orders that he should send to have us arrested and that from Castile he would give him all assistance for doing so.

Diego Velázquez assembled a fleet of nineteen ships and fourteen hundred soldiers, more than twenty guns, much powder, every sort of provision of stones and balls, two artillerymen, eighty horsemen, ninety crossbowmen and seventy escopeteros, placing them all under the command of Pánfilo de Narváez with orders "to take Cortés and all of us prisoner or, at least, not to leave any of us alive."

The Royal Audiencia of Santo Domingo and Jeronymite friars, who were acting as governors, heard about the fleet and decided to send a licentiate named Lucas Vázquez de Ayllón, a judge of the same Royal Audiencia, to stop Diego Velázquez's fleet and not let it sail. Velázquez ignored the judge. The judge himself went with Narváez to make peace and bring about agreements between Narváez and Cortés, but the judge favored Cortés's claims, and Narváez "seized the king's judge and sent him away by ship as a prisoner." The judge convinced the captain of the ship to take him to Santo Domingo where he reported his bad treatment to the Royal Audiencia.

Pánfilo de Narváez, after his arrival on the mainland, set up camp in Cempoala where he took from the fat cacique many of the gifts of Indian women, gold, and cloaks that Cortés had given him. The fat cacique said he would send a complaint to Cortés. "When they heard that, they made fun of what he said, and the auditor Salvatierra, the one who spoke most boastingly, said to his other friends and to Narváez himself: 'Didn't you hear what fear all these caciques have of this little nobody Cortés?'" Narváez also established contact with Montezuma,

saying that Cortés and all the men with him were traitors to the
king. Montezuma responded with gifts and ordered the towns
in the area to support Narváez with food, clothing, and gold.
Cortés learned of all this, prepared to meet Narváez and his men
in battle, had a final conversation with Montezuma in which
neither one divulged all he knew, and left Pedro de Alvarado
behind in charge of Montezuma and a garrison of eighty Span-
iards. With that, Cortés and men marched off to meet Narváez's
much larger contingent. Narváez made preparations for a major
confrontation with Cortés.

[CXXI] Narváez ordered all his artillery, horsemen, escopeteros, crossbowmen, and soldiers taken out to a field about a quarter of a league from Cempoala to wait for us and not to let any
of us escape death or capture. As it rained a great deal that day,
Narváez's men were already sick of waiting for us in the rain, and
as they were not used to rain and hardships and his captains did
not think very much of us, those captains let him know they
would return to their lodgings; that it was an affront to be there
as they were waiting for two or three little men, as they said we
were; that he should put his artillery, eighteen large guns, in front
of their lodgings; that forty of the horsemen should be waiting
all night on the road by which we had to come from Cempoala;
that he should have at the ford of the river, where we would have
to come, his lookouts, who should be good horsemen and foot
soldiers and fast runners to carry messages; and that in the courtyards of the lodgings of Narváez twenty horsemen should be on
patrol the entire night.

This agreement they presented to him was to persuade him to
return to the lodgings. His captains also said to him: "What then,
sir, do you take Cortés for, that he'd dare, with his three cats, come
to this camp based on what this fat Indian says? Don't believe it,
sir, but rather that he's made this uproar and show of coming so
that you might arrive at a better agreement with him." In this way,
Narváez returned to his camp, and after his return he promised
publicly that he would give two thousand pesos to whoever might

kill Cortés or Gonzalo de Sandoval. He at once posted lookouts at the river, and the watchword, countersign, and secret signal that he gave for when they were battling against us in his camp was to be: "Santa María, Santa María!" In addition to this arrangement, Narváez ordered that many soldiers, including escopeteros, crossbowmen, and others with halberds, sleep in his lodging, and he ordered as many others to be in the lodgings of the auditor Salvatierra, Gamarra, and Juan Bono.

[CXXII] When we arrived at the little stream with some good meadows about a league from Cempoala, after having sent out our trustworthy scouts, our captain Cortés, on horseback, summoned us, captains as well as all the soldiers. When he saw us together, he asked us please to be quiet, and he began a speech in such a beautiful style, with words so well spoken that it was certainly more delightful and filled with promises than I will know how to write it here. In it, he reminded us of everything that happened to us from when we left the island of Cuba until that time, and he said to us:

"You know well, gentlemen, that Diego Velázquez, governor of Cuba, chose me as captain general, not because there weren't among you many who were worthy of it. You know that you believed that we were coming to settle, for so it was published and proclaimed, but, as you've seen, he was sending us to trade. You know what we went through about my wanting to return to the island of Cuba to give an account to Diego Velázquez of the charge he gave me, in accordance with his instructions, but you ordered and persuaded me to settle this land in the name of His Majesty, and, thanks to Our Lord, we've settled it, and it was a very wise thing to do. In addition, you made me your captain general and chief justice of the settlement until His Majesty might be pleased to order differently. As I've already said, among some of you there were discussions about returning to Cuba, but I don't want to go into it further, for, so to speak, it happened yesterday, and our staying was holy and good, for we have done a great service to God and His Majesty, and that much is clear. You already know what we promised in our letters to His Majesty after having given him an account and report of all our deeds, which didn't leave out a thing, that this land is, so far as we've seen and known of it, four times larger than Castile, with great towns, very rich in gold and mines, with other provinces nearby; how we sent to beg His Majesty that he not give the governorship of it nor any other kind of authority over it to anyone at all, (because we believed and knew for certain that the bishop of Burgos, don Juan Rodríguez de Fonseca, who was at that time president of the Indies and had great authority, would ask His Majesty for it for Diego Velázquez or some relative or friend of the bishop himself). Because this land is such and so good that it would be appropriate for an infante[62] or great lord, we decided not to give it to anyone until His Majesty hears our representatives and we see his royal signature. Seeing it, we would, in all humility, do what he's pleased to order. With those letters you know we sent and served His Majesty with all the gold, silver, jewels, and everything we'd gotten."

He said he did not want to tell other things he should speak of in detail, for there would not be time to finish the discussion; it was late and night was coming. He said more: "Let us say further, gentlemen, Pánfilo de Narváez is coming against us with great fury and desires to get his hands on us; he hadn't yet disembarked before he was calling us traitors and evil people, and he sent a message to the great Montezuma, not the words of a wise captain but an agitator. Beyond that, he had the audacity to arrest a judge of His Majesty, and for this crime alone he deserves to be very fully punished. You will have already heard how he's proclaimed war in his camp against us, with free plundering as if we were Moors." Then, after having said this, Cortés began to praise us and our courage in past wars and battles, saying that we were fighting then to save our lives, but that now we had to fight with all our strength for life and honor, for they are coming to seize us, throw us from our homes and steal our property. Beyond that, we do not yet

---

62. The title and rank given to a king's sons who are not heirs to the throne.

know if Narváez brings decrees from our king and lord or only pronouncements of the bishop of Burgos, our opponent.

He said that if we should fall into the hands of Narváez, which God forbid, all our services we have done for God first and His Majesty will become disservices, and they will bring lawsuits against us, saying that we have killed and robbed and destroyed the land, whereas they are the robbers and agitators and do disservice to our king and lord. They will say they have served him; and he said we could see with our own eyes everything he had said, and as good gentlemen, we are obligated to favor His Majesty's honor and our own and our homes and property. With this intention he left Mexico, having confidence in God and in us, that he put everything first in the hands of God and after that in ours, and let us see how it seems to us.

Then all of us as one answered him, together with Juan Velázquez de León, Francisco de Lugo, and other captains, that he should feel certain that, with the help of God, we would conquer or die trying; and he should be careful that they not convince him with personal gain because if he should do anything improper, we would stab him. Then, as he saw our strong will, he rejoiced greatly and said that he had come in that confidence. Then he made us many offers and promises that we would all be very rich and powerful. When this was done, he again asked us please to maintain silence, saying that in wars and battles, prudence and knowledge were more necessary to conquer the enemy fully than excessive boldness, and because he knew of our great bravery, and that in order to win honor each one of us would want to push forward first to meet the enemy, we should put ourselves in order and companies. As the first thing we had to do was take their artillery, eighteen guns positioned before the lodgings of Narváez, Cortés ordered that a relative of his named Pizarro should go as captain. Pizarro was a swift young man, and Cortés assigned him sixty young soldiers, and I was among them. He ordered that, after taking the artillery, we should all go to the lodging of Narváez, which was on a very high cu, and to seize Narváez he designated as captain Gonzalo de Sandoval with another sixty companions; as Sandoval was chief constable, Cortés gave him an order which said: "Gonzalo de Sandoval, chief constable of this New Spain in the name of His Majesty, I order you to seize Pánfilo de Narváez, and if he should resist, kill him, for so the service of God and the king our lord requires, inasmuch as Narváez has done many disservices to God and His Majesty and arrested a judge. Given in this camp, and signed Hernando Cortés, countersigned by his secretary, Pedro Hernández." After giving the order, he promised that to the first soldier who laid a hand on Narváez he would give three thousand pesos, to the second two thousand, and to the third a thousand, and he said that what he promised was just a tip so we might well see the wealth that was within our grasp.

He then designated Juan Velázquez de León to seize the youth Diego Velázquez with whom he had had a quarrel,[63] and he gave him another sixty soldiers; likewise he designated Diego de Ordaz to seize Salvatierra and gave him another sixty soldiers, for those two captains were in their fortress and high cus. With another twenty soldiers, Cortés himself, for emergencies, was to go where there was most need, and what he had in mind was to be present at the seizure of Narváez and Salvatierra. Once the lists were given to the captains, Cortés said: "I know well that Narváez's men are, in all, four times more than we; but they're not accustomed to arms, and as the greater part of them are on bad terms with their captain and many sick, we'll take them by surprise. I have had the belief that God will give us victory, that they will not persist much in their defense because we'll do them more good than their Narváez. So, then, gentlemen, because our lives and honor depend, after God, on your courage and your strong arms, I have no other favors to ask of you and nothing

---

63. The youth Diego Velázquez was a nephew of the governor of Cuba, Diego Velázquez, and also served as one of Narváez's captains. At a dinner in Narváez's camp, Juan Velázquez de León, who had been sent as an emissary by Cortés, and the young Diego Velázquez almost came to blows arguing about Cortés and which of the two of them was a "good" Velázquez.

more to remind you, except that this is the touchstone of our honor and fame forever onward, and it's worth more to die as good men than to live dishonored." Because at that time it was raining and it was late, he said no more.

Something I have thought about since is that never did he say to us: I have made such and such an agreement in the camp, or that so and so or so and so is on our side, or anything of that kind, but only that we should fight like brave men. Not telling us he had friends in the camp of Narváez was the act of a very astute captain, because for that reason we would not fail to fight like very courageous men and would have no hope in them, but only, after God, in our own great courage. Let us leave this and talk about how each one of our captains was with his designated soldiers telling them how and in what way we had to fight and giving one another courage. Then my captain Pizarro, with whom we were to take the artillery—which was the matter of greatest danger for we had to be the first to break through to the guns—also said with much courage how we were to enter and lower our pikes to the on-guard position until we had the artillery in our power; and as soon as we had taken it, our artillerymen, Mesa the Sicilian, Usagre, and Arvenga, should attack the people in the lodging of Salvatierra with those same guns and the balls that were ready to be discharged.

Also I want to talk about the great need we had of arms, that for a breastplate or headpiece or helmet or iron chin guard we would that night have given whatever they asked for it and all we had already gained. Then, secretly, they told us the battle cry we had to use while doing battle, which was Holy Spirit, Holy Spirit! They said that this is usually kept secret in the wars so they can recognize and call each other by the battle cry opponents and the others would not know. Narváez's men had as their battle cry and shout, Santa María, Santa María! With all of this done, as I was a great friend and supporter of the captain Sandoval, he begged me that night as a favor that after we had taken the artillery, if I was still alive, I would always be with him and follow him, and I promised him I would and so I did.

Let us talk now about what we were doing for a while in the night, preparing and thinking about what lay ahead of us, for we had nothing at all for our supper; our scouts left right away, and lookouts and the watch were posted. They put another soldier and me on watch, and before long a scout came to ask me whether I had heard something, and I said no. Then a squad leader came and said that Galleguillo, who had come from the camp of Narváez, had disappeared, that he was a spy sent by Narváez, and that Cortés ordered us to march on the road to Cempoala right away. We heard our fifer play and our drummer beat, and the captains prepared their soldiers and we began to march. Galleguillo was found sleeping under some cloaks, for as it was raining and the poor man was not accustomed to being wet or cold, he went there to sleep. Then, going along at our fast pace, without playing the fife or beating the drum, the captains cautioning their soldiers, we began to march. With our scouts reconnoitering the land, we arrived at the river where the lookouts of Narváez were, who were named Gonzalo Carrasco and Hurtado, and they were off their guard so we had time to seize Carrasco, and the other went shouting to the camp of Narváez: "To arms, to arms, Cortés is coming!"

I remember that when we crossed that river, as it was raining, it had become somewhat deep and the stones somewhat slippery, and the pikes and our arms hindered us greatly. I also remember that when Carrasco was seized, he said to Cortés in a loud voice: "Look out, señor Cortés, don't go there, for I swear that Narváez is waiting for you in the field with his whole army." Cortés gave him to his secretary Pedro Hernández to guard. As we saw that Hurtado went to give warning, we did not delay at all. Rather Hurtado's shouting and giving the warning, "To arms, to arms!" Narváez calling to his captains, and we lowering our pikes to the ready and closing in on the artillery all happened at once. Their artillerymen had time only to fire four guns; some of the balls passed overhead, but one of them killed three of our companions. Then in that instant, all our captains arrived, our fifer and drummer sounding the call to arms, but as many of Narváez's men were on horseback, our men were delayed somewhat by them, but they brought down six or seven of them. We who had taken the artillery did not dare abandon the guns because Narváez was shooting at us with crossbows and escopetas from his lodging, and he wounded seven of our men. At that moment, the captain Sandoval arrived and rushed up the steps, and in spite of the strong resistance Narváez put up with his crossbows, escopetas, with halberds and lances, the captain Sandoval and his soldiers still ascended. Then, as soon as we soldiers saw that we had captured the artillery, that there was no one to defend it, we turned it over to our artillerymen, and the captain Pizarro and many of us went to help Sandoval, for Narváez's men made them back down two steps in retreat, but with our arrival they again climbed up. We were fighting for some time with our pikes, which were long, and when I least expected it, we heard Narváez shouting: "Holy Mary, protect me, for they've killed me and put out one of my eyes!" When we heard that, we immediately shouted: "Victory, victory for those of the name of the Holy Spirit, for Narváez is dead! Victory, victory for Cortés, for Narváez is dead!" But for all this, we could not enter the cu where they were until one Martín López, he of the brigantines, because he was tall, set fire to the thatch on the high cu, and all Narváez's men came tumbling down the steps. Then we seized Narváez, and the first who had his hands on him was Pedro Sánchez Farfán; I gave him to Sandoval and the other captains with him, who were still shouting and crying: "Long live the king, long live the king, and in his royal name Cortés, Cortés! Victory, victory, for Narváez is dead!"

Let us leave this combat; let us go to Cortés and the rest of the captains who were each still battling with the captains of Narváez, who had not yet given up despite the shots the artillerymen shot at them, our shouts, and the death of Narváez, because they were in very high cus. As Cortés was very shrewd, he immediately ordered it proclaimed that all of Narváez's men should come at once to submit themselves beneath the banner of His Majesty and Cortés, in his royal name, on pain of death. Even with all this, the men of Diego Velázquez the younger did not give themselves up nor those of Salvatierra, because they were in very high cus, which could not be entered until Gonzalo de Sandoval went with half of us who were with him; with that, the guns and the proclamations, we entered where they were and so Salvatierra and those with him were taken as well as Diego Velázquez the younger. Then Sandoval came with all of us who had gone to seize Narváez to put him in a safer place. After Cortés, Juan Velázquez and Ordaz had taken as prisoners Salvatierra, the young Diego Velázquez, Gamarra, Juan Juste, Juan Bono the Biscayan, and other important people, Cortés came unrecognized, accompanied by our captains, to where we had Narváez. With the heat, which was great, loaded with his arms, going from one place to another, calling to our soldiers and giving proclamations, he became very sweaty and tired, such that he was out of breath. He spoke to Sandoval twice, but he did not succeed in saying what he wanted because of the trouble he was having, but somewhat relieved, he said: "Hey, stop! What about Narváez? What about Narváez?" Sandoval said: "Here he is, here he is, and very well guarded." And Cortés, still out of breath, spoke again: "Take care, my son Sandoval, that you don't leave him, you and your companions, so he doesn't escape from you, while I go to take care of other things, and see to it that those captains captured with him are guarded carefully."

Then he went and made other proclamations, that, under pain of death, all the men of Narváez should come right that minute to surrender under the flag of His Majesty, and in his royal name Hernando Cortés, his captain general and chief justice, and that none of them should carry any arms, but all should give them up and turn them over to our constables. All this was at night, for it had not yet dawned, and it still rained from time to time; then the moon came out, but when we had arrived there it was very dark and it was raining. The darkness helped, however, for as it was so dark, there were many fireflies, which give light at night, and the men of Narváez believed they were the matches of the escopetas.

Let us leave this and move ahead. As Narváez was very badly wounded and had lost an eye, he asked permission from Sandoval that the surgeon he had brought in his fleet, Master Juan, might take care of his eye and the other captains who were wounded, and Sandoval gave permission. While they were being tended to, Cortés came close by, disguised so they would not recognize him, to see Narváez being treated. They said quietly to Narváez that Cortés was there; and as they said it to him, Narváez said: "Señor captain Cortés, you must consider this a great victory that you've had over me, taking me prisoner." Cortés replied to him that he gave great thanks to God for giving him the victory and for his courageous gentlemen and companions who had part in it, but taking him prisoner and defeating the man who had the audacity to arrest a judge of His Majesty was one of the least important things he had done in New Spain. As soon as he had said this, he left, and said nothing more to Narváez, but he ordered Sandoval to post very good guards on Narváez and not to leave, keeping responsible people with him. We had already put two pairs of shackles on him, and we carried him to a building and posted soldiers to guard him. Sandoval selected me as one of them and privately ordered me not to allow any of Narváez's men to speak with him until it was daytime and Cortés could put him in a safer place.

As Cortés and his men were battling and defeating Narváez, news came that Mexico was in revolt, that Pedro de Alvarado was besieged, that the Mexicans had set fire to the Spaniards' lodgings, killed seven soldiers, and wounded many others. "When we heard such terrible news, God knows how much it upset us, and by forced marches we began to go in the direction of Mexico."

Chapter 12

La Noche Triste, the Night of Sorrows

[CXXV] As I recall, when the news arrived that Pedro de Alvarado was besieged and Mexico had revolted,[64] Cortés spoke to Narváez's men, saying he was sorry they would not come with us of their own goodwill to help with the relief effort, and he beseeched them to set aside past hatreds over what had happened with Narváez, offering to make them rich and give them posts. Because they had come to seek a living, he said, and were in a land where they could serve God and His Majesty and become rich, their chance was now. He spoke to them so skillfully that, to the last man, they all offered to go with us. Had they known the strength of Mexico, however, it is certain none of them would have gone. We were soon on our way, moving very rapidly until we reached Tlaxcala. There we learned that Montezuma and his captains had continued attacking Pedro de Alvarado, killing seven of his soldiers and burning his lodgings, until they found out how we had routed Narváez. But when they found out about our victory, they stopped attacking him. We also learned that Alvarado and his men were exhausted from lack of food and water; Montezuma had never ordered that food be given to them. Indians of Tlaxcala brought this news the very moment we arrived there.

Cortés then ordered a review of the men, and he counted more than thirteen hundred soldiers, including ours and Narváez's, and more than ninety-six men with horses, eighty crossbowmen, and an equal number of escopeteros, which seemed to Cortés to be enough men to allow us to enter Mexico very safely; besides this,

---

64. The claim that the Mexicans were in revolt, or had rebelled, rests on the Spaniards' belief that Montezuma, on behalf of the Mexican people, had declared fealty to the Spanish Crown and they were therefore subject to it and its proper representatives, which Cortés declared and represented himself to be.

in Tlaxcala the caciques gave us two thousand Indian warriors. We then went rapidly to Texcoco, a large city, where they paid us no honor at all, nor did any lord appear; on the contrary, everything was abandoned and in bad shape. We arrived in Mexico on St. John's Day, June 1520. Neither caciques nor leaders nor any Indians we knew appeared in the streets; rather, all the houses were empty. When we arrived at the lodgings where we used to stay, the great Montezuma came out to the courtyard to speak to Cortés and embrace him, to welcome him, and talk about his victory over Narváez. But because Cortés was arriving victorious, he did not want to listen, and Montezuma went into his lodging, very sad and pensive.

After we were all lodged where we had been before we left Mexico to deal with Narváez, and Narváez's men were lodged elsewhere, we saw and spoke with Pedro de Alvarado and the soldiers who had stayed with him. They told us about the attacks the Mexicans had made on them and the difficulty in which it put them, and we reported on our victory over Narváez.

[CXXVI] It seems that, on the way to Mexico, Cortés had boasted to Narváez's captains of the great respect and command accorded to him, of how the Indians would come out to greet him on the road, hold celebrations, and give him gold, of how in Mexico he commanded the great Montezuma as absolutely as he commanded all his captains, and of how they would give him presents of gold as they were used to doing; but now, seeing that everything was very much the opposite of his expectations, that in Texcoco they had not welcomed us, nor even given us anything to eat except bad food and leftovers, and that everything was going from bad to worse, and no chieftains were there with whom to speak, and he found everything in bad shape, that it was the same when he came to Mexico, that they were not holding the tianguez but it was abandoned, and having heard from Pedro de Alvarado about the disorderly way he attacked the Mexicans, Cortés became very angry and irritable with the many Spanish men he brought with him and very sad and sulky. At this very moment the great Montezuma sent two of his chieftains to beg

Cortés to come see him because he wanted to speak with him. Cortés's reply was: "The hell with the dog, when he will not even hold a tianguez nor order any food to be given to us."[65] When our captains, Juan Velázquez de León, Cristóbal de Olid, Alonzo de Ávila, and Francisco de Lugo, heard Cortés say that, they said: "Sir, temper your anger and look how much good and honor this king of these lands has done us, this king who is so good that, if not for him, we would already be dead and they would have eaten us, and look how he has even given you his daughters."

When Cortés heard this, he was even more indignant at their words, as they seemed to be a scolding, and he said: "What courtesy should I show a dog who has been dealing secretly with Narváez, and who you now see doesn't even give us anything to eat?" And his captains said, "It seems to us that you must do this, and it's good advice." Because Cortés had so many Spaniards there in Mexico, both ours and those of Narváez, he did not care about anything and spoke so angrily and rudely to the chieftains. So he spoke to the chieftains again, saying they should tell their lord Montezuma to order immediately that the tianguez and market be held. If this was not done, Montezuma would see what would happen. The chieftains clearly understood the insulting words that Cortés said about their lord and even the scolding that our captains gave Cortés about it, because they knew the captains well as the ones who used to guard their lord, and they knew that these men were great servants of their Montezuma. As far as they understood everything, they told Montezuma about it. Then from anger, or perhaps because the Mexicans had already agreed to attack us, not even a quarter of an hour later a soldier came in great haste, very badly wounded, from a town near Mexico called Tacuba. He had been bringing some Indian women who belonged to Cortés, one of them a

---

65. *Perro* (meaning "dog") was one of the primary and strongest insult words among the Spanish of that time. It had been used relative to the Muslims (Moors) and Jews in Spain and carried over to the indigenous people of the New World, where it was often used to diminish the stature of indigenous people of high rank.

daughter of Montezuma; it seems, when we went to deal with Narváez, Cortés had left them in the care of the lord of Tacuba because they were that lord's relatives. The soldier said that the entire city and road by which he came was filled with warriors with all types of arms, that they took from him the Indian women he was bringing and wounded him in two places, that they had seized him and if he had not gotten loose, they were going to put him in a canoe and carry him off to be sacrificed, and they destroyed a bridge.

When Cortés and some of us heard that, we were certainly very sorry because we were very well aware, those of us who were used to fighting Indians, of the great multitude they normally gathered together, and that however well we might fight, even if we now had more soldiers, we were going to be at great risk for our lives and hunger and hardships, especially because we were in so strong a city.

Trapped in their lodgings without provisions, the Spaniards made numerous focused attempts to fight their way out of the city. In describing the ferocity of the attacks on them, Bernal Díaz writes, "some three or four soldiers there with us swore many times to God that they had never seen such fierce wars in any they had experienced among Christians and against the artillery of the king of France, nor of the great Turk."

We decided to ask for peace to leave Mexico. At daybreak, many more squadrons of warriors came, and indeed they surrounded our lodgings on all sides, and if they hurled many stones and arrows before, this day they came more densely and with greater yells and whistles; and other squadrons from other sides tried to enter, against whom neither cannons nor escopetas were of use even though they did great damage. Seeing all this, Cortés decided that the great Montezuma should speak to the Mexicans from a rooftop and tell them they should stop their warring, that we would like to leave their city. When the great Montezuma was told this on behalf of Cortés, they say he said with great grief:

"What does Malinche want from me now, for I do not want to live or to listen to him, for because of him my fate has brought me to such a state." He refused to come, and they say he said that he did not want to see or hear Cortés anymore, or his false words, or promises and lies. Then the Mercedarian father and Cristóbal de Olid went and spoke to Montezuma with much respect and very affectionate words. Montezuma said: "I do not believe I will be able to do anything useful to end this war, for they have already raised up another lord and have proposed not to let you leave here alive; and so I believe that all of you will have to die."

Let us return to the great battles they were waging against us. Montezuma took a position at the parapet of a rooftop with many of our soldiers guarding him, and he began to speak in very affectionate words, saying they should stop the war and we would leave Mexico. Many Mexican chieftains and leaders recognized him and ordered their men to be quiet and not to hurl spears or stones or arrows; and four of them came closer so that Montezuma could speak to them, and, weeping, they said to him: "Oh Lord, our great lord, how sorry we are for your misfortune and the harm to you, your children, and relatives! We now inform you that we have already elevated one of your relatives as our lord." The speaker gave his name, which was Coadlavaca, lord of Iztapalapa; it was not Guatemuz, who became lord later. They also said that they were going to finish the war, that they had promised their idols not to end it until all of us were dead and that they begged Huichilobos and Tezcatepuca each day to keep him, Montezuma, free and safe from our power. They also said that should it turn out as they wanted, they would not fail to hold him in even greater esteem than before as their lord, and they asked that he pardon them. They had barely finished this speech when, at that moment, the Mexicans hurled so many stones and spears that he was hit by three stones, one in the head, another on the arm, and another on the leg. Our men who were surrounding him had neglected for one moment to protect him because they noticed that while he was speaking with the Mexicans, they were not attacking. Although they begged him to care for himself and to eat something and said good words about it to him, he would not, and, when we least expected it, they came to tell us he was dead. Cortés cried for him, as did all our captains and soldiers, and there were those among us who knew and dealt with him who were as tearful as if he were our father, and we should not wonder at this, seeing how good he was. They said that he had reigned for seventeen years, that he was the best king there had ever been in Mexico, and that he had won in three personal challenges he had met over the lands he subdued.

[CXXVII] I have already told of the sadness we felt when we saw that Montezuma had died, and we thought badly of the Mercedarian friar who was always with him for not being able to convince Montezuma to become Christian; but he gave as his reason that he did not believe Montezuma would die of those wounds, except that he should have ordered them to give Montezuma something to deaden the pain. In short, not to talk more about it, Cortés ordered a papa and a chieftain from among the prisoners to be freed so they could go tell the cacique named Coadlavaca, whom the Mexicans had raised up as lord, and his captains that the great Montezuma was dead, that they had seen him die and of the way he had died from wounds his own people had given him, that they should say how very sorry we all were about it, that they should bury him as the great king he was, that they should raise up as king Montezuma's cousin, who was with us, because the inheritance belonged to him or to Montezuma's other sons, that the one they had raised up as lord did not come by it rightfully, and that they should negotiate a peace so we could leave Mexico. If they did not do that, Cortés said, now that Montezuma was dead, for whom we had respect and for whose sake we had not destroyed their city, we would come out to attack them, burn all their houses, and do them much harm. So they could see that Montezuma was dead, Cortés ordered six Mexicans, high chieftains, and the rest of the papas we were holding as prisoners to carry him on their shoulders, deliver him to the Mexican captains, tell them what Montezuma commanded at the time of his death, and tell them that the ones who carried Montezuma on their shoulders had been present at his death. They told Coadlavaca the entire truth, that Montezuma's own people killed him with three blows from stones. When the Mexicans saw him dead, they made a very great lament, and we heard clearly their crying and wailing for him. But even with all of this, their great, continuous battering of us did not stop. They were on us with spears and stones and arrows, and they came on yet more forcefully, with greater fury, and they said to us: "Now you will truly pay for the death of our king and lord and the dishonor of our idols; and as for the peace you wanted, come out here and we will discuss how it must be."

The Mexicans said so much about this and other things that I cannot now remember it all, and so I will stop here. But they said they had already chosen a good king, and he would not be so weak of heart that he could be tricked with false words as their good Montezuma had been. They also said that we should not concern ourselves about the burial but about our lives, that in two days none of us would be left alive to send them such messages. With these words came very great cries, whistles, showers of stones and spears and arrows, and many other squadrons were still trying to set fire to many parts of our lodgings.

[CXXVIII] Day by day we saw our forces growing smaller and those of the Mexicans increasing, and we saw many of our people dead and most of the rest wounded. Although we were fighting courageously, we could not make the Mexicans retreat nor free ourselves of the many squadrons that day and night were attacking us; our gunpowder was dwindling and also the food and water; the great Montezuma was dead, and they were not accepting the peace and truces we were requesting. In short, we saw our deaths before our very eyes, and the bridges were raised. Cortés and all our captains and soldiers decided that we should leave at night when the warrior squadrons should be least watchful. To distract them further, we sent a papa who was a prisoner, a man important among them, and some other prisoners, with a message saying that they should let us leave in peace in a week from then, and we would give them all the gold; all this was done to distract them so we could leave that night.

Now I will tell how it was arranged that a bridge be made of very strong timbers and boards that we could carry to put over the destroyed bridges, and four hundred Tlaxcalan Indians and one hundred fifty soldiers were designated to carry and place it and guard the way until all the baggage and the army had passed; two hundred Tlaxcalan Indians and fifty soldiers were designated to bring the artillery; Gonzalo de Sandoval and Diego de Ordaz were designated to be in front, fighting; Francisco de Saucedo, Francisco de Lugo, and a company of one hundred young, fast soldiers were divided into two groups to go where they were most needed in the fighting; Cortés himself, Alonso de Ávila, Cristóbal de Olid, and the other captains were designated to be in the middle; in the rearguard Pedro de Alvarado and Juan Velázquez de León, and inserted in the middle, between the captains and Narváez's soldiers, three hundred Tlaxcalans and thirty soldiers were designated to take charge of the prisoners and doña Marina and doña Luisa.

This agreement made, it was already night and time to get out the gold to take it away or distribute it. Cortés ordered his chamberlain Cristóbal de Guzmán and other soldiers who were from his household to bring out all the jewels and silver and gold, and with the help of many Tlaxcalan Indians he had given them for the purpose, they put it in the hall. Then he said to the king's officials, Alonso de Ávila and Gonzalo Mejía, that they should take the king's share, and he gave them seven wounded and lame horses and a mare and more than eighty Tlaxcalan friends. They loaded as much of it in bulk as they could carry, for it had been made into very wide bars, but much gold was left in piles in the hall. Then Cortés called his secretary and other king's notaries, and he said: "Give me written testimony that I can't do anything more to guard this gold; here in this building and hall we have more than seven hundred thousand gold pesos, and as you have seen, it can neither be weighed nor put in a safer place; I hereby give it to those soldiers who would like to take some of it, otherwise it's going to be left here lost among these dogs." When many of Narváez's soldiers and some of ours heard that, they loaded themselves with the gold. As for me, I coveted nothing but my life, although I did not fail to grab, from some small boxes, four chalchiuis, which are stones very much prized by the Indians. I immediately put them on my chest under my armor; later, their value served me well for healing my wounds and buying food.

When we learned of Cortés's arrangement for how we were to leave and go to the bridges that night, and as it was somewhat dark, misty, and drizzling, we began before midnight to carry the bridge and move the baggage, the horses, the mare, and the Tlaxcalans loaded with gold. The bridge was quickly put in place, and Cortés, with those he took with him, went over first, as did many of the horsemen. While this was going on, the Mexicans' voices, horns, cries, and whistles sounded, and they called out in their language to the people of Tlatelolco: "Come out with your canoes immediately because the teules are leaving; cut them off so that none of them is left alive." When I was not expecting it, we saw so many squadrons of warriors on us and the entire lake solid with canoes that we could not defend ourselves, and many of our soldiers had already gone over.

With us in this situation, a great multitude of Mexicans charged to get rid of the bridge and wound and kill our men, who were unable to lend each other a hand. Misfortune is compounded in such times, and one evil follows on another; as it was raining, two horses slipped and fell into the water. When I and other of Cortés's men saw that, we got to safety on the far side of the bridge, but so many warriors were charging that no matter how well we fought, no further use could be made of the bridge. Thus, that passage and the opening in the water were quickly swollen with dead horses, Indian men and women, *naborías*,[66] baggage, and trunks. Fearing they would kill all the rest of us, we pushed ahead along our causeway and encountered many squadrons waiting for us with long lances.

---

66. A term the Spaniards used to designate a household servant.

They hurled insults, among which were: "Oh, *cuilones*,[67] are you still alive?"

With sword thrusting and slashing we got through, although they wounded six who were with us. Was there some order like what we had planned? Not a sign of it, for Cortés and the captains and soldiers on horseback who passed over first, so as to protect themselves and get to dry land and save their lives, spurred on forward along the causeway and they did the right thing, and the horses with the gold and the Tlaxcalans also got out safely; but I say that if we had waited on the bridge for one another, and this is as true for the horsemen as for the soldiers, all of us would have perished, not one of us would have been left alive, and the reason is this: passing along the causeway, assaulting the Mexican squadrons, with water on one side and flat-roofed houses on the other, the lake filled with canoes, we could do nothing. The escopetas and crossbows all stayed on the bridge, and because it was night, what could we do other than what we had done, which was to charge, slashing a bit at those who came to take hold of us, and go forward until we left the causeways. Had it been daytime, it would have been worse; and even those of us who escaped did so only because it pleased Our Lord. For anyone who did not see the huge number of warriors that were on us that night and the canoes full of them coming to seize our soldiers, I say to you, it was terrifying.

While we were advancing along our causeway into the town of Tacuba, where Cortés and all his captains already were, Gonzalo de Sandoval and Cristóbal de Olid and other horsemen who had gone ahead were calling loudly: "Señor captain, wait for us, because they say we are running away and leaving them to die on the bridges. Let us go back to help them in case some have been left behind, for no one is coming out or getting here."

---

67. This is a sexual term used derisively to call into question an enemy's manliness and courage; in Nahuatl it is *cuiloni*, the passive partner in male homosexual relations.

Cortés's response was that it was a miracle any of us had got out. Then he went back with the horsemen and soldiers who were not wounded, but they did not go any distance, because soon Pedro de Alvarado appeared, badly wounded, on foot with a lance in his hand because the Mexicans had killed his sorrel mare. He brought with him four soldiers as badly wounded as he was and eight Tlaxcalans, all streaming blood from many wounds. While Cortés was on the causeway with the rest of the captains, we made a halt in the courtyards of Tacuba. Many squadrons had already arrived there from Mexico crying out to inform Tacuba and another town called Escapuzalco, so they began to hurl spears, rocks, and arrows, and attack with their large lances. We made some assaults, defending ourselves and attacking them.

Let us return to Pedro de Alvarado. When Cortés and the rest of the captains found him in that condition and saw that no more soldiers were coming, tears sprang to his eyes, and Pedro de Alvarado said that Juan Velázquez de León had died at the bridge with more than eighty other gentlemen, both ours and Narváez's. He said that, after the Mexicans killed their horses, he and the four soldiers he brought with him passed with great danger at the bridge over dead bodies, horses, and trunks, for the area around the bridge was packed solid with them. He also said that all the bridges and causeways were filled with warriors.

While we were in Tacuba, many Mexican warriors came together from all the towns around and killed three of our soldiers. We decided to leave that town as rapidly as we could with five Tlaxcalan Indians, who discovered a way to go to Tlaxcala without using the road. They carefully guided us until we arrived at some groups of houses on a hill next to a cu, their fort-like adoratorio, where we made a halt. We were followed by the Mexicans who were hurling arrows, spears, and stones from slings, and they surrounded us, always charging; it was a terrifying thing. I have said this many times, and I am tired of saying it, but readers should not see it as long-windedness, because each time the

Mexicans pressed us, wounded us, and made strong attacks on us, I must mention the squadrons that followed and killed so many of us.

We took shelter in that cu and fortress and tended to the wounded, but even with the many fires we made, there was nothing to eat by any stretch of the imagination. After the great city of Mexico was won, we built a church in that cu and ado-ratorio called Our Lady of Los Remedios, now much vener-ated, and many citizens and gentlemen of Mexico now go there on pilgrimage and make many novenas.[68] But let us leave this and return to discussing how pitiful it was to see our wounds treated and dressed with cloths from blankets, and because they were chilled and swollen, they were very painful. But more to weep for were the missing gentlemen and brave soldiers, Juan Velázquez de León, Francisco de Saucedo, Francisco de Morla, and one Lares, the good rider, and many others of us men of Cortés. I name only these few, because to write the names of so many of us who were missing would not allow me to finish very soon. As for Narváez's men, most of them were left on the bridges loaded down with gold.

Let us note that the sons and daughters of Montezuma as well as the prisoners we were bringing and Cacamatzin, lord of Tex-coco, and other kings of provinces were left behind, dead, on the bridges.

We were all thinking about what we were facing ahead; all of us were wounded, and only twenty-three horses had escaped; we saved none of the guns, artillery, or powder; the crossbows were few, and we immediately repaired their cords and made bolts. And the worst of all was that we did not know the mood we were going to find in our friends in Tlaxcala. In addition, that night, still surrounded by Mexicans and their cries, their spears and arrows and stones shot from slings, we decided to leave at midnight. With our Tlaxcalan guides in front, we went on

---

68. A devotion in the Catholic church that lasts nine days and is dedi-cated to a specific intent.

our way in good order, the wounded in the middle, the lame with staffs, some who could not walk and were very ill on the haunches of lame horses not fit for battle, and the horsemen who were not wounded in front and distributed on either side. In this way, all of us who were fit faced the Mexicans; the wounded Tlaxcalans were inside the body of our squadron, but the rest who were fit faced the enemy with us, because the Mexicans were still harassing us with loud shouts and cries and whistles, and they were saying, "You are going where none of you will be left alive." We did not understand why they said that, but you will see further on.

I have forgotten to write about the joy we felt in seeing alive our doña Marina and doña Luisa, the daughter of Xicotenga, who some Tlaxcalans had saved at the bridges, and also a woman named María de Estrada, for she was the only Spanish woman we had with us in Mexico. Those who had escaped and gotten away from the bridges first were some sons of Xicotenga, brothers of doña Luisa, but the rest of the naborías given to us in Tlaxcala and in Mexico City itself were dead.

Chapter 13

The Battle of Otumba and the Return to Mexico

[CXXVIII] Let us return to talking about how we arrived that day at some outlying settlements and groups of houses belonging to a large town called Gualtitan,[69] which was given to Alonso de Ávila after we won Mexico; and although the Indians yelled and shouted at us and hurled stones, spears, and arrows, we stood up to it all. From there we went past some houses and small towns,

---

69. Cuauhtitlan.

the Mexicans always following us, and, as many of them were now gathered, they tried to kill us. They began to surround us and hurl many stones from slings and spears and arrows, and used their broadswords, and they killed two of our soldiers in a place hard to get through. They also killed a horse and wounded many of our men, but with sword thrusts and stabs we also killed some of them, and the horsemen did the same. So we slept in the houses and ate the horse they killed. Early the next day we began to move with the same arrangement as before, and even better, with half the horsemen always in front. A little more than a league from there, on a plain, just when we believed we were out of danger, our scouts who were reconnoitering returned from the countryside and reported that the fields were filled with Mexican warriors waiting for us. When we heard this, we were very fearful, but not so much that we lost heart or failed to meet them in a fight to the death. We stopped there for a while and it was arranged that the horsemen were to charge and return at slack rein, that they should not stop to lance but point their lances at the Mexicans' faces until their squadrons were thrown into confusion, that we soldiers should all thrust our swords so that they passed through the Mexicans' entrails, and that we would do everything in a way to avenge our dead and wounded very well so that, if it pleased God, we might escape with our lives. After commending ourselves completely to God and to Saint Mary and invoking the name of señor Santiago, when we saw that the Mexicans were beginning to surround us, the horses, in groups of five, broke through them, and all of us charged together. Oh, what a thing it was to see, this so dreadful and fierce battle! How we moved, all mixed up with them at close quarters, how we slashed and thrust at them with our swords, with what fury the dogs fought and how they wounded and killed us with their lances and war clubs and two-handed swords, and, because the field was flat, how the horsemen lanced at will, charging and returning, and although both they and their horses were wounded, they did not stop battling as the bravest of men! All of us who did not have horses seemed to put forth a double effort, for although we

Four Aztec warrior-priests wearing regalia and, bound to their backs, standards appropriate to their level of experience, achievement, and leadership in battle. The least accomplished is on the right and the most senior warrior is on the left, bearing the image of a mountain lion on his helmet. *Codex Mendoza.*

were wounded, and we received new wounds, we did not bother to tighten our bandages in order not to have to stop, for it was not the time to, but with great energy we came to grips with the enemy to give them sword thrusts. I want to mention Cortés, Cristóbal de Olid, Gonzalo de Sandoval, Gonzalo Domínguez, and one Juan de Salamanca, who, although they were badly wounded, rode from one side to the other breaking up squadrons; and I want to note also the words Cortés said to us who were in the midst of the enemy, that the thrusts and slashes of our swords should be aimed at the notable lords, because all wore great plumes of gold and carried rich arms and devices. Then to see how the brave and spirited Sandoval encouraged us and said: "Come on gentlemen, for today is the day we'll win; have faith in God that we'll come out alive for some good purpose!" And I will note once more that they killed and wounded many of our soldiers. Let us return to Cortés, Cristóbal de Olid, Sandoval, Gonzalo Domínguez, and the others on horseback I do not name here, and Juan de Salamanca. All of us soldiers gave Cortés great courage to fight, and Our Lord Jesus Christ and Our Lady, the Holy Virgin Mary, put that courage in our hearts, as did señor Santiago, who certainly helped us.

It pleased God that Cortés and the captains I have already named went together to a place where the captain general of the Mexicans was, with his banner unfurled, with rich arms of gold and great plumes decorated with silverwork. When Cortés saw him with many other Mexican chieftains, all of whom wore great plumes, he said to Gonzalo de Sandoval, Cristóbal de Olid, Gonzalo Domínguez, and the rest of our captains: "Come on gentlemen! Let's break them up and not leave a single one without wounds." Commending themselves to God, Cortés, Cristóbal de Olid, Sandoval, Alonso de Ávila, and other horsemen charged. Cortés ran his horse into the Mexican captain, which forced him to lower his banner, and the rest of our captains finished breaking through the squadron of many Indians. It was Juan de Salamanca who was following the captain with the banner, who had not yet fallen from the blow Cortés had given him; Salamanca was riding with Cortés, mounted on a good cream-colored mare, and lanced him, took the rich plumed headdress he was wearing, and right away then gave it to Cortés, saying that, as it was Cortés who first engaged the Mexican captain and made him lower the banner, which caused his men to lose their will to fight, the plume was his. But three years later His Majesty gave it to Salamanca for his coat of arms, and his descendants have it on their armorial banners.

Let us return to our battle. It pleased Our Lord God that with the death of that Mexican captain carrying the banner and many others who died there, the Indians' fighting grew weaker, and all the horsemen were pursuing them. We were neither hungry nor thirsty, but it seemed instead that we had endured or experienced neither suffering nor hardship, and we followed up the victory killing and wounding. Our friends, the Tlaxcalans, became like lions with their swords, broadswords, and other arms they had seized there, using them effectively and courageously. When the horsemen returned from following up the victory, we all gave great thanks to God for having escaped from so great a multitude, for there had never been seen nor encountered in battle in all the Indies so large a number of warriors together; and because they were the flower of Mexico, Texcoco, and all the towns around the lake and many other bordering towns, as well as the towns of Otumba, Tepetezcuco, and Saltocan,[70] they thought that this time not a trace of us would be left. What rich arms they carried, with so much gold and plumes and devices, and so many captains and important people! Near where this hard-fought and famous battle took place, in a town called Otumba, this battle as well as many other battles we had with the Mexicans up to the time we conquered Mexico, is very well painted with carved portraits of the Mexicans and Tlaxcalans.

Curious readers might appreciate being reminded that when we went to the aid of Pedro de Alvarado in Mexico we were, in all, more than thirteen hundred soldiers, counting those on horse, which amounted to ninety-seven, and eighty crossbowmen, as many escopeteros, and more than two thousand Tlaxcalans and much artillery. We entered Mexico on St. John's Day, June of 1520; we left fleeing the tenth of July of the same year, and this battle, called the Battle of Otumba, occurred on July 14. Now that I told how we escaped from all the close calls I have mentioned, I would like to give another count of how many of us were killed, not only in Mexico, but also on the bridges and causeways, in all the clashes, in this Battle of Otumba and along the roads: In about five days, more than eight hundred sixty soldiers were killed and sacrificed, as well as seventy-two in a town called Tustepeque, and five Spanish women; the ones killed in Tustepeque were Narváez's men; more than twelve hundred Tlaxcalans were killed.

They also killed a Juan de Alcántara the elder with three other citizens of Villa Rica, who were coming for the shares of gold coming to them, so they lost both the gold and their lives. If we think about it, in general, none of us had much pleasure from the shares of gold they gave us, and if on the bridges many more of Narváez's men died, it was because they left loaded down with

---

70. Xaltocan.

gold, and because of its weight, they could neither swim nor get out of the water.

> *Having survived the escape from Mexico and the subsequent attacks by well-organized and determined groups of Mexicans on their journey to Tlaxcala, Cortés and his men, initially concerned about what reception they would receive at the hands of the Tlaxcalans, were warmly greeted and taken in when they arrived at the head town. After resting and healing, Cortés determined to punish the towns that had supported Mexico in its effort to wipe out his men and those of Narváez. Cortés moved first against the people of Tepeaca, where the Mexicans had posted their first garrison. The joint force of Mexicans and Tepeacans were defeated, and the Spaniards and Tlaxcalans enslaved many of the people. The Spaniards renamed the town of Tepeaca the "Villa de Segura de la Frontera." From there, in about forty days, numerous towns in the surrounding area were pacified and punished. In addition, Cortés and his men were reinforced by the arrival of several ships of fully provisioned and armed Spaniards.*

At that time in Mexico, they had elevated another lord, because the lord who had driven us out of Mexico had died of smallpox. The lord they raised up was a nephew or very close relative of Montezuma named Guatemuz, a young man of about twenty-five years, very much a gentleman for an Indian, very courageous, and he made himself so feared that all his people trembled before him. He was married to a daughter of Montezuma, a very beautiful woman for an Indian. When this Guatemuz, lord of Mexico, learned we had defeated the Mexican squadrons in Tepeaca, that the people there had given their obedience to His Majesty, were serving us and giving us things to eat, that we had settled there, he feared we would raid Oaxaca and other provinces and attract them to our friendship; so he sent his messengers through all the towns so that they would be very ready with all their weapons, and to the caciques he gave golden jewels, and he pardoned others from their tribute. Above all, he ordered very great captaincies and garrisons of warriors to see that we did not enter his lands, and he sent to say that they should fight very vigorously with us.

Let us talk about how, with all the towns in the neighborhood of Tepeaca at peace, Cortés decided that Francisco de Orozco would stay in the town of Segura de la Frontera as captain with some twenty soldiers who were wounded and ill, and with all the rest of our army we went to Tlaxcala. Arrangements were made for wood to be cut to make thirteen brigantines in order to go against Mexico again, because we were certain we could not master the lake without brigantines, nor could we attack, nor again enter the causeways to that great city except with great risk to our lives. He who was the master of cutting the wood, making the frames, and calculating and planning everything, explaining how they had to be fast and light for their purpose, and making them, was one Martín López, who certainly, besides being a good soldier in all the wars, served His Majesty well in this matter of the brigantines and did a strong man's work on them. It seems to me that if he had not been fated to be among the first to come in our company, having to send to Castile for another master would have wasted much time, and none might have come because of the great obstacles that the bishop of Burgos put in our way.

I will return to our subject and talk about how, when we arrived at Tlaxcala, our great friend and very loyal vassal of His Majesty, Maseescaci, had died of smallpox; his death made all of us very sad, and Cortés felt it, as he said, as if he were his father, and he wore black cloaks in mourning as did many of our captains and soldiers. Cortés and all of us paid much honor to the children and relatives of Maseescaci; and because in Tlaxcala there were disagreements about the command and office of cacique, Cortés ordered and commanded that it be one of the legitimate sons of Maseescaci himself, because his father had ordered that before he died. Maseescaci had also told his sons and relatives that they should see that they did not stray from the command of Malinche and his brothers, because we were certainly the ones who would be masters over these lands, and he gave them much other good advice. Let us stop talking now about Maseescaci, because he is dead, and let us talk about Xicotenga the elder, Chichimecatecle, and all the other caciques of Tlaxcala, who offered to serve Cortés both in cutting wood for the brigantines and all other things he might order for the war against the Mexicans. Martín López was so fast in cutting the wood with the great assistance of the Indians, that in a few days he had it all cut and each piece of wood marked with the place it was supposed to go in the way that the officials, master craftsmen and ships' carpenters make their marks. Also another good soldier named Andrés Núñez assisted him and an old carpenter who was lame from a wound, who was called Ramírez the elder.

In chapters CXXXVI through CXLVI Bernal Díaz recounts several activities and events as Cortés, his captains, and men, leaving Martín López in Tlaxcala to finish cutting the word for the brigantines, made their way from Tlaxcala to Mexico.

To determine the place to finish assembling the brigantines and to prepare for the siege of Mexico, Cortés and his men went to Texcoco, "because it was near many towns, and when we had that city on our side, we could make expeditions into the lands neighboring Mexico, and once we were in that city we would have a better idea how things might go." Accompanying them were reinforcements that had just arrived from Castile and ten thousand Tlaxcalan warriors under Chichimecatecle.

Once they entered Mexican territory, they met some resistance from the Mexicans, the most significant encounter occurring at Texcoco itself. The lord of Texcoco feigned an offer of peace to Cortés, even having his caciques lower their banner and bow down, which was a sign of peace. The Spaniards quickly came to understand that the offer of peace was a sham; "nevertheless, Cortés accepted the banner, which was worth about eighty pesos." When Cortés understood that the lord of Texcoco who offered the false peace had fled to Mexico, he called together the other caciques in the town and together they agreed that "there were other lords to whom the kingdom of Texcoco came more justly than the one who now had it, in particular a youth who at that time, with great solemnity, became Christian, and he was named don Hernando

Cortés because our captain was his godfather." This new lord of Texcoco provided Cortés with many Indian laborers to broaden and deepen the canals and ditches so the brigantines could enter the lake of Mexico when they were finished. *"I want to say that there was not a single day that seven or eight thousand Indians failed to work on the ditch and canal, and they opened and broadened it very well so that ships of large size could have floated in it."*

The Tlaxcalans who, after twelve days in Texcoco, had nothing to do and no resources, wished to fight against the Mexicans to avenge the Tlaxcalans the Mexicans had killed and sacrificed in recent defeats. So Cortés decided that he, Andrés de Tapia, Cristóbal de Olid, Spanish soldiers, and Tlaxcalan Indians would march against Iztapalapa, about four leagues from Texcoco. The Mexicans and the people of Iztapalapa devised a strategy for defeating the Spanish and Tlaxcalans: They would lure the Spanish and Tlaxcalans into houses on dry land near the lake, allow them to think they had had a victory, and *"when we least expected it, so much water flowed through all the town, that if the chieftains we had brought from Texcoco had not cried out and warned us to get out of the houses and onto dry land right away we all would have been drowned; they had released two canals of fresh and salted water and opened a causeway, whereupon everything was suddenly completely swollen with water."* A follow-up attack by the Mexicans was just short of disastrous for the Spaniards and Tlaxcalans, *"and we returned to Texcoco half humiliated."*

While Cortés and his men were in Texcoco after the expedition against Iztapalapa, several towns came in peace to ask pardon for the past wars and the death of Spaniards they had killed, saying they had done these things by order of the lord of Mexico. Cortés pardoned them, and they pledged to be vassals of the Spanish king. In addition, whenever he could, Cortés sent men to protect towns being harassed by the Mexicans, if they requested it.

Cortés continued to send to Guatemuz (Cuauhtemoc), who had been elevated to the caciqueship of Mexico after Coadlavaca, to ask for peace. Cortés said he would pardon the deaths and damage the Spaniards had suffered when in that city, and *"that Guatemuz*

*should see that war is easy to remedy at the beginning but dif-
ficult in the middle and end, and that in the end they would be
destroyed." Guatemuz sent no response but continued war preparations and attacks against the towns that had accepted Spanish
friendship.*

*Martín López arrived in Texcoco with eight thousand Tlax-
calan Indians carrying wood for the brigantines, eight thousand
more as a guard, and two thousand more carrying food. Cortés
gave Martín López an order to have the brigantines ready in fifteen days, then went with Chichimecatecle and the Tlaxcalans on
a series of expeditions against a number of Mexican towns, finding
many of them deserted. They finally met the Mexicans in Tacuba,
where they had battles and encounters with them for five days.
The Indians tricked Cortés, leading him into an ambush, but
Cortés narrowly escaped and returned with his army to Texcoco.
The Tlaxcalans, now rich and loaded with spoils from the many
expeditions, asked to return to their lands, and Cortés gave his
permission.*

*Another ship came from Castile bringing as His Majesty's trea-
surer Julián de Alderete, fray Pedro Melgorejo, a number of other
Spaniards, and supplies of weapons and powder. "In short, as a
ship coming from Castile, it came loaded with many things, and
we rejoiced at that and at the news it brought from Castile."*

*Even as the plans for besieging Mexico were developing, Cortés
continued to support the towns that had pledged friendship to
him. "As Cortés had told the people of Chalco that he would go to
help them so that the Mexicans would not come to attack them,
for we were tired of coming and going each week to rescue them,
he decided to ready all the soldiers and army." When he arrived
in Chalco, he called together the caciques of the province and
told them they were going to bring some towns around the lake
to peace in preparation for besieging Mexico. Cortés received a
strong, positive response. More than twenty thousand Indians
joined the Spaniards, inspiring Bernal Díaz to write, "so many
came that, in all the expeditions on which I had been since I
came to New Spain, never did I see so many warriors from our*

friends as came in our company then. So great a multitude of them went because of the spoils they would get, and certainly in order to gorge themselves on human flesh if there were battles, because they knew well that there would be battles. It is the same as when in Italy an army marched from one place to another, crows and kites and other birds of prey would follow it to nourish themselves on the dead bodies that were left on the field after a very bloody battle; so I believe this is the reason so many thousands of Indians followed us."

The Spaniards had victories over several strongholds and towns, including one particularly hard-fought victory in a stronghold they called the "rocky crags," where the Indians assaulted them by rolling boulders down from above. One of the major battles was at Xochimilco where the Mexicans carried off four Spaniards alive to Mexico. "When they carried those four soldiers to Guatemuz, he managed to find out how very few we were, those who came with Cortés, that many were wounded, and he learned everything he wanted to know about our journey. When he was fully informed, he ordered the feet, arms, and heads of our unfortunate companions to be cut off, and they sent them to many towns of our friends who had come to us in peace." Cortés and his men then moved from Xochimilco to Coyoacan and from there to Tacuba. During the move, the Mexicans seized two of the young squires who served Cortés and carried them off to Guatemuz, who sacrificed them, which nearly brought Cortés to tears.

While Cortés was positioning his forces for the move against Mexico, some of the men he had left behind were plotting against him. "It seems that a great friend of the governor of Cuba, Antonio de Villafaña, native of Zamora or Toro, planned with other soldiers among Narváez's men, who I will not name here for the sake of their honor, that when Cortés returned from that expedition [to Tacuba], they would kill him with dagger stabs." This plot became known to Cortés, who went with his captains and some judges and supporters to Villafaña's lodging and took him prisoner. Cortés immediately undertook proceedings against Villafaña, who confessed to the conspiracy. "After Villafaña confessed to the

father Juan Díaz, they hanged him from a window of the build-
ing where he was staying. Cortés did not want anyone else to be
defamed in that terrible affair, although at that time they made
prisoners of many in order to frighten them and to signal that he
wanted to bring others to justice."

[CXLVII] When Antonio de Villafaña had been brought to
justice and those quieted who together with him were conspiring
to kill Cortés, Pedro de Alvarado, Sandoval, and those of us who
would go to their defense, and, seeing that the brigantines were
now finished, their rigging and sails and very good oars in place,
more oars than necessary for each brigantine, and the waterway
through which they were to go out to the lake very wide and
deep, Cortés sent to tell all the towns close to Texcoco that were
our friends that each town should make eight thousand copper
tips for crossbow bolts patterned after others from Castile that
they took to them as a sample. Likewise, he ordered that each
town should make and trim another eight thousand bolts of a very
good wood, for which they also brought a sample. He gave them
a deadline of a week to bring them, both the bolts and the bolt
tips, to our camp, which they brought within the time he ordered,
more than fifty thousand bolt tips and as many thousand bolts,
and those bolt tips were better than the ones from Castile.

Then Cortés ordered Pedro Barba, who at that time was
captain of the crossbowmen, to divide both bolts and bolt tips
among the crossbowmen and to order them to continue trim-
ming the supply and feather them with a glue made of some
roots called *zacotle*, which sticks better than that from Castile.
Likewise, he ordered Pedro Barba to see that each crossbowman
had two very smooth and well-prepared cords for their crossbows
and as many spare nuts, so that if a cord should break or the nut
fail, another could immediately replace it. He also ordered that
they should be shooting at a target to see how far the crossbow
would carry, and he gave them a great deal of Valencia thread for
the cords, because the ship from Castile that I said came a few
days before, which belonged to Juan de Burgos, brought a great

deal of thread, a large quantity of powder and crossbows, many other arms, horseshoes, and escopetas. Cortés also ordered the horsemen to have their horses shod and their lances ready and to mount their horses each day, run them, and train them very well to turn and skirmish.

This done, he sent messengers and letters to our friend Xicotenga the elder who, as I have already said other times, had now become a Christian and was called don Lorenzo de Vargas, and to his son Xicotenga the younger, and to his brothers, and to Chichimecatecle, informing them that when the day of Corpus Christi had passed, we were going to leave that city to go against Mexico to besiege it. He asked that they send him twenty thousand of their warriors from Tlaxcala and those of Guaxocingo and Cholula, for all were friends and brothers in arms, and they already knew the time and plan through their own Indians who were always going from our camp loaded with spoils from the expeditions we had made. Also he cautioned the people of Chalco and Tamanalco and their subjects that they should be prepared for when we might summon them, and he let them know the arrangements for besieging Mexico, and at what time we were going to go. He also told don Fernando, lord of Texcoco, and his chieftains and all his subjects, and all the rest of the towns that were our friends. All to a person replied that they would do fully what Cortés ordered them and that they would come, and the people of Tlaxcala came when the Feast of the Holy Spirit had passed. This done, it was agreed to make muster on one of the feast days.

[CXLVIII] After things were arranged, and messengers and letters were sent to our friends, the people of Tlaxcala and the people of Chalco, and notice was given to the rest of the towns, Cortés decided with our captains and soldiers that, on the second day of the Feast of the Holy Spirit of the year 1521, he would muster the men. The muster was held in the great courtyards of Texcoco, and there were eighty-four horsemen, six hundred fifty soldiers with swords and shields, many with lances, and one hundred ninety-four crossbowmen and escopeteros. From those were selected for the thirteen brigantines the following:

For each brigantine, twelve crossbowmen and escopeteros; these men did not have to row. Besides these men, another twelve rowers were selected, six for each side, plus a captain for each brigantine, so each brigantine would go out with twenty-five soldiers counting the captain. There were thirteen brigantines of twenty-five soldiers, which comes to two hundred eighty-eight, and with the artillery-men given to them besides the twenty-five soldiers, there were in all the brigantines three hundred soldiers, according to the account I have given. Also, he divided among them all the brass guns and falconets we had and the powder it seemed they needed.

This done, he ordered proclaimed the ordinances we all had to follow.

First, that no person should dare blaspheme Our Lord Jesus Christ nor Our Lady, his blessed mother, nor the Holy Apostles nor other saints, under pain of heavy penalties.

Second, that no soldier should treat our friends badly, because they were there to help us, nor should they take anything at all from them, even if it should be things they had acquired in war, neither an Indian man nor woman, nor gold, nor silver, nor chalchiuis.

Another, that no soldier should dare go out, night or day, from our camp to go to any town of our friends nor anywhere else to get food or anything else, under pain of heavy penalty.

Another, that all soldiers should wear very good armor, well quilted, a gorget, visor, leggings, and shield; as we knew how great would be the number of spears, stones, and arrows and lances, against all that it was necessary to wear the armor the proclamation declared.

Another, that no person should gamble for horses or arms on any account, with great penalty.

Another, that no soldier, horseman, crossbowman, or escopetero should sleep without being dressed in all his armor and with his hemp sandals on, unless it was from great need because of wounds or being ill, so that we might be very ready for whatever time the Mexicans came to attack us.

Besides this, the laws were proclaimed that are normally observed in the military matters, which is that anyone who falls asleep on watch or leaves his post, punishment of death, and that no soldier should go from one camp to another without permission of his captain, under pain of death.

Another, for the soldier who deserts his captain in war or battle, punishment of death.

[CXLIX] After having held the review I have talked about before, Cortés saw that there were not enough seamen who knew how to row the brigantines, even though those we had brought in our ships that we wrecked when we came with Cortés were well known, and likewise the sailors from the ships of Narváez and those from Jamaica were known. All were placed on a list and were warned that they would have to row, but even with all of them, there were not enough for thirteen brigantines, and many of them objected and even said they would not row. Cortés made inquiries to find others who were sailors or had been seen going fishing, and if they were from Palos, Moguer, Triana, Puerto, or any other port or area where there were sailors, he ordered them under heavy penalties to go into the brigantines; and however much they might say they were gentlemen, he made them row. In this way he gathered one hundred fifty men to row, and they came off much better than we who were on the causeways fighting, and they got rich from spoils, as I will say later on.

After Cortés had given the order regarding those who would go into the brigantines and divided the crossbowmen and escopeteros, powder, guns, crossbow bolts, and all the rest needed among them and ordered them to put in each brigantine a royal banner and another banner with the name given to each brigantine, and other things that were needed, he named as captains for each one of them: García Holguín; Pedro Barba; Juan de Limpias Carvajal, the deaf; Juan Jaramillo; Jerónimo Ruiz de la Mota; his companion Carvajal, who is now very old and lives on San Francisco Street; one Portillo, who had just come from Castile, a good soldier, who had a beautiful wife; one Zamora, who was ship's mate and who lives now in Oaxaca; one Colmenero, who was a sailor, good soldier; one Lema; Ginés Nortes; Briones, native of Salamanca; I do not remember the name of the other captain; and

Miguel Díaz de Ampiés. After he had named them and ordered all the crossbowmen, escopeteros, and the other soldiers who had to row to obey the captains whom he was placing over them and not to leave their commands under heavy penalties, he gave instructions for what each captain was to do and in which position he had to go along the causeways and with which of the captains on the land he would coordinate. When he had finished arranging everything as I have said, they came to tell Cortés that the captains of Tlaxcala were coming with a large number of warriors and that as their captain general came Xicotenga the younger, the one who was captain during the wars of Tlaxcala and who was planning the treason against us in Tlaxcala when we were fleeing from Mexico. They said he was bringing in his company two of his brothers, sons of the good old man don Lorenzo de Vargas, and was also bringing in his company a large number of Tlaxcalans under Chichimecatecle as captain, and another captaincy from Guaxocingo and another of Cholutecas, although they were few, because as far as I could ever see, after we had punished the people in Cholula, they never were with the Mexicans, nor with us either, but never committed themselves, and even when we were driven out of Mexico, they did not oppose us. Let us leave this and return to our story. When Cortés learned that Xicotenga, his brothers, and other captains were coming, and they came a day earlier than he had told them they should come, Cortés went out to receive them a quarter of a league from Texcoco with Pedro de Alvarado and others of our captains, and when he met Xicotenga and his brothers, Cortés paid them much respect and embraced them and all the rest of the captains. They were coming in great order, all very brilliant with great devices, each captaincy by itself, its banners unfurled, with the white bird they have as their badge that looks like an eagle with its wings outspread, their standard-bearers waving their banners and standards about, and all of them with their bows and arrows, two-handed swords, and spears with spear-throwers. Others carried war clubs and large lances and others small lances, and they wore their feathered headdresses; they were positioned in good order, shouting, crying and whistling, calling

out: "Long live the emperor our lord!" "Castile, Castile!" "Tlaxcala, Tlaxcala!" They took more than three hours entering Texcoco. Cortés ordered them to be lodged in good buildings and fed
from everything there was in the camp. After many embraces and
promises that he would make them rich, he took leave of them
and told them that the next day he would give them orders as to
what they had to do but that now they were tired and should rest.

*Cortés divided his army into four groups; one was led by Pedro de
Alvarado, and he was sent to Tacuba. A second under Cristóbal de
Olid was sent to Coyoacan. A third under Gonzalo de Sandoval
went to Iztapalapa. Finally, Cortés took command of the thirteen
brigantines.*

Let us talk about how Cortés gave instructions to each captain.
As we were to leave the next day, and so that there would not
be so many impediments along the way, we sent ahead all the
captaincies of Tlaxcala until they should reach Mexican territory.
As the Tlaxcalans were moving along carelessly with their captain
Chichimecatecle and other captains with their men, they did not
notice that Xicotenga the younger, who was their captain general, had left, and when Chichimecatecle questioned and inquired
what had happened to him, where he could be, they learned that
he had returned secretly that night to Tlaxcala and was going to
take by force the caciqueship, vassals, and land of Chichimecatecle himself. The Tlaxcalans said that the reasons for it were that
when Xicotenga the younger saw the captains of Tlaxcala going
to war, especially Chichimecatecle, he knew he would have no
opposition, because he did not fear Xicotenga the blind, who, as
his father, would help him, and our friend Maseescaci was now
dead, so the only one he feared was Chichimecatecle. They also
said they always knew that Xicotenga had no desire to go to war
against Mexico, because they heard him say many times that all of
us and all of them were going to die in such a war.

When the cacique Chichimecatecle heard and understood that,
he turned back from the journey quickly and came to Texcoco to

inform Cortés of it. Cortés ordered that five chieftains from Texcoco and another two from Tlaxcala, friends of Xicotenga, go at once to make him return and tell him that Cortés begged him to come back immediately to go against his enemies the Mexicans, to consider that if his father don Lorenzo de Vargas were not old and blind as he was, he would come against Mexico himself, and that since all the people of Tlaxcala were and are very loyal servants of His Majesty, he should not want to defame them with what he was doing now. He also made many offerings and promises to give him gold and cloaks so he would come back. The reply Xicotenga sent was that if the old man, his father, and Maseescaci had believed him, Cortés would not have dominated them so much and made them do everything he wanted, and so as not to waste more words, he said he would not return. When Cortés heard that response, he immediately gave an order for a constable to go very quickly with four horsemen and five chieftains of Texcoco, and wherever they reached Xicotenga, they should hang him. He said: "There's no cure for this cacique; he'll always be a traitor, evil-minded and with evil plans," and it was no time to put up with him any longer nor to tolerate what had happened. When Pedro de Alvarado learned of it, he pleaded strongly for Xicotenga, and Cortés gave him a good response, but secretly he ordered the constable and horsemen not to leave Xicotenga alive. So it was done, and in a town subject to Texcoco, they hanged him, and that is what his treasons led to. There were some Tlaxcalans who said that don Lorenzo de Vargas, Xicotenga's father, sent to tell Cortés that that son of his was bad, that he would not trust him, and that Cortés should try to kill him.

Let us leave this conversation thus, and I will say that for this reason we halted that day without setting out for Texcoco. The next day, which was May 13, 1521, we set out, both captaincies together, because Cristóbal de Olid and Pedro de Alvarado had to go the same way. We spent the night in a town subject to Texcoco. The next day we went on our journey, both captaincies together, and we spent the night in a town that was deserted, because it was now Mexican territory. The next day too we spent the night in another large town called Gualtitan, which I have mentioned other times, and it was also without people. The next day we passed through two towns called Tenayuca and Escapuzalco, also deserted. At the hour of vespers, we arrived at Tacuba and right away lodged ourselves in some large houses and lodgings, because this town was also deserted, and all our friends the Tlaxcalans also lodged themselves, and that very afternoon, they went through the outlying settlements of those towns and brought things to eat. We slept that night with good watches, sentinels, and scouts, because I have already said other times that Mexico is near Tacuba. As night fell, we heard great cries that they were giving out to us from the lake, yelling many words of contempt, saying that we were not men enough to come out to fight them. They had many canoes filled with warriors and the causeways filled with warriors too, and those words were intended to offend us so that we would come out that night to fight. But as we had learned our lesson from the experience of the causeways and bridges, we did not want to go out until the next day, which was Sunday. After having heard mass, which Father Juan Díaz said for us, and after commending ourselves to God, we decided that both captaincies together would go and cut off the water from Chapultepec, from which the city was supplied, which was a half league from Tacuba. As we were going to break the pipes, we came upon many warriors who were waiting for us on the road because they had understood well that that would be the first thing by which we could do them harm. So when they met us near some bad passes, they began to shoot arrows and throw spears and stones from slings, and they wounded three of our soldiers; but we quickly made them turn their backs, and our friends the Tlaxcalans pursued them so that they killed twenty and captured seven or eight of them. When those squadrons had been put to flight, we broke the pipes through which the water went to the city, and from then on it never went to Mexico as long as the war lasted.

When we had done that, our captains decided that we should go right away to look around and enter along the causeway of Tacuba and do what we could to take a bridge from them. When we had arrived at the causeway, there were so many canoes on the lake filled with warriors, and warriors on the causeways themselves, that we were amazed at it. And they threw so many spears, arrows, and stones from slings that in the first engagement they wounded more than thirty soldiers. Still we kept advancing along the causeway toward a bridge; and as I understand it, they allowed us to in order to get us on the other side of the bridge. When they had us there, I say that such a multitude of warriors charged at us that we could not hold out against them, because on the causeway, which was eight paces wide, what could we do against such a great power that was on one side and the other of the causeway and used us as a target? Although our escopeteros and crossbowmen did nothing but load and shoot at the canoes, they did them only very little damage, because they had the canoes very well reinforced with wooden shields. And when we attacked the squadrons that were fighting on the causeway itself, they immediately threw themselves into the water, and there were so many of them that we could not prevail. The horsemen did no good at all because the enemy wounded their horses from both sides in the water, and when they charged against the squadrons, the enemy threw themselves into the water. They had made barricades where other warriors were waiting with some long lances they had made like scythes from the weapons they took from us when they drove us from Mexico and we left fleeing. We were fighting with them for about an hour in this way, and they pressed us so that we could not defend ourselves against them; and we even saw that from other directions a great fleet of canoes was coming to cut off our passage and attack us from the rear. Knowing this, our captains and all of us soldiers warned that our friends the Tlaxcalans, whom we had brought, were blocking the causeway and that they should leave it, because it was clear they could not fight in the water. So we decided to retreat in good order and not advance anymore.

When the Mexicans saw us retreating and sending the Tlaxcalans away, what cries, howls, and whistles they gave us and how they came up to join us hand to hand. I say that I do not know how to write about it, because they filled the entire causeway with spears, arrows, and stones they had hurled at us, and those that fell in the water were many more. When we found ourselves on dry land, we gave thanks to God for having delivered us from that battle. But eight were left dead at that time and more than a hundred were wounded. Even with all this, they gave us cries and yelled out words of contempt from the canoes, and our friends the Tlaxcalans yelled at them that they should come on land, and even if the enemy were double their number, they would fight them. This was the first thing we did: take away their water and take a look at the lake, although we won no honor with them by doing so. That night we stayed in our camp and tended the wounded, and one horse even died, and we placed watchmen and sentinels for good security.

A dispute between Cristóbal de Olid and Pedro de Alvarado led to Olid's leaving Tacuba and going to Coyoacan, where Cortés had originally ordered him to go; Pedro de Alvarado stayed in Tacuba. Gonzalo de Sandoval went to Iztapalapa from Texcoco. Thus, the three groups were positioned for the siege on Mexico. Meanwhile, Cortés and the brigantines held off many attacks from the Mexicans, protecting the three groups of men on the causeways from attacks by canoes on the lake, although Cortés made his base with Cristóbal de Olid in Coyoacan. Cortés ordered Sandoval to leave Iztapalapa and go by land to besiege the other causeway from Mexico to Tepeaquilla, "which they now call Our Lady of Guadalupe, where she makes and has made many and holy miracles." During this time, all three groups were attempting to fight down the causeways in order to enter Mexico, and they were under constant attack by the Mexicans.

[CLI] As Cortés and all our captains and soldiers understood that without the brigantines we could not invade along the causeways to fight against Mexico, he sent four of them to Pedro de Alvarado, he left six in his camp, which was that of Cristóbal de Olid, and to Gonzalo de Sandoval, on the causeway of Tepeaquilla, he sent two brigantines and ordered that the smallest brigantine not go about on the lake for fear the canoes might overturn it because it was not very steady; he ordered the men and sailors who were in it to be divided among the other twelve, because there were already twenty very badly wounded men among those who were in them.

When we found ourselves assisted by the brigantines in our camp at Tacuba, Pedro de Alvarado ordered two of them to go along one side of the causeway and the other two on the other side; we began to fight in earnest because the brigantines routed the canoes, which had been fighting us from the water, so we had an opportunity to take some bridges and barricades from them. When we were fighting with them, they were hurling at us so many stones from slings, spears, and arrows that despite all the soldiers being well armored, they injured and wounded us, and we did not stop the fighting and combat until night separated us.

Well, I want to say that the Mexicans were moving their squadrons around and relieving them from time to time; we knew this from their devices and insignias on their armor. As for the brigantines, what they did to them from the rooftops! They hurled spears, arrows, and stones on them thicker than hail. I do not know how to say it here, nor will anyone be able to understand it except those who were with us in it, that such a multitude of them came, more than like hailstones, that soon they covered the causeway. Then, when, with much difficulty, we took some bridge or barricade and left it without guarding it, that same night they would take it and deepen it, and they built much better defenses and even made hidden pits in the water so that the next day when we were fighting and it was time to retreat, we would become entangled and fall into the pits; with the canoes they would then be able to rout us because they also had prepared many canoes for this purpose, positioned in places where our brigantines could not see them, so that when we were in difficult straits in the pits, some by land and others by water would come after us. So that our brigantines could not come to help us, they had put many stakes hidden by the water so our brigantines would run up on them. This is the way we were fighting every day.

Let us talk about how, when we separated at night, we tended our wounds by burning them with oil, and a soldier named

Juan Catalán blessed them and used spells on them, and I say truly we found that Our Lord Jesus Christ was pleased to give us strength in addition to the many mercies he gave us each day, for they healed quickly. Wounded and bandaged with rags, we fought from morning to night, and if the wounded had stayed in the camp without going out to fight, there would not have been twenty healthy men in each captaincy to go out. When our friends the Tlaxcalans saw that the man I have discussed was blessing all our wounds and injuries with the sign of the cross, they all went to him, and there were so many of them that he had plenty to do all day long treating them. Well, I want to talk about our captains, standard-bearer, and other flag bearers, who were covered with wounds and their banners ragged; and I say that every day we had need of a new standard-bearer, because we all came out in such a condition that they could not go back to the fight carrying the flags again. Well, with all of this, do you think we had enough to eat? I am not talking about lacking maize tortillas, of which we had plenty, but of some refreshment for the wounded, of which we had not the slightest. What kept us alive were some *quelites*, herbs that the Indians eat, and native cherries as long as they lasted, and afterward, prickly pear fruits, which came into season at that time. Things were the same in the camp where Cortés was and in Sandoval's as they were in ours. Never for a single day did there fail to be great captaincies of Mexicans that continuously attacked them from dawn until night. To achieve that, Guatemuz had designated the captains and squadrons that were to go to each causeway, and Tlatelolco and the towns on the lake had been alerted that when a signal came from the great cu in Tlatelolco,[71] some should come by canoes and others by land. The Mexican captains had been prepared for this, with careful arrangement, how, when and to what places they were to go.

Let us leave this and say how we changed our order and way of fighting: When we saw that whatever openings in the water we

---

71. The cu was not in Tlatelolco, the site of the great market, but at Tenochtitlan.

gained by day, and in gaining them had our soldiers killed and the rest of us wounded, the Mexicans stopped them up again, we decided that we would go station ourselves in the causeway in a small plaza where there were some towers of idols we had already taken, where there was room to make our soldiers' shelters, even though they were quite miserable, for when it rained we all got very wet, and they were only good for covering us against the evening dew. We left the Indian women who made bread for us in Tacuba, and all the horsemen and our friends the Tlaxcalans were left to guard them and to watch and guard the passes so the enemy would not come from the neighboring towns to attack us in the rear on the causeways while we were fighting. So when we had set up our huts where I have said, from then on we tried to destroy the houses or blocks of them right away and fill in the openings in the water we took from them. We knocked the houses to the ground, because if we set them on fire, it would take too long for them to burn and one house would not catch fire from another, because every house stood in the water and one could not go from one to the other without crossing bridges or going in canoes. If we wanted to cross by swimming, they would do us much harm from the flat roofs, so we were more secure destroying the houses.

As soon as we had taken some barricade or bridge or bad pass where they put up much resistance, we tried to guard it day and night. In this way all our captaincies kept the night watch together, and the agreement that was made was that the first captaincy took the watch from nightfall to midnight, and they were more than forty soldiers; from midnight until two hours before dawn, another captaincy of forty men took the watch, but the first captaincy did not leave the post, rather we slept there on the ground, and this watch is called the *modorra*, the time of heavy sleep and dreams; then came another forty soldiers and they had the dawn watch, which is those two hours before daylight, but those who had the modorra watch could not leave either but had to stay there, so that when dawn broke there were more than one hundred twenty soldiers on the watch together. Some nights, when we sensed great danger, we even kept watch

together from nightfall to daybreak, waiting for the great impe-
tus of the Mexicans for fear they might break through, for we
had warnings from some Mexican captains we had captured in
battles that Guatemuz had the idea, and had brought it up in
conversation with his captains, that they would try either in the
night or by day to break through us on our causeway, and, defeating us on our side, he could quickly defeat and rout those on
the other two causeways where Cortés was and where Gonzalo
de Sandoval was. He had also arranged that the nine towns on
the lake and Tacuba itself and Escapuzalco and Tenayuca would
unite, and on the day when they wanted to break through and
attack, the nine towns would hit us from the rear on the causeway, and that one night they would quickly carry off the Indian
women who were making bread for us in Tacuba and our baggage. When we became aware of this, we warned the horsemen
who were in Tacuba to watch and be on the alert all night, and
also our friends the Tlaxcalans. Thus, as Guatemuz had planned
it, he put it into effect. On several nights great squadrons came
to break through us and attack at midnight, others during the
modorra, and others during the dawn watch, and they came
sometimes without making any noise and other times with great
yells and whistles, and when they arrived where we were keeping watch at night, what spears, stones, and arrows they hurled,
and many others were there with lances, and although they
wounded some of us, we resisted them and many of them went
back wounded. Many other warriors who came to fall on our
baggage were routed by our horsemen and Tlaxcalans, because
as it was night, they did not stay around long. And in the way
I have said we kept watch, no matter whether it rained or was
windy or cold, even if we were in the middle of pits of mud and
wounded, we were going to stay there; even with those miserable
tortillas and grass that we had to eat or prickly pear, something
extra over and above the job of fighting, as the tradesmen say, it
was going to be that way.

Well, even with all these precautions we took, they would
reopen the bridge or causeway that we had taken from them, and

we could not keep them from doing it by night, so the next day we took it from them again and filled it in, and they opened it again and made it stronger with barricades, until the Mexicans changed their way of fighting, which I will talk about at the appropriate time. Let us stop talking about all the battles we had every day, and the same thing in the camp of Cortés and in that of Sandoval, and let us talk about what little good it did to have taken the water of Chapultepec from them, nor did it do any more good to prevent them from getting provisions and water by the three causeways, neither were our brigantines of any use staying in our camps, serving only to protect our backs in the fighting against the warriors who were in canoes and fighting from the roof terraces. The Mexicans received much water and provisions from the nine towns on the lake, which supplied them by canoes at night, and from other friendly towns they received maize, hens, and everything they wanted. To prevent these supplies from getting to them, it was decided by all three camps that two brigantines should go by night around the lake to give chase to the canoes that came loaded with provisions and capture all the canoes they could and destroy them or bring them to our camps. When this arrangement was made, it was good, although we were without the two brigantines at night to help us when we were fighting, but they were of great use in preventing provisions and water from entering. Even with all this, many canoes loaded with provisions were able to get in, and as the Mexicans went without caution in their canoes carrying supplies, there was not a day that the brigantines did not capture canoes with many Indians hanging from the yards of the brigantines.

Let us talk about the clever ruse the Mexicans had for taking our brigantines and killing those who were in them. It was like this: As I have said, every night and in the mornings, our brigantines went searching for enemy canoes around the lake, overturned them, and captured many of them, so the Mexicans decided to equip thirty pirogues, which are very large canoes, with very good rowers and warriors, and by night they positioned all thirty canoes among reed beds in an area where the brigantines could not see them and covered them with branches; before nightfall, they sent out two or three canoes with good rowers as if they were carrying provisions or bringing in water; and in a place where it seemed to the Mexicans the brigantines would go when they were fighting with them, they had driven in many thick pieces of wood made into stakes so the brigantines would run up on them; then as the canoes went around the lake showing signs of being fearful, drawing close to the reed beds, two of our brigantines went out after them, and the two canoes made as though they were retreating to land and went to the area where the thirty pirogues were lying in wait, the brigantines following them, and when they arrived at the ambush, all the pirogues together came out and fell upon the brigantines; they quickly wounded all the soldiers, rowers, and captains, and the brigantines could not go in either direction because of the stakes the Mexicans had put in place. In this way, they killed the captain, who was called somebody de Portilla, an excellent soldier who had been in Italy, and they wounded Pedro Barba, who was a very fine captain, and three days later he died of the wounds, and they captured one of the brigantines. These two brigantines were from the camp of Cortés, and he was very distressed over it. But a few days later, they paid for it very fully in some other ambushes they set.

> *At this point, four main activities occurred. First, the routine of the Mexicans opening bridges the Spaniards had captured during the day and the Spaniards returning during the following day to recapture and fill up the newly made gaps was broken when the Mexicans made a much deeper and wider ditch full of stakes and traps. Under Pedro de Alvarado, this obstacle was crossed temporarily but with much danger and loss. Bernal Díaz himself was seized, calling on God and the Virgin in that moment, and had forcefully to pull his arm away, all the while thrusting mightily with his sword. Even so, he got a bad wound in the arm, emerging from it senseless and out of breath from the effort. Cortés reprimanded Alvarado and warned him in the future by no means to advance without having filled in any intervening water obstacle. Second, the Mexicans continued using their pirogues*

to lure the brigantines that were giving them chase into areas in which they had placed stakes for the brigantines to run up on, but, in response, the Spaniards devised their own ambush, luring the pirogues into a trap by hiding six brigantines in reed beds at night to fall upon the pirogues that were in pursuit of the brigantine that was fleeing an Indian ambush; after that, the Indians gave up the ambush strategy. Third, every day the Mexicans massively attacked all three camps. Finally, more and more towns south of the city came to Cortés to seek peace.

[CLII] As Cortés saw that it was not possible to fill in all the openings, bridges and ditches of water we took each day, because at night the Mexicans came back to open them and make the barricades stronger than they had been before, and that it was a great hardship fighting and filling bridges and all of us together keeping watch, especially as most of us were wounded and twenty soldiers had died, he decided to start conversations with the captains and soldiers in his camp; he also wrote to us in the camp of Pedro de Alvarado and that of Sandoval to get the opinion of all our captains and soldiers. What he asked was whether it seemed to us that we should enter the city at one rush to reach Tlatelolco, the great marketplace of Mexico, much wider and larger than that of Salamanca, and that having arrived there, whether it would be good to establish all three camps in it, because from there we would be able to battle through the streets of Mexico without having such difficulties in retreating nor having so much to fill in nor keep watch on the bridges. As usually happens in such discussions and consultations, there were many viewpoints; some of us said that it was neither advisable nor reasonable to put ourselves right in the heart of the city, but that we should keep doing as we were, battling and pulling down and leveling houses. Those of us who were of this opinion gave as the most obvious reason that if we stationed ourselves in Tlatelolco and left the causeways and bridges unguarded and deserted, that the Mexicans, who had so many warriors and canoes, would break the bridges and causeways again, and we would no longer be masters of them. They would attack night and day with their great forces, and as they always had many stakes prepared, our brigantines could not help us. With what Cortés suggested, we would be the ones besieged, and the Mexicans would have the land, countryside, and lake for themselves; we wrote to him about the proposal so that what happened to us before, when we fled Mexico would not happen to us again, as the saying from "Mazagatos"[72] goes.

After Cortés had heard everyone's opinion and the good arguments we gave for them, what resulted from the whole discussion was that the next day we were to go out from all three camps with all the strength we could, horsemen as well as crossbowmen, escoperos, and soldiers, and we were to push forward as far as the main plaza, which is Tlatelolco. With everything ready in all three camps, and with our friends the Tlaxcalans as well as the people of Texcoco and those from the towns of the lake, who had recently given obedience to His Majesty and were to come with their canoes to aid the brigantines, one Sunday morning, after having heard mass, we set out from our camp with Pedro de Alvarado, and Cortés also set out from his, and Sandoval with his captaincies, and with great strength, each captaincy pushed forward capturing bridges and barricades; the enemy fought like brave warriors, and Cortés on his side was victorious, and likewise Gonzalo de Sandoval on his side. As for our position we had already captured another barricade and a bridge with much difficulty because large forces of Guatemuz were guarding them, and we came out of it with many of our soldiers wounded, and one later died of the wounds, and more than one thousand of our friends the Tlaxcalans came out badly injured, but still we followed up our victory very satisfied.

Cortés and his contingent now fell into another Mexican trap. The Mexicans pretended to flee, and Cortés followed. In the confusion of the Mexican counterattack, Cortés's contingent fled, their backs turned.

---

72. Mazagatos is an allusion to a difficult or dangerous situation.

When Cortés saw them turning back defeated, he encouraged them and said: "Stop, stop, gentlemen! Stop short! What is this that you're doing turning your backs?" But he could not stop them. In a passage Cortés's men had neglected to fill in, and on the causeway, which was narrow and bad there, they put Cortés to rout with the canoes and wounded him in the leg; they carried away alive more than sixty-six soldiers and killed eight horses. Six or seven Mexican captains had already grabbed Cortés, but it pleased Our Lord God to help him and to give him strength to defend himself even though he was wounded in one leg, because at that moment a very brave soldier named Cristóbal de Olea, a native of Old Castile, came quickly to him, and when he saw so many Indians holding on to Cortés that way, the soldier fought so fiercely that he quickly killed with sword thrusts four of the captains who had seized Cortés, and another very valiant soldier named Lerma helped him. The personal bravery of the two men was so great that the Indian captains let Cortés go, but in defending Cortés, Olea lost his life there, and even Lerma was at the point of death. Soon many soldiers hurried to help, and although badly wounded, they got hold of Cortés and helped him get out of that danger and the mud in which he was standing. Then Cristóbal de Olid, the maestre de campo, came in haste, and they took Cortés by the arms and helped him get out of the water and mud, and they brought him a horse on which he escaped death. At that instant, one of the *mayordomos* named Cristóbal de Guzmán came and brought him another horse. From the roof terraces, the Mexican warriors kept fighting very fiercely and victoriously and in a very evil way so that they captured Cristóbal de Guzmán and carried him alive to Guatemuz. Still the Mexicans continued pursuing Cortés and all his soldiers until they reached their camp.

Even after that disaster, when Cortés and his men found themselves in safety, the Mexican squadrons did not cease following them, chasing them down and screaming, yelling out many insults and calling them cowards. Let us stop talking about Cortés and his defeat and return to our army, that of Pedro de Alvarado, in the causeway of Tacuba. As we went forward victoriously, and when we did not expect it, we saw coming against us many Mexican squadrons with great cries and very beautiful devices and plumes, and they threw in front of us five heads running with blood that they had cut off from the men they had taken from Cortés, and they said: "So will we kill you as we have killed Malinche and Sandoval and everyone they brought with them, and these are their heads, so look at them well." Saying these words to us, they closed in on us to the point of laying hands on us, and neither slashing nor thrusting with our swords nor crossbows nor escopetas were of any use; they just came at us as if at a target. Even so, we did not lose a bit of our order in retreating, because right away we ordered our friends the Tlaxcalans to remove themselves from the streets, causeways, and bad passes. This time they did so willingly, because when they saw the five heads of our companions running with blood and heard the Mexicans say they had already killed Malinche and Sandoval and all the teules they brought with them and that they were going to do the same to us, the Tlaxcalans were very frightened; they believed it was true, and for this reason I say that they cleared off from the causeway in all earnest.

Let us return to talking about how, when we were retreating, we heard drumbeats coming from the great cu, which is where the idols Huichilobos and Tezcatepuca were and which, from its height, dominated the whole city; they played a large drum with the most doleful sound, in short like a demonic instrument, and it thundered so that it could be heard for two leagues, and together with it, many little drums, shell trumpets, horns, and whistles. At that moment, as we learned later, they were offering ten hearts and much blood from our companions to the idols I have mentioned. Let us leave the sacrifice and return to our retreat and the great war they were waging on us from the causeway, the terraced roofs, and the canoes on the lake. In that instant, many squadrons Guatemuz was sending out anew came against us, and he ordered his cornet sounded, which was a signal that his captaincies and warriors had to fight in such a way that they would take prisoners or die in the attempt, and the sound it made resounded in the

ears. When the squadrons and captaincies heard it, I do not know
how to express here how terrifying the fury and strength was with
which they came at us to lay hands on us; and now that I stop to
think about it, it is as if I am actually seeing it and am in that war
and battle. But I affirm again that Our Lord Jesus Christ saved us,
for if he had not given us strength, because we were all wounded,
we could not have managed otherwise to get to our huts, and I
give him much thanks and praise that I escaped that and many
other times from the hands of the Mexicans.

Returning to our story, the horsemen made charges there, and
with two heavy guns we put near our huts, some firing and others
loading, we held out; the causeway was full from one rim to the
other with enemies, and they came at us up to the houses, as if
we were already conquered, to throw spears and stones at us, and
with those guns we killed many of them. The one who helped
most that day was a gentleman named Pedro Moreno Medrano,
who now lives in Puebla, because he served as the artilleryman;
the artillerymen we usually had were dead, some of them, and
others wounded, and Pedro Moreno, besides having always been
a very courageous soldier, was a great help to us that day.

Because we were in that condition, greatly distressed and
wounded, and we knew nothing of Cortés or Sandoval and their
armies, we did not know whether or not they had been killed or
defeated, as the Mexicans told us when they threw the five heads
before us, which they held by their hair and their beards; and they
said they had already killed Malinche and all the teules and that
they were going to kill us in that way that same day. We could
not know anything about them because we were battling about
half a league from each other, and where they defeated Cortés
was farther away; for this reason we were distressed, but with all
of us keeping together as a single body, both the wounded and
the sound, we held out against the fury of the Mexicans who were
on us, who believed that none of us would be left alive, neither
the weak nor the strong, after the war they were waging against
us. They had already captured one of our brigantines, killed three
soldiers, and wounded the captain and most of the soldiers in it,

but another brigantine, with Juan Jaramillo as captain, came to its aid. Another brigantine had run up on the stakes in a place from which it could not go out, and its captain was Juan de Limpias Carvajal, who at that time became deaf and now lives in Puebla. He fought so valiantly himself and so encouraged all the soldiers who were rowing in the brigantine that they broke the stakes and got away, all of them badly wounded, but they saved their brigantine. This brigantine was the first that broke the stakes, which was a good thing for the future.

Let us return to Cortés. As he and all his men were for the most part killed or wounded, the Mexican squadrons went to his camp to attack. They even threw down before his soldiers who were resisting the Mexicans as they were fighting, four other heads streaming with blood, heads of the soldiers they had carried off from Cortés himself, and they told the soldiers that they were the heads of Tonatio, who is Pedro de Alvarado, Sandoval, and that of Bernal Díaz and of other teules and that they had already killed all of us who were at Tacuba. Then they say Cortés was much more disheartened than he ever was before, and tears were coming from his eyes and the eyes of all those with him, but not in such a way that they could sense too much weakness in him. Then he ordered Cristóbal de Olid, who was maestre de campo, and his captains to take care that the many Mexicans who were coming at them did not break through to the camp and that both wounded and sound should keep together in one body. He ordered Andrés de Tapia to go as quickly as possible with three horsemen, risking their lives, to Tacuba, which was our camp, to find out whether we were alive, and if we were not defeated, to tell us to keep a very good watch in the camp, and that all together we should make one body by day and night on watch; what he was ordering us to do we already customarily did. The captain Andrés de Tapia and the horsemen who were with him came very quickly, even though Tapia and two of those in his company were wounded, and their names were Guillén de la Loa, Valdenebro, and one Juan de Cuéllar, brave men. When they arrived at our camp and found us battling with the Mexican force that was still close to us, they rejoiced in their hearts and told us all that had happened with the rout of Cortés and what he had sent to tell us, but they did not want to let us know how many were dead, so they told us about twenty-five and that all the rest were well.

Let us return to Sandoval and his captains and soldiers, who were victoriously advancing in the section and streets of their conquest. When the Mexicans had routed Cortés, they turned on Sandoval and his army and captains in such a way that they could not defend themselves. They killed six of his soldiers and wounded all those he had brought with him, and they wounded him in three places: the thigh, the head, and the left arm. As he was battling with the enemies, they put before him six heads of those of Cortés's men they had killed, and they said those heads were of Malinche and Tonatio and other captains and they were going to do the same to Sandoval and those who were with him, and they fought him most fiercely. When Sandoval saw that, he ordered all his captains and soldiers to show great spirit, not to be disheartened, and to take care that in retreating there not be any disorder on the causeway, which was narrow; the first thing he did was to order our friends, who were many, to leave the causeway, so they would not hinder them, and with his two brigantines, his escopeteros and crossbowmen, he retreated with great difficulty to the place he was staying, all his men very badly wounded and even fainting and six dead. When he found himself clear of the causeway, although he was surrounded by Mexicans, he encouraged his men and his captains and strongly charged them to keep together in one body, both day and night, and to guard the camp so the Mexicans would not defeat them. When he learned from the captain Luis Marín that he could do so very well, wounded and bandaged though he was, Sandoval took with him two other horsemen and went very quickly by land to the camp of Cortés. When Sandoval saw Cortés he said to him: "Oh, señor captain! What is this? Are these the counsels and ruses of war that you've always given us? How has this disaster happened?" Cortés answered him, the tears flowing from his eyes: "Oh, my son Sandoval, it's been permitted because of my sins, but I'm not so guilty in it as all our captains and soldiers make me, but it's the treasurer Julián de Alderete, to whom I gave the instruction to fill in that passage where they defeated us, and he didn't do it as he isn't used to fighting nor even receiving orders from captains!" Then the treasurer himself replied. He was there next to Cortés and had come to see and speak to Sandoval to find out whether his army was dead or routed. He said that Cortés himself was to blame, not he, and the reason he gave was that, as Cortés was going forward in victory, in order better to follow it up, he said: "Forward, gentlemen," and did not order them to fill in either the bridge or the bad passage, that if he had ordered it, he would have done it with his captaincy and the friends. He also blamed Cortés for not ordering the many friends he brought with him to clear off the causeways in time. Because there were many other discussions between Cortés and the treasurer and they were spoken with anger, they will be left untold, and I will talk about how, in that instant, two brigantines that Cortés had in his company and on his causeway arrived; they had not come nor was anything known of them since the rout. It seemed they had been stopped and run up on some stakes, and, according to what the captains said, they had been held back and surrounded by canoes that attacked them, and they were all wounded. They said that God, first of all, helped them, and with a wind and the great strength they put into rowing, they broke the stakes and saved themselves, which greatly delighted Cortés, because until then—although he did not publicize it because he did not want to dishearten the soldiers, as he knew nothing about them—he took them for lost.

Let us return to Cortés, who then strongly instructed Sandoval to go immediately, rapidly, to our camp of Pedro de Alvarado, the Tacuba camp, to see if we were routed or how we were, and if we were alive, to help us put up resistance in the camp so they could not break through. He told Francisco de Lugo to accompany him because he knew well that there were Mexican squadrons on the road; and he told him he had already sent Andrés de Tapia with three horsemen to find out about us, and he feared he might have been killed on the road. When he had said this to him and took his leave, he went to embrace Sandoval and said to him: "Look, my son, since I'm not able to go everywhere, for you see that I'm wounded, I entrust these tasks to you so that you might see to the safety of all three camps; I know well that Pedro de Alvarado and all his captains, brothers and soldiers I gave him must have battled bravely and acted like gentlemen, but I fear the great power of these dogs might have defeated him. As for me and my army, you see how I am."

Sandoval and Francisco de Lugo quickly came to where we were, and when he arrived, it was a little after the time of vespers, because the rout of Cortés seems to have been before the time of the main mass. When Sandoval arrived, he found us battling with the Mexicans, who were trying to get into our camp by way of some houses we had pulled down, others by the causeway, many canoes by the lake; they already had one brigantine run up on the ground, and they had killed two of the soldiers who were in it and wounded most of all the rest. Sandoval saw me with six other soldiers waist high in the water helping the brigantine get into deeper water, many Indians coming at us with swords they had taken from us in the rout of Cortés, others with broadswords with knife-like blades—and they gave me an arrow wound and a knife cut in the leg—so that we would not help the brigantine, which they wanted to carry off with their canoes judging by the effort they were putting into it, for they had tied many ropes to carry it off and take it inside the city. When Sandoval saw us in that condition, he said to us: "Oh, brothers, use all your strength to keep them from carrying off the brigantine!" We put forth such strength that we soon pulled it to safety, although as I have said, all the sailors came out wounded and two soldiers dead.

At that time many captaincies of Mexicans came to the causeway and wounded both the horsemen and all of us, and they even gave Sandoval a strong blow in the face with a stone. Then Pedro de Alvarado came to his aid with the other horsemen. As so many squadrons were coming, and I and twenty other soldiers were facing them, Sandoval ordered us to retreat little by little so they would not kill the horses, and because we did not retreat as quickly as he wanted, he said to us with fury: "Do you want them to kill me and all these horsemen because of you? For my sake, brother Bernal Díaz, fall back all of you." Then they again wounded him and his horse. At that time we sent our friends off the causeway and, little by little, we retreated facing the enemy and not turning our backs, just going along checking them, some crossbowmen and escopeteros shooting and others loading their escopetas, for they did not shoot them all at once; the horsemen made some charges, and Pedro Moreno Medrano setting up and firing his guns, but no matter how many Mexicans the cannon balls carried off, we could not get them away from us, but they kept coming after us constantly with the idea that they would carry us off to sacrifice that night. Well, when we were retreating close to our lodgings and had already crossed a large opening where there was much water, and the arrows, spears, and stones could not reach us, and Sandoval, Francisco de Lugo, and Andrés de Tapia were standing with Pedro de Alvarado, each telling what had happened to him and what Cortés ordered, the very mournful drum of Huichilobos sounding again, along with many other shell horns, cornets, and others like trumpets, and the sound of all of them was terrifying. We all looked to the high cu where they were making the sounds, and we saw them taking our companions up the steps by force, the same ones they had captured when they defeated Cortés, and they were taking them to be sacrificed. When they had taken them up to a small plaza where the adoratorio was in which their cursed idols were, we saw them put plumes on the heads of many of them and they made them dance with something like fans before Huichilobos, and as soon as they had danced, they put them on their backs on top of some stones, rather narrow, that they had made for sacrifices, and with some flint knives, they sawed them open at their breasts and pulled out their beating hearts and offered them to the idols there, and they kicked their bodies down the steps; Indian butchers who were waiting below cut off their arms and feet, flayed the faces, preparing them afterward like glove leather, and they kept them with their beards to celebrate with when they had drunken festivals, and they ate the flesh with *chilmole*.[73] They sacrificed all the others in the same way, eating their arms and legs and offering the hearts and blood to their idols, as I have said, and the bodies, that is the bellies and entrails, they threw to the tigers, lions, and snakes they kept in the house of the beasts.

Well, when we saw those cruelties, all of us in our camp, and Pedro de Alvarado, Gonzalo de Sandoval, and all our other captains—the curious readers who should see this can imagine how sorry we felt for those killed—said to each other: "Thank God they didn't take me to be sacrificed today!" The curious readers should also note that we were not far from them, but we could not help them; rather we prayed to God to guard us from this most cruel death. Well, in the very instant they were making the sacrifices, great squadrons of warriors suddenly fell on us and gave us a great deal to do from all directions, and neither in one way nor in another could we prevail, and they shouted at us: "See the way you are all going to die, for our gods have promised it to us many times." Then the threatening words they yelled at our friends the Tlaxcalans were so hurtful and so evil that they disheartened them, and they threw roasted legs of Indians at them and the arms of our soldiers and yelled at them: "Eat the flesh of these teules and of your brothers, for we have already had our fill of them, and you can stuff yourselves with what is left over from us, and we will take you to the houses you have knocked down so that you can build them again much better with white stone and well-worked stonemasonry. So help those teules very well, for you will see them all sacrificed."

Well, another thing Guatemuz ordered them to do was that when he won that victory, he sent the feet and hands of our soldiers, their flayed faces with their beards, and the heads of the horses they killed to all the towns of our allies, friends, and their relatives, and he sent word to them that more than half of us were already dead and that he would finish us off soon, that they should give up our friendship and come to Mexico, that if they did not give it up immediately, he would come to destroy them. He sent to tell them many

---

73. Chilmole is sauce made from chilies.

other things so they would leave our camp and us, because we would quickly be killed at his hand. As they were continuing to attack us day and night, all of us in the camp kept watch together, Gonzalo de Sandoval, Pedro de Alvarado, and the rest of the captains keeping us company on the watch, and although great captaincies came at us at night, we resisted them. Half the horsemen were in Tacuba all day and night and the other half on the causeways. Well, they did another greater evil to us; no matter how much we had filled in after getting onto the causeway, they opened it again, and they built barriers much stronger than before. Then the friends from the cities of the lake, who had recently accepted our friendship and came to help us with their canoes, believed "they took wool and came back shorn," because many of them lost their lives and more than half the canoes they brought, and many others returned wounded; but even with all this, from then on they did not help the Mexicans because they were on bad terms with them, but they never committed themselves.

Let us stop speaking about misfortunes and go back to talking about the caution and the manner of it that we used from then on and about how Gonzalo de Sandoval, Francisco de Lugo, Andrés de Tapia, Juan de Cuéllar, Valdenebro, and the rest of the soldiers who had come to our camp thought it would be good to return to their posts and report to Cortés how and in what way it was with us. So they went rapidly and told Cortés how Pedro de Alvarado and all his soldiers were exercising great care, both in fighting and in keeping watch, and Sandoval, as he considered me a friend, even told Cortés that he found me and the other soldiers battling waist high in the water defending a brigantine that had run aground, that if it were not for us, the enemies would have killed all the soldiers and the captain who were in it, and because he said other things praising me personally when he ordered me to retreat, I am not going to say them here; other people talked about it and it was known in both our camp and that of Cortés, so I do not want to recite it here.

Cortés then told the soldiers in all three camps not to undertake offensive fighting but simply to defend themselves while they recuperated from their wounds and losses and decided what to do.

Chapter 14

The Fall of Tenochtitlan

[CLIII] The attacks on all three camps continued incessantly day and night. The sacrifices of the captured Spaniards also continued; it took ten days to sacrifice all the soldiers, and they saved for last Cristóbal de Guzmán, whom they kept alive twelve or thirteen days. The verbal threats and taunts at both the Spaniards and Tlaxcalans also continued. To one taunt, "Look how bad and vile you are; even your flesh is bad to eat, it tastes as bitter as gall, so bitter we cannot swallow it," Bernal Díaz comments that it seemed "Our Lord willed their [the Spaniards'] flesh to become bitter." Perhaps most damaging was that many of the Indian friends left to return to their lands. Bernal Díaz notes that "of more than twenty-four thousand friends that we brought, only about two hundred friends stayed in all three camps, and all went away to their towns." A turning point seemed to come when a lord of Texcoco, Ixtlilxochitl (don Carlos), told Cortés that it was all right to stay in the camps but he should send the brigantines out every day and night to make sure water and provisions were not brought into the city, "because inside this great city there are so many warriors that the food they have will run out, and the water they are now drinking, from some springs they have made, is brackish. What can they do if you keep the food and water from them?" According to Bernal Díaz, Cortés was elated by the advice. The three camps went back to filling in the causeways, supported by the brigantines, which were now able to break through any stakes set for them. Mexican attempts to use the crossbows they had taken failed. Some Indian friends began to return.

Because I am tired of writing about battles, and I was more tired and wounded when I was in them, it will seem wearisome to the readers that I talk about them so much, but I can do nothing else, because for ninety-three days we were constantly battling. From here on, if I may be excused, I will not bring it up so much in this story. Let us return to our tale. As in all three camps we were entering their city, Cortés on his side, Sandoval on his, and Pedro de Alvarado on ours, we reached the spring from which they were drinking the brackish water, and we tore it down and took it apart so they could not use it. Many Mexicans were guarding it, and we had a good skirmish with spears, stones, arrows, and many long lances with which they were waiting for the horses, because now we were moving through all parts of the streets we had taken, because now they were level and without water and openings and the horses could run very easily.

[CLIV] When Cortés saw that we were taking many bridges, causeways, and barricades in the city and knocking down houses, as he had as prisoners three chieftains who were captains of Mexico, he ordered them to speak to Guatemuz about making peace with us, but the chieftains said they would not dare go with such a message because their lord Guatemuz would order them killed. But, in short, so much did Cortés beg them, and with promises he made them and cloaks he gave them, that they went. What he ordered them to say to Guatemuz was that because he liked him very much, because he was such a close relative of Montezuma his friend, married to his daughter, because from pity Cortés did not want the destruction of so great a city to be completed, and in order to avoid the great slaughter that occurred each day on its inhabitants and visitors, he begged him to come in peace, and in the name of His Majesty he would pardon all the deaths and damage they had done to us and would do them many favors; he said they should take into account that he had already sent this message four times, and that Guatemuz—whether because he was young, or because of his advisors, and most of all because of his accursed idols and papas who gave him bad advice—had refused to come and had wanted only to wage war; but because he had now seen so many deaths that had occurred in the battles they fought against us, and we had on our side all the cities and towns of that whole area, and every day more new ones were coming against them, that he should take pity because of such ruin of his vassals and city; and also he sent to say that we knew they had used up the provisions, that they had no water, and many other well-chosen words.

The three chieftains understood this very well through our interpreters, and they asked Cortés for a letter, not because they would understand it, but because they already knew clearly that when we sent some message or things we were ordering them, it was on a paper like those they call amales, a sign that it was an order. When the three messengers appeared before their lord Guatemuz, with great tears and sobbing they told him what Cortés ordered them, and Guatemuz, when he and his captains who were with him heard it, according to what we learned, was furious at first that they had dared come to him with those messages; but Guatemuz was a young man, a fine figure of a man for an Indian, of good disposition and joyful countenance, and even his color had something more of a tinge of white than the shade of Indians; he was about twenty-five or twenty-six years old and was married to a very beautiful woman, daughter of the great Montezuma, his uncle, and, as we came to know later, he wanted to make peace. In order to discuss the message, he ordered all the chieftains, captains, and papas of the idols to come together, and he told them that he wanted not to fight against Malinche and all of us; what he said to them was that he had already tried everything that was possible to do in the war and changed the way of fighting many times, but we were of such a nature that when he thought he had us conquered, we would return much more vigorously against them; that at present he knew about the great forces of friends who had newly come to us, that all the cities were against them; that the brigantines had already broken their stakes; that the horses were galloping unrestrained through all the streets of his city; and he put before them many other problems they had regarding provisions and water. He begged or ordered each of them to give his opinion, and the papas should also give theirs and what they had heard their gods, Huichilobos and Tezcatepuca, say and promise, that no one should fear saying truthfully what they believed. It appears that they said to him: "Lord, and our great lord, we already have you for our king, and you were a good choice to rule, for in everything you have shown yourself manly, and the kingdom comes to you by right; the peace you mention is good, but reflect and think: Since these teules entered this land and city, how things have gone from bad to worse for us; look at the services and gifts that our lord, your uncle the great Montezuma, gave them, how he ended up; then your cousin Cacamatzin, king of Texcoco, with the same result; then your relatives, the lords of Iztapalapa, Coyoacan, Tacuba, and Talatcingo, what became of them; then the sons of our great Montezuma all died; then all the gold and riches of this city are gone; then you already see that they have made slaves and branded the faces of all your subjects and vassals of Tepeaca and Chalco, and even Texcoco, and all your cities and towns. Look first at what our gods have promised you, give it full consideration and do not trust Malinche and his friendly words, which are all lies and wickedness; it is better that we all die in this city fighting than see ourselves in the hands of those who would make slaves of us and torture us for gold."

At that time, the papas also told him that their idols had promised them victory three nights in a row when they were sacrificing. Then Guatemuz, half-angry, said: "Because you want it to be so, be very watchful of the maize and provisions that we have, and let us all die fighting, and from now on no one must dare ask me for peace; otherwise I will order him to be killed." Then, everyone promised to fight night and day or die in defense of their city. Then with this finished, they negotiated with the people of Xochimilco and other towns to bring them water in canoes, by night, and they opened other springs in places that had water, although brackish. Let us now talk about how Cortés and all of us were two days without entering the city awaiting their reply, and when we did not expect it, a great many squadrons of Indian warriors fell on us in all three camps, attacking us furiously and coming to engage with us like very fierce lions, believing they would carry us off conquered. What I am talking about was on our side, that of Pedro de Alvarado; on that of Cortés and that of Sandoval, they also said that the enemy arrived at their camps, that they could not keep them back however much they killed and wounded them, and when the enemy were fighting, the cornet of Guatemuz sounded, and then we had to keep close order so they would not rout us because they pushed themselves onto the very points of our swords and lances to lay hands on us. As we were already accustomed to these encounters, because every day they wounded and killed some of us, we held out against them hand to hand, and in this way they fought six or seven days in a row, and we killed and wounded many of them, and even with all this, they cared nothing at all about dying fighting.

I remember that they said to us: "What is Malinche up to, asking us for peace every day? Our idols have promised us victory, we have plenty of food and water, and we are not going to leave any of you alive; so do not talk any more about peace, for words are for women and arms are for men!" Saying this, they would come on us like mad dogs, all of them, and we would fight them until night separated us; then we would retreat with great order because great captaincies of them were coming in pursuit of us. We would get our friends off the causeway because now many more had come than before, and we would return to our huts and at once altogether go on watch. On the watch, we would eat our scant quantity of quelites, which are grasses, and in the early morning we began to fight because they did not give us much resting time. This is the way we were for many days. While we were in this situation, another very troublesome thing arose, and it is that they gathered together from three provinces, Matalzingo, Malinalco, and another town called Tulapa, and I do not remember now the names of the rest, which were about eight or ten leagues from Mexico, to come against us in our rear and in our camps while we were battling with the Mexicans, and then the Mexican forces would come out, some on one side and some on the other, and they thought they would rout us.

[CLV] So that this might be understood well, it is necessary to go back to talking about when they defeated Cortés and carried off to sacrifice the seventy-odd soldiers, and I may as well say seventy-eight, because there were that many when they were counted well. I have also said that Guatemuz sent the heads of the horses and faces they had flayed and the feet and hands of the soldiers they had sacrificed to many towns and to Matalzingo and Malinalco and Tulapa. He sent them word that they had already killed more than half our men and begged them, so they could finish killing us, to come help him and attack our camps day or night, so that, of necessity, we would have to fight with them to defend ourselves; when we were fighting, they would come out from Mexico and attack us on the other side so that they would conquer us and have many of us to sacrifice to their idols, and they would satiate themselves on our bodies. He sent this word to them in such a way that they believed it and took it as true. In Matalzingo and Tulapa, Guatemuz had many relatives on his mother's side; and when they saw the faces and heads of our soldiers and heard what he sent word to them to say, they immediately set about gathering all the forces they could to come to the aid of Mexico and of their relative Guatemuz. They were already in fact coming against us, and along the road where they went were three towns friendly to us, and they began to attack and rob the settlements and maize fields, and they killed children for sacrifice; the towns sent to let Cortés know about it at once so that he would send them aid and relief.

He immediately sent Andrés de Tapia, who, with twenty horsemen, one hundred soldiers, and many Tlaxcalan friends, helped them very much; he made the enemies go back to their towns, and he returned to the camp, at which Cortés was very pleased. In that moment also other messengers came from the towns of Cuernavaca to ask for help, for the same people of Matalzingo, Malinalco, Tulapa, and other provinces were coming down on them, and they asked Cortés to relieve them. To do that, he sent Gonzalo de Sandoval with twenty horsemen and eighty soldiers, the soundest there were in all three camps, and I went with him, and many friends. God knows that those who stayed were at great personal risk in all three camps, because most of them were wounded, and they had no nourishment at all. Although there is much to say about what we did in Sandoval's company, how we defeated the enemies, I will omit talking about it except to say that we came back immediately to relieve Sandoval's camp, and we brought two chieftains from Matalzingo with us, and we left those towns in peace. That expedition we made was very useful. For one thing, it kept our friends from receiving more damage than they had received. For another thing, it kept the enemy from coming against our camps to attack us, as in fact they were coming to do. Also Guatemuz and his captains could see that they no longer had aid or support from those provinces, nor could they say, when we were fighting with the Mexicans, that they were going to kill us with the help of Matalzingo and other provinces and that their idols had promised it to them.

Let us return to talking about how Cortés sent to Guatemuz to make peace, that he would pardon him everything that was past, and he sent word that the king our lord had recently sent to order him not to destroy more of that city; for this reason, the past five days he had neither attacked nor entered the city fighting. He said they should consider that they no longer had food or water, that more than two-thirds of their city was flattened, and that as for the relief they were awaiting from Matalzingo, he should inform himself from those two chieftains that Cortés now sent him, how it had gone for them in their expedition. He also sent to make them other promises. With those messengers went the two Indians from Matalzingo and six Mexican chieftains who had been taken prisoner in recent battles. When Guatemuz saw the prisoners from Matalzingo and they told him what had happened, he gave them no response at all except to tell them to return to their town, and he ordered them to leave Mexico at once.

Let us leave the messengers who departed immediately. The Mexicans came at us in three directions with the greatest fury we had seen up to that time and fought very strongly in all three camps, and given that we wounded and killed many of them, it seems to me they wanted to die fighting. Then when they were going most furiously against us hand to hand and killed ten of our soldiers, whose heads they cut off, hastening martyrdom for them like the rest they had killed, they brought the heads and threw them in front of us. They said: *"Tlen quitoa, rey Castilla, tlen quitoa."* This means in their language: "What does the king of Castile say now?"[74] With these words, they hurled spears, stones, and arrows, which covered the ground and causeway.

Let us leave this, for now we were winning a large part of the city from them, and we sensed that even though they were fighting very manfully, not so many squadrons were coming in relief as before, nor were they opening ditches or causeways; but another thing they did most certainly, which was that, when we were retreating, they came pursuing us until they laid hands on us. I also want to say that we now had used up the powder in all three camps, and at that moment a ship had arrived at Villa Rica, which was from the fleet of Licentiate Lucas Vásquez de Ayllón, which was lost or destroyed in the island of Florida, but the ship showed up at that port, and some soldiers, powder, and crossbows came in it. The deputy governor who was in Villa Rica, Rodrigo Rangel, who was guarding Narváez, immediately sent powder, crossbows, and soldiers to Cortés.

To be brief, let us return to our conquest. Cortés arranged with all the other captains and soldiers that we should advance as much as we could until we reached Tlatelolco, which is the great market-place, where their high cus and adoratorios were. Cortés on his side, Sandoval on his and we on ours went on taking bridges and barri-cades. Cortés advanced as far as a little plaza where there were other adoratorios and some small towers. In one of those houses were some beams put on end, and on them many heads of our Spaniards whom they had killed and sacrificed in recent battles, and they had very long hair and beards, much longer than when they were alive, and I would not have believed it had I not seen it. I recognized three soldiers, my companions, and when we saw them like that, it saddened our hearts. At that time, they were where they were, but

---

74. The actual translation is, "What does the king of Castile say, what does he say?"

twelve days later they were removed, and we buried those heads and others they had offered to idols in a church we built, which is now called The Martyrs, near the bridge they call Alvarado's Leap.

Let us talk about how those of us in the captaincy of Pedro de Alvarado went forward fighting; we arrived at Tlatelolco, and so many Mexicans were guarding their idols and high cus, and they had so many barricades that we were unable to enter or take them for a good two hours, but as the horses, even though most of them were wounded, could now enter, they helped us very much, and the horsemen speared many Mexicans. As so many enemies were in three places, we two captaincies went to battle with them, and Pedro de Alvarado ordered the captaincy of a captain named Gutierre de Badajoz to climb to the top of the cu of Huichilobos, which has one hundred fourteen steps, and they fought very well against the enemies and the many papas in the cus and adoratorios. The enemies attacked Gutierre de Badajoz and his captaincy in such a way that they made him tumble down ten or twelve steps, and we immediately went to help him. As we were advancing, the squadrons with which we were fighting followed us, and we ran great risk of our lives, but we still climbed the steps, which are one hundred and fourteen.

Here there would be much to tell about the danger in which we all found ourselves in capturing those fortresses, which were very high, and in those battles they again wounded us all very badly; still, we set them on fire, the idols were burned, we raised our banners; and setting it on fire, we were battling on level ground until nighttime, but we could not prevail against so many warriors.

The next day Cortés and his captains saw from where they were advancing, battling on their sides in other neighborhoods and streets far from the high cu, the flames that were burning the great cu, for they had not been put out; they saw our banners on top, and he rejoiced greatly and wanted also to be on it, but he could not—and they even said he was envious—because it was a quarter of a league from one place to the other and he had many bridges and water openings to take. Wherever he went they waged furious war on him, and he could not advance as quickly as he wanted into the heart of the city, as we in Alvarado's company had. But within four days he joined us, Sandoval as well as Cortés, and we could go from one camp to the other through the streets and houses that were pulled down, bridges, barricades that were destroyed, and water openings now all filled in. In this instant Guatemuz with all his warriors were already retreating to a part of the city within the lake, because the house and palace in which he lived had now been leveled to the ground, but with all this, they did not cease to come out every day and attack us, and at the time for us to withdraw they continued following even more closely than before.

When Cortés saw this and that many days were going by and they were not coming to seek peace nor had any such thought, he decided with all our captains that we would set up some ambushes, and it was in this way: From all three camps, about thirty horsemen and one hundred soldiers joined together, the most nimble and warlike that Cortés knew; Cortés summoned one thousand Tlaxcalans from all three camps, and very early in the morning we put ourselves in some large houses that had belonged to a lord of Mexico, and Cortés advanced with the rest of the horsemen, his soldiers, crossbowmen, and escopeteros through the streets and causeways, fighting in the usual way and making as though he was filling in a water opening and bridge. Then the Mexican squadrons that were prepared for it were fighting with him, as well as many others Guatemuz sent to guard the bridge. When Cortés saw that there was a great number of enemies, he made as if he was retreating and ordered the friends to get off the causeway so the enemy might believe our men were retreating. They pursued him, at first little by little, but then, when they saw that he was really making as though fleeing in fact, all the forces in that causeway went after him, attacking him. When Cortés saw that they had passed somewhat beyond the houses where the ambush was, he ordered two cannons discharged close together, which was the signal for us to come out of the ambush. The horsemen came out first, and then all our soldiers came out and we fell on the enemy at leisure. Then immediately Cortés turned around with his men, and our friends the Tlaxcalans, and they did much damage to the enemies so that many were killed and wounded, and from then on they did not follow us when it was time for us to withdraw.

Let us say how we were all now in Tlatelolco, and Cortés ordered all the captaincies to be there with him and keep watch, because we were coming more than a half league from the camp to do battle. We were there three days without doing anything of note, because Cortés ordered us not to advance any further into the city nor to tear down any more houses, because he wanted to ask for peace again. During those days when we were in Tlatelolco, Cortés sent to Guatemuz begging him to give himself up and not to have fear; he made great promises that he would respect and honor his person very much and that Guatemuz would govern Mexico and all his lands and cities as usual, and he sent him food and treats, which were tortillas, hens, cherries, prickly pear fruit, and cacao, for he had nothing else. Guatemuz entered into counsel with his captains, and what they advised him was to say that he would like peace but that they would wait three days to give the response, that at the end of the three days, Guatemuz and Cortés would see each other and would make the agreement for peace, because in those three days they would have time to know more fully the will and reply of their Huichilobos. What he did not say is that they would have time to repair bridges; open causeways; prepare spears, stones, and arrows; and make barricades. Guatemuz sent four chieftains with that answer. We believed that the peace was genuine, and Cortés ordered that the messengers be given plenty to eat and drink, and he sent them back to Guatemuz; with them he sent more refreshments, the same as before. Guatemuz again sent other messengers and with them two rich cloaks, and the messengers said that Guatemuz would come when everything was arranged. But so as not to waste more words on this, he never agreed to come because they had advised him not to believe Cortés and reminded him about the end of his uncle, the great Montezuma, and his relatives and the destruction of the entire noble Mexican lineage; they told him he should say he was ill and they should all go out to fight, and it would please their gods to give them victory, for so many times they had promised it to them.

Well, as we were waiting for Guatemuz and he did not come, we understood the cunning, and at that moment so many battalions of Mexicans came out with their devices and attacked Cortés so fiercely that he could not hold out, and it was the same thing in our camp and in Sandoval's. They did this in such a way that they seemed to be beginning all over again, and as we were somewhat careless, believing they were already at peace, they wounded many of our soldiers, and three died from their very severe wounds, and two horses; but they did not go away boasting very much, because they paid for it fully. When Cortés saw this, he ordered us to go back to attacking them and to advance into the part of their city where they had taken refuge. When they saw that we were taking the entire city from them, Guatemuz sent two chieftains to tell Cortés that he would like to speak to him from across a water opening, Cortés on one side and Guatemuz on the other, and they designated the time for the next morning. Cortés went to speak with him, but Guatemuz did not come for the appointment; rather he sent chieftains, and they said their lord did not dare to come for fear that when they were speaking our men would fire escopetas and crossbows at him and kill him. Cortés promised him on his oath that he would not harm him in any way, but it was of no use, for they did not believe him, and they said they already knew about his promises.

At that time, two chieftains who were speaking with Cortés took out some tortillas from a large bag they were carrying and the leg of a hen and cherries, and they sat down in a very leisurely manner to eat so that Cortés would see this and believe they were not hungry. When Cortés saw that, he sent to tell them that, because they did not want to come to make peace, we would soon go into their houses and see if they had maize, much less hens. We were another four or five days in this way, and we did not attack them, but at this time many poor Indians who had nothing to eat would come out of Mexico every night, and they came to our camp desperate from hunger; when Cortés saw that, he ordered us not to attack them, because perhaps they would change their mind about coming in peace. But they would not come, although he sent to them to request peace.

[CLVI] Seeing that Guatemuz and his captains did not want to make peace at all, Cortés ordered Gonzalo de Sandoval to enter with the brigantines into the place in the city where Guatemuz had retreated with the flower of his captains and most noble people in Mexico, but he ordered them not to kill or wound any Indians unless they attacked him, and, even if they did attack him, he should only defend himself and not do them any other harm, but he should knock down their houses and the many platforms they had made in the lake for fighting. Cortés climbed the great cu of Tlatelolco to see how Sandoval was advancing with the brigantines, and also with Cortés were Pedro de Alvarado, Francisco Verdugo, Luis Marín, and other soldiers. As Sandoval advanced vigorously with the brigantines on that place where the houses of Guatemuz were, and when Guatemuz saw himself surrounded, he was afraid they would capture or kill him, and he had ready fifty large pirogues with good rowers so that when he saw himself in trouble, he could save himself by placing himself in some reed beds and get from there to land and hide in other towns. He had also ordered his captains and people of most importance who were with him in that part of the city to do the same. When they saw that the brigantines were entering among the houses, they embarked in the fifty canoes where they had already placed his property, gold, jewels, and entire family and women, and he put himself in them and shot out onto the lake, accompanied by many captains. As many other canoes were leaving at that moment, the lake full of them, and Sandoval immediately got news that Guatemuz was fleeing, he ordered all the brigantines to stop demolishing houses and fighting platforms and pursue the enemy in the canoes and take care that they kept close track of where Guatemuz was going, that they not harm him or anger him at all but do their best to capture him peacefully.

As one García Holguín, a friend of Sandoval, was captain of a brigantine, a very fast sailing vessel with good rowers, Sandoval ordered him to follow in the direction they told him Guatemuz was fleeing with his large pirogues; and he ordered that if he caught up with Guatemuz he should do him no harm at all beyond capturing him. Sandoval continued in another direction with other brigantines that accompanied him. It pleased Our Lord God that García Holguín caught up with the canoes and pirogues in which Guatemuz was going, and from the style and richness of it, its awnings and the seat in which he sat, he knew it was Guatemuz, the great lord of Mexico. He signaled them to stop, but they would not, so he made as if he was going to shoot with the escopetas and crossbows. When Guatemuz saw that, he was frightened and said: "Do not shoot me, for I am king of this city and they call me Guatemuz; what I beg of you is that you do not touch the things I am taking with me, nor my wife nor relatives, but take me immediately to Malinche." When Holguín heard him, he was greatly delighted, and with much respect he embraced him and put him in the brigantine along with his wife and thirty chieftains, and he had him sit in the stern on some mats and cloths and gave him what they had brought to eat; he did not touch the canoes carrying his property, but brought them along with his brigantine.

At that time, Gonzalo de Sandoval had ordered all the brigantines to gather together, and he learned that Holguín had captured Guatemuz and was taking him to Cortés.

When Cortés learned this, he immediately dispatched the captain Luis Marín and Francisco Verdugo to summon Sandoval and Holguín to come just as they were in their brigantines, and, with much respect, bring Guatemuz's wife and all the rest. While they were summoning him, Cortés ordered a dais prepared, the best there could be in the circumstances, with mats, cloaks, other things to sit on, and a great deal of food from what Cortés had for himself. Soon Sandoval and Holguín came with Guatemuz, and the two captains brought him before Cortés; when he was in front of Cortés, he paid him much respect, and Cortés joyfully embraced him and showed much affection to him and also his captains. Then Guatemuz said to Cortés: "Señor Malinche, I have done what I was obligated to do for my city and vassals, and

I can do no more, so I come by force and a prisoner before your person and power; take that dagger you have in your belt and kill me with it right away." When he said this, he wept many tears and sobbed, and other great lords he had with him also wept. Cortés answered him through doña Marina and Aguilar, our interpreters, very affectionately, and he told him that because he had been so valiant in defending his city, he thought much more highly of him personally, that he did not deserve any blame at all, but his defense should be seen as more good than bad; but what he wanted was that Guatemuz had come for peace of his own will when they had been nearly defeated, before so much of that city had been destroyed and there were so many deaths among his Mexicans; but now both had occurred, and there was no remedy or solution for it, so let his spirit be at rest and that of all his captains, and he will rule Mexico and its provinces as before. Guatemuz and his captains told Cortés that they were grateful.

Cortés asked after his wife and the other great ladies, wives of the other captains they told him came with Guatemuz. Guatemuz himself replied and said that he had begged Gonzalo de Sandoval and García Holguín to allow them to stay in the canoes while he came to see what Malinche ordered. Cortés sent for them at once and ordered them given the best food they had in the camp, and then, because it was late and beginning to rain, Cortés arranged for them to go immediately to Coyoacan, and he took with him Guatemuz and all his household and family and many chieftains, and he also ordered Pedro de Alvarado, Gonzalo de Sandoval, and the rest of the captains each to go to his own shelters and camp; and we went to Tacuba, Sandoval to Tepeaquilla, and Cortés to Coyoacan. Guatemuz and his captains were captured on the thirteenth of August, at the hour of vespers, on the day of Sr. San Hipólito in the year 1521. Thanks to Our Lord Jesus Christ and to Our Lady, the Virgin Saint Mary, his blessed mother. Amen.

It rained and thundered with lightning that afternoon until midnight, with much heavier rain than at other times. After Guatemuz had been taken prisoner, all of us soldiers were left as deaf as a man standing at the top of a belfry with many bells clanging, which all stopped in a single instant. I say this on purpose because all ninety-three days that we were besieging this city night and day, Mexican captains gave out so many yells and shouts while they were readying the squadrons of warriors who were going to battle on the causeways; others calling to those in the canoes who were going to fight with the brigantines and with us on the bridges; to others driving in palings and opening and deepening the water openings and bridges and making barricades; to others preparing spears and arrows, and the women making rounded stones to cast with the slings; then from the adoratorio and towers of idols the accursed drums and cornets and mournful great drums never stopped sounding. In this way, night and day, we had so much noise, we could not hear each other, but after the capture of Guatemuz, the shouts and all the noise stopped; that is why I have said it was as if we had been standing in a belfry before.

Let us talk about the dead bodies and heads in those houses where Guatemuz had retreated. I say, and I swear, Amen, that all the houses and fighting platforms in the lake were filled with heads and dead bodies, and I do not know how to write about it, for in the streets and in the very courtyards of Tlatelolco, it was all the same, and we could not walk except among bodies and heads of dead Indians. I have read about the destruction of Jerusalem, but I do not know if there was greater slaughter than here, because so many people in this town were missing, most of the warriors from all the provinces and towns subject to Mexico who gathered there died, and the ground and lake and fighting platforms were all full of dead bodies; they smelled so bad that there was no man who could bear it, and for this reason as soon as Guatemuz was taken prisoner, each of our captains went to his own camp, and even Cortés was sick from the stench that penetrated into his nostrils and from headache during those days he was in Tlatelolco.

Let us talk about how the soldiers who went about in the brigantines were the ones who fared best, and they had good spoil because they could go to the houses in certain areas of the lake where they believed there would be clothing, gold, or other riches; they also went to search in the reed beds where the Mexicans were carrying the wealth to hide when we took some areas and houses. Also, under the pretext that they were chasing the canoes that carried provisions and water, when they came upon some of them in which some chieftains were fleeing to dry land to go among the towns of Otomis, who were nearby, they stripped them of everything they carried with them. I want to say that we soldiers who fought on the causeways and on land had no profit whatsoever except many arrow wounds, [and wounds from] lance thrusts, knife slashes, spears, and stones, because when we took some houses, the residents had carried off all the possessions they had and we could not go by water until we had first filled in the openings and bridges. For this reason I have said that when Cortés was searching for sailors to go in the brigantines, they fared better than those of us who battled on land. It also came out clearly because the Mexican captains and even Guatemuz told Cortés, when he demanded the treasure of Montezuma from them, that those who were in the brigantines had stolen the greater part of it.

Let us say that, as there was such a bad stench in that city, Guatemuz begged Cortés to give permission for all the forces of Mexico that were in the city to go outside to the neighboring towns, and he immediately ordered them to do so. I say that for three days and nights, all three causeways were crammed with men, women, and children, never ceasing, and they were so thin, yellow, dirty, and bad smelling that it was pitiful to see them. When they had cleared the causeway, Cortés went to see the city, and we saw the houses full of dead people, and among them even some poor Mexicans who could not leave, and what they excreted from their bodies was a filthiness such as very thin pigs that only eat grass excrete. The entire city was as if plowed up and the roots of the good herbs pulled out, and they had eaten them and even cooked the bark of some trees. We found no fresh water there, but brackish. I want also to say that they did not eat the flesh of their Mexicans but only our flesh and that of the Tlaxcalans whom they had captured, and there had not been a people for a long time that had suffered so much from hunger, thirst, and continual fighting.

Now that I am away from the combats and fierce battles we had day and night with the Mexicans, for which I give many thanks to God who delivered me from them, I want to tell something that happened to me after I saw the sixty-two soldiers from the men of Cortés who were carried off alive, sacrificed, and cut open at their breasts, their hearts offered to the idols. What I will now say will seem to some people to be because of a lack of spirit on my part for fighting, but on the other hand, if one considers it well, it is from the excessive daring and great courage with which I had to put myself into the most ferocious of the battles those days, because at that time it was presumed of a good soldier and was necessary for his reputation that he do what the most daring soldiers were obliged to do. As every day I saw my companions being carried off to sacrifice, and I had seen how they were sawing through their chests to pull the beating hearts from them and to cut off their feet and arms and eat them, the sixty-two of them, and as previously they had killed eight hundred fifty of our companions, I feared that one day or another they would do the same to me, because they had already had me in their grasp twice to carry me off to sacrifice, but it pleased God that I should escape their hands. Remembering those very ugly deaths, and as the proverb goes, the little pitcher that goes often to the well, etc., for this reason, from then on, I always feared death more than ever. I have said this because, before going into the battles, I felt a sort of horror and great sadness in my heart, and I urinated once or twice, but commending myself to God and to His blessed mother, going into battle it was always the same, that dread immediately left me. I also want to say what a strange and new thing it was to me to feel that unaccustomed fear, when I had been in many battles and very dangerous encounters of war, and here at the end, my heart should have been hardened and spirit more deeply embedded than ever. For I can recall and recount things back to when I came to discover with Francisco Hernández de Córdoba and with Grijalva and returned with Cortés. I took part in the affair at Cape Catoche and in that of Lázaro, also called Campeche, and at Potonchan and at Florida, which I have written about more fully when I came to discover with Francisco Hernández de Córdoba.

Let us go back and mention the expedition of Grijalva, and in the same expedition the affair of Potonchan, and then with Cortés in the matter of Tabasco and that of Cingapacinga and in all the battles and encounters of Tlaxcala and Cholula, and when we defeated Narváez, they designated me to be among those who went to capture their artillery, eighteen cannons loaded with stones and balls that we took from Narváez, and this was a moment of great danger; and I was in the first defeat, when the Mexicans drove us from Mexico, when they killed more than eight hundred fifty of our soldiers in about a week; and I took part in the expeditions of Tepeaca and Cachula and their surroundings, and in other encounters we had with the Mexicans when we were in Texcoco harvesting the maize fields; and I was in the affair of Iztapalapa when they tried to drown us, and I was there when we were climbing the rocky crags, as they now call the forts or fortresses that Cortés captured, and in the affair of Xochimilco, four battles, and in many other encounters; and I was among the first to enter with Pedro de Alvarado to lay siege to Mexico when we cut off the water from Chapultepec; and I took part when we first entered the causeways with Alvarado, and afterward, when they defeated us in the same place and carried off eight of our soldiers and laid hold of me and were carrying me off to be sacrificed; and I took part in all the rest of the battles I have already mentioned that we had every day, up to when I saw the cruel deaths they inflicted on our companions before my eyes. I have already said that all these battles and dangers of death had gone by without my having had such fear as I felt now at the end; let those gentlemen who understand military matters and have found themselves in danger of death in critical situations say to what cause they attribute my fear, whether to weakness of spirit or to great courage, because as I have said, I felt in my thoughts that when I was battling I had to put myself into such dangerous places that, of necessity, I had to fear death then more than at other times, and for this reason my heart trembled, because it feared death. All these battles in which I found myself, which I have talked about here, they will see in my story.

EPILOGUE

As Bernal Díaz indicates, his story and the story of the Spanish conquest of New Spain do not end with the fall of Tenochtitlan. That part of the conquest was only the first and most focused step in the process of settling the land. Almost immediately upon the fall of Mexico, Cortés began to send his captains and their men off to New Spain's other major population centers in search of further treasure, lands to occupy and distribute in encomienda, and peoples to overcome and subject to Spanish domination. His reasons for sending off his several captains varied according to circumstance: With some, he was fulfilling promises he had made in the course of conquering Mexico; in others he was rewarding people who had served him particularly well; in yet others he was putting people he distrusted at a distance so as to avoid revolts and attempts on his life. Thus, as reward for loyal service, he sent Gonzalo de Sandoval to settle the territory of the Zapotecs, that is, Oaxaca; Pedro de Alvarado to settle Guatemala; and Cristóbal de Olid to Honduras, an assignment Cortés would come to regret; but, for example, he sent Alonso de Ávila to Gualtitlan precisely because Cortés knew him to be "a very bold person and was uneasy with regard to him," particularly as he had "served the bishop of Burgos,... and for that reason Cortés tried to keep Ávila at a distance from him" (CLIX). However, Cortés was not simply attempting to fulfill his promises to those who had served him in the overthrow of Mexico or keep his friends close and his enemies at a distance, but was, at the same time, attempting to consolidate his position as governor-general of New Spain, along with the status and economic benefits that pertained to such a position, against the opposition of his enemies, representatives of the Spanish Crown and those who simply wanted to take advantage of the chaos that arises in the midst of such social upheaval as the new situation created. Finally, Bernal Díaz del Castillo remains loyal to Gonzalo de Sandoval and Cortés, serving them as asked and required, even though his experience of Cortés convinces him that the latter is more interested in his own fame and fortune than the well-being of those who accompanied him on the trek to and siege of Mexico.

Among the signal events to which Bernal Díaz bears witness in the last part of his history are Cristóbal de Olid's betrayal of Cortés and the execution that follows, the nearly two-and-one-half-year trek with Cortés to Guatemala with its disastrous results, Cortés's fight to secure recognition and compensation for service to the Spanish Crown, as well as Cortés's lack of regard for those who served him, the chaotic state in which Cortés found Mexico upon his return, first, from the Guatemala expedition and then from his trip to Spain. Finally, Bernal Díaz recalls those who were in the company that overthrew Mexico, providing portraits of them, which he concludes with a final statement of his reasons for writing his history.

The Spanish Crown had urged Cortés to take possession of Higueras and Honduras in part to search out all the gold and other treasure possible and because it sought a passage to the Spice Islands. Cortés commissioned Cristóbal de Olid with this task because he had performed so valiantly during the siege of Mexico, because "he was made by the same hand . . . and because he had given Cristóbal de Olid a good share of Indians around Mexico, therefore believing he would be loyal" (CLXV). Olid was to go by sea from Villa Rica to Havana to secure provisions, particularly horses, from where he was to proceed to Higueras to invade Honduras. Among the company Olid took with him was a person named Briones, who was a "disruptive man and enemy of Cortés" (CLXV). Briones cajoled Olid into a conspiracy to meet with Diego Velázquez, who, when Olid's fleet reached Cuba, "came to where the fleet was and reached an agreement with Cristóbal de Olid that together they would take the land of Higueras and Honduras in his royal name and that

Diego Velázquez would do what was necessary to make it known to His Majesty in Castile" (CLXV). When Cortés discovered the conspiracy and Olid's revolt, he determined to take revenge. He sent a relative, Francisco de Las Casas, with a well-armed fleet of five ships to Higueras and Honduras to take the territory back and punish Olid. As Las Casas's fleet arrived and anchored at the port of Higueras, a storm came up that wrecked most of the ships, and Las Casas with most of his men had to abandon their ships and were captured and imprisoned by Olid, who, it turns out, ended up not guarding Las Casas and his companion Gil Gonzales de Ávila closely, even entertaining them at dinner. One night, while at dinner talking about old times, Las Casas "grabbed him [Olid] by the beard and slashed at his throat" and Ávila, along with other supporters of Cortés, "rapidly gave Olid so many wounds that he could not defend himself" (CLXXII). Olid managed to escape and hide, but Las Casas and Ávila soon discovered where he was, captured him, and "brought charges against, sentenced, and beheaded him in the plaza at Naco. And so he died because he rebelled, having followed bad counselors" (CLXXII).

In the meantime, Cortés, opposed by some of his bitterest enemies, especially the bishop of Burgos and archbishop of Rosano, Diego Velázquez and Pánfilo Narváez, had petitioned the pope and the Spanish Crown to confirm him as governor of New Spain and grant him both lands and rights to make grants of lands and Indians to those he saw fit. After a protracted hearing in Spain, a specially appointed panel of judges sequestered itself for five days and unanimously found for Cortés and the conquistadors who accompanied him:

> First, they found Cortés and all of us, the true conquistadors who came over with him, very good and loyal servants of His Majesty, and they thought highly of our great fidelity, and they lauded and praised most highly our daring in the great battles we had had with the Indians and did not fail to mention how few we were when we

defeated Narváez, and they immediately silenced Diego
Velázquez's claim to govern New Spain, although if he had
spent on outfitting the fleets, he could sue Cortés for it in
the courts. Next, they declared by formal judgment that
Cortés should be governor of New Spain in accord with
the order of the high Pontiff and that they affirmed in the
name of His Majesty the encomiendas Cortés had made
and gave him power to divide the land from then on; and
they approved of all he had done because it was clearly
in the service of God and His Majesty. . . . And they ordered that all the conquistadors should receive preference
and that they should give us good encomiendas of Indians
and that we should be given the most prestigious seats,
both in churches and in other places. (CLXVIII)

Upon hearing news of the judgment, Diego Velázquez fell
ill and died within a few months. For his part, when Cortés heard the news, he began to allocate lands and Indians
to those who were then in his favor and were supporting his
current efforts, but not to the conquistadors who had been
with him through the siege of Mexico, nor did he plead their
case to the Spanish Crown. Bernal Díaz repeatedly states that
Cortés turned a blind eye and deaf ear to the conquistadors'
complaints except when he was under duress and required
their loyalty and service.

In the meantime, with the intention of settling areas in the
northern part of Oaxaca, Bernal Díaz and a number of other
captains and conquistadors went off on an expedition under the
command of Gonzalo de Sandoval. After one less-than-successful
foray, they made their way to Coatzacoalcos, about seventy leagues
from Veracruz. When they came to the Coatzacoalcos River, a
large river that required care in crossing, in part because in doing
so they would have to divide their party and thus weaken themselves in case of an attack, they summoned the local caciques and
sought their help, which the caciques initially gave only reluc-
tantly. Having crossed the river, however, they found the area to

be well populated, with rich soil and abundant food, and, Bernal Díaz writes,

> We settled in the town that was near the river, and it was a good place for trade by sea because there was a port about four leagues downstream from there, and we named it the Villa de Espíritu Santo. We gave it that sublime name, first, because we defeated Narváez on the Feast of the Holy Spirit; also because that holy name was our battlecry when we captured and defeated him; further because we crossed that river [Coatzacoalcos] on that same day; and, finally, because all those lands came peaceably, without making war on us. There the flower of the gentlemen and soldiers who had come from Mexico with Sandoval settled. (CLX)

Upon settling, Sandoval allocated the lands among those who came with him, but with time and the imposition of new laws, Bernal Díaz expresses the view that "it would have been better that I had not stayed there because, as it latter turned out, the land was poor, and we brought many lawsuits against the three towns that were settled later" (CLX).

At this point, leaving the government of Mexico in the charge of certain of the king's officers and the conversion of the Indians to fray Turibio Motolinia, Cortés determined to go overland to Honduras in search of Cristóbal de Olid, Francisco de Las Casas, and the others he believed to be there, undertaking what turned out to be an arduous trek that lasted, according to Bernal Díaz, more than two years. Once again, Cortés called on those who had been with him since arriving on the coast of New Spain. Bernal Díaz writes,

> [Cortés] ordered all of us citizens of that town [Coatzacoalcos] to accompany him . . . [so that] at the time when we should have been resting up from our great hardships and acquiring some great property and enterprises, he ordered us to go on a campaign of more than

five hundred leagues, going through lands nearly all on a war footing, leaving behind in ruin all we had, and we were on that journey more than two years and three months. (CLXXV)

On the one hand, this was another journey of discovery, with Cortés and his men making their way through territory not previously traveled by Europeans, mountainous territory marked by dense forests, mostly hostile Indian peoples able to attack and then slip silently away, and many streams and rivers, many of which required the Spaniards to build bridges in order to make their way across. It was also territory in which food was notably scarce, and Cortés's men spent a great deal of time on the edge of starvation. It seems also to have been the first expedition on which Cortés commissioned Bernal Díaz del Castillo as a captain to lead Spanish soldiers and Indians, although Bernal Díaz does not report events of particular danger or importance while he was doing so. However, during this grueling journey, one that led to several near revolts against Cortés's leadership, one singularly significant event did occur. For reasons that are not entirely clear, Cortés had decided to bring Cuauhtemoc and other important Indian caciques from Mexico with him on this journey. At a certain point, they conspired to kill Cortés and his men while they were vulnerable crossing some river or other difficult territory, return to Mexico, unite the remaining Indians, and kill all the Spaniards who stayed in the city. Cortés became aware of the plot, seized Cuauhtemoc and the cacique of Tacuba, and forced a confession from them. Bernal Díaz writes,

> Cuauhtemoc confessed that it was as the others had said; nonetheless, the plan was not his idea and he did not know whether everyone was in on it or if it would be carried out, that he had never thought of actually doing it, but had only been in on the talk about it. The cacique of Tacuba said that he and Cuauhtemoc had said that it would be better to die right away than to die each day on

the road, seeing the great hunger their vassals and kinsmen were going through. Without further legal procedures, Cortés ordered Cuauhtemoc and the lord of Tacuba, his cousin, to be hanged.... When they were about to hang him, Cuauhtemoc said, "Oh, Malinche: Long since I had understood that you were going to kill me in this way and I had recognized your false words, for you kill me unjustly! God demands it of you for I did not kill myself when I was delivered to you in my city of Mexico." The lord of Tacuba said that in dying with his lord Cuauhtemoc, he took his death as a good thing. . . . Truly, I was greatly saddened by the deaths of Cuauhtemoc and the lord of Tacuba, for I knew them to be very great lords.... And this death they were given was very unjust, and it seemed bad to all who came with us. (CLXXVII)

One cannot fix the precise date of Cuauhtemoc's execution, nor can one locate it precisely in the two years and three months of Cortés's expedition to Honduras. But the journey continued from this point, and even though Cortés seems to have accomplished the tasks important to him, and the cost on the road in terms of the hardships his men endured and their sense of losing important time and opportunities to settle and begin to acquire land and wealth wore at their morale, they continued to honor and support him. On the other hand, both morale and order were also beginning to decline in Mexico under the governorship of those on whom Cortés had settled authority for governance, and from Cuba Diego de Ordaz had even written those in charge that Cortés and all who were with him were dead, leading to further instability, so much so that Gonzalo de Sandoval and others finally confronted Diego de Ordaz, asking "him with great bitterness why he had written this, given that he neither knew nor had evidence for it, adding that his letters . . . were so evil that New Spain might have been lost because of them" (CXCII). All of this occurred at a time when Cortés's delegated governorship of New Spain had begun to fray and was being passed from individual to individual and various of Cortés's enemies began leveling complaints about and charges against Cortés both as a person and as governor, causing him to decide to return to New Spain proper and Mexico in particular. Just after he arrived in Veracruz, Licentiate Luis Ponce de Leon also arrived to "take the *residencia* of Cortés" (CXCI), but even this event turned chaotic when the licentiate took ill and died shortly after having arrived in Mexico. As a consequence of the continuing turmoil, in the face of repeated threats to his governorship, and in hope of securing even greater titles, rights and privileges, Cortés went to Spain to seek preferment from Emperor Charles V, which, in fact, he received, including the title Marquis de Valle. Cortés did return to New Spain and supported a number of significant activities on behalf of the Spanish Crown, but none was as successful as his leadership of the conquest of New Spain itself. Finally, he returned to Spain, where he died and was first interred in his nearby parish church. Eventually, his body was disinterred, taken to Mexico, and laid to rest.

Bernal Díaz del Castillo, having unsuccessfully pursued a number of different strategies for securing good lands with grants of Indians—his main reason for participating in the discovery and conquest of New Spain—eventually settled in Guatemala, going there in 1541 to live permanently. He wrote his *True History of the Conquest of New Spain* from there, in part to establish his merit as a participant in the conquest, in part to secure rights to lands and Indians in perpetuity for his children, rights that were being challenged in Spain. He also wanted to set the record straight, as his references to Gómara and other chroniclers indicate, a fact he emphasizes as he completes his account of those conquistadors who people his epic story:

> My name is Bernal Díaz del Castillo, and I am a citizen and member of town council of the city of Santiago de Guatemala, and a native of the very noble and famous and celebrated town of Medina del Campo, son of Francisco Díaz del Castillo, member of its town council, who

was also known as el Galant, may he rest in holy glory; and I give great thanks and praise to Our Lord Jesus Christ and our Lady the Holy Virgin Mary, his blessed mother, who has protected me from being sacrificed, for in those times they sacrificed most of my companions who I have named, so that now our heroic deeds should be revealed most clearly and who those valiant captains and tough soldiers were who won these regions of the New World and not attribute the honor due all of us to one captain alone. (CCV)